Christ-
Centered
Sermons

Christ-Centered Sermons

MODELS *of*
REDEMPTIVE PREACHING

Bryan Chapell

B
Baker Academic
a division of Baker Publishing Group
Grand Rapids, Michigan

Published by Baker Academic
a division of Baker Publishing Group
P.O. Box 6287, Grand Rapids, MI 49516-6287
www.bakeracademic.com

Printed in the United States of America

Library of Congress Cataloging-in-Publication Data
Chapell, Bryan.
    Christ-centered sermons : models of redemptive preaching / Bryan Chapell.
        pages cm
    Includes bibliographical references and index.
    ISBN 978-0-8010-4869-2 (pbk.)
    1. Sermons, American. 2. Preaching. I. Title.
BV4253.C478 2013
252—dc23   2013013145

13   14   15   16   17   18   19   7   6   5   4   3   2   1

Contents

Preface

Why Christ-Centered Sermons

I love to teach preaching. Nothing brings me more joy than the "aha!" moment when a devoted student or dedicated preacher says, "Now I understand how I can proclaim God's Word better." This book is a simple quest for more such "aha!" moments. When *Christ-Centered Preaching* was first published two decades ago, I could not have anticipated, or even dared hope, that the Lord would use it so extensively to help others learn principles of preaching the gospel from all Scripture. I also did not anticipate how often I would be asked to provide examples of those principles.

The book that follows provides two kinds of examples: (1) sermons that exemplify the types of messages taught in *Christ-Centered Preaching*, and (2) structures that demonstrate a variety of preaching techniques and practices that aid expository communication.

Part One of *Christ-Centered Sermons* focuses on structure, with examples of formal, informal, expository, and inductive sermon structures. Instructive notes and references inserted throughout the example sermons describe principles or practices being employed at each stage of the message. My goal, as much as possible, is to create the effect of sitting at the elbow of each reader to say, "Now here I am applying this principle, or using this structure, for this reason."

Part Two explores various approaches to redemptive interpretation of texts. Each sermon is an example of a different approach to biblical theology, demonstrating how to preach texts that predict, prepare for, reflect, or result from the ministry of

Christ. The instructive notes and references continue to expand readers' exposure to a variety of communication considerations and techniques.

Part Three provides sermons that demonstrate how the redemptive truths excavated from Scripture apply to our lives. Important discussion of how grace motivates and enables Christian dedication unfolds with varying emphases in the different examples. In addition, messages in this portion of the book explore the supernatural aspects of our union with Christ and the power of the Word in order to provide preachers the hope and boldness they need to preach in challenging circumstances.

The introduction following this preface is a summary of the principles of *Christ-Centered Preaching* that lays the foundation for the examples that follow. My prayer is that these principles will combine with the concrete examples in the remainder of the book to provide readers clear guidance and confidence for a lifetime of preaching Christ-centered sermons.

Introduction

Christ-Centered Sermons

Expository preaching has a simple goal: to say what God says. Expository preachers presume that true spiritual health can only be produced by the Spirit of God. That Spirit inspired the Word of God as his only infallible witness to the minds and hearts of his people (2 Tim. 3:16–17). As the Spirit works by and with the Word in our hearts, God teaches us the truths needed for us to understand, experience, and honor him.[1] Thus, the chief goal of preachers who desire to proclaim God's truths should be to say what the Holy Spirit has said in the Bible. The most dependable way to do this is to explain the meaning of biblical texts and show how they apply to the lives of believers. Such explanation drives the preacher to serious study of God's Word for careful articulation of both its original meaning and its present significance. Making sure God's people know what God has said and why he has said it is the tandem goal of expository preaching.[2]

Preaching with God's Goals

We need to understand that the preacher's concern should not only be instructive. God is active in his Word, convicting the heart, renewing the mind, and

---

1. *Westminster Confession of Faith*, I.5, 7; hereinafter *WCF*.
2. This chapter is used with permission and adapted from the author's "The Necessity of Preaching Grace for Progress in Sanctification," in *All for Jesus: A Celebration of the 50th Anniversary of Covenant Theological Seminary*, ed. Robert Peterson and Sean Lucas (Ross-shire, UK: Christian Focus, 2006).

strengthening the will. This means that preaching is not simply an instructive lecture; it is a redemptive event. If we think of the sermon only as a means of transferring information, then we will prioritize making the message dense with historical facts, moral instruction, and memory-retention devices that seem designed to prepare listeners for later tests of formal doctrine or factual knowledge. Such tests are rare. And most people's inability to remember a sermon's content in following days can devastate the ego of a preacher whose primary goal is the congregation's doctrinal or biblical literacy.

The needed reordering of priorities will not come by emptying the sermon of biblical content but by preparing it with the goals of equipping God's people for spiritual warfare and welfare. Our primary goal is not preparing people for later tests of mind or behavior but rather humbling the heart and strengthening the will of each listener in the present moment. Because God is active in his Word, we should preach with the conviction that the Spirit of God will use the truths of his Word *as we preach* to change hearts now! As hearts change, lives change—even when sermon specifics are forgotten (Prov. 4:23).

Preparing for hearts to receive the transforming truths of any biblical passage requires careful study of God's Word and caring insight into God's people (2 Tim. 2:15). Simply reciting commentary information is not preaching. The faithful preacher must marshal facts, doctrine, illustrations, and applications together with the dynamics of pastoral *logos, pathos,* and *ethos* to address both what listeners need to hear and what they are capable of hearing (1 Thess. 2:2–13).[3] Organizational tools that help communicate biblical truths with these means predominate the early chapters of my book *Christ-Centered Preaching,* and the sermon examples in Part One of this companion volume highlight such. These examples feature both formal and informal structures, along with comments about techniques that will help listeners understand and remember messages.

These organizational aids are not the core of any sermon but help communicate the content that is. If our sermons are not interesting, clear, or organized, then we put our credibility into question and may undermine the truths we speak. So it is important to learn the tools of language and structure that make our messages

---

3. See thoughts regarding the "necessities and capacities of the hearers" in the *Westminster Larger Catechism,* question 159. Relevant discussion of *logos, pathos,* and *ethos* appears in chap. 1 of the author's *Christ-Centered Preaching: Redeeming the Expository Sermon,* 2nd ed. (Grand Rapids: Baker Academic, 2005); hereinafter CCP. Chaps. 4 and 6 of CCP deal primarily with issues of organization and structure.

fire the imagination, illumine understanding, and glow in memory. But again, these effects—as desirable and helpful as they may be—are not our chief concern. The ultimate goal of the sermon is not to create fascination, inform the mind, or impact memory but rather to confront the mind and heart with biblical truth in order to conform the will of the hearer to the purposes of Christ. Our preaching should not be judged primarily by what people sense, learn, or remember from the sermon but by how they live in the wake of our message.

The preacher's obligation to *transform* as well as *inform* should compel us to ensure that our sermons are instruments of empowering grace and conduits for needed truth. My concern for excavating principles of grace from all Scripture has an intensely personal origin. The inadequacies of my preaching were torturing me, and I wondered whether I should leave the ministry. I could not figure out what was wrong. Church members complimented my preaching, but their lives were consistently plagued by depression, addictions, and anger with each other. I had to question, "If I am such a good preacher, then why are the people I serve doing so badly?" Ultimately, I determined that a central reason for their despair, their escapist compulsions, and their judgmental impatience with one another was a pattern of thought that I was unintentionally encouraging.

Preaching God's Whole Counsel

The pattern of thought that I reinforced was not immediately apparent to me because I believed that my preaching was faithful to the commands of God's inerrant Word. The same Bible that attests to my Savior's virgin birth, sinless life, substitutionary atonement, physical resurrection, Great Commission, and sovereign rule also calls God's people to holiness. I knew that I could not embrace all that is dear to me in God's Word without also embracing its commands. So I preached the whole counsel of God as I understood it.

Week after week, I told the imperfect people in my church to "do better." But this drumbeat for improvement, devoid of the encouragements and empowerments of grace, actually undermined the holiness that I was seeking to exhort. When God's people hear only the imperatives of the Word, they are forced to conclude that their righteousness is a product of their efforts. There are only two possible reactions to such preaching: despair or pride. Some will reason, "I will never meet God's requirements," leading them to hopelessness; others will assert, "I have measured up to what God requires—at least, compared to other people," leading to spiritual arrogance and intolerance.

Preaching the Redemptive Context

I recognized that these reactions were symptoms of spiritual sickness, but I did not know the cure. I had to learn that the remedy was preaching not less of Scripture but more. In particular, I needed to learn to preach each text in its redemptive context. Paul writes in Romans, "For whatever was written in former days was written for our instruction, that through endurance and through the encouragement of the Scriptures we might have hope" (Rom. 15:4). Scanning the scope of the law and the prophets, the apostle is able to say that all Scripture was intended to give us hope. All Scripture has a redemptive purpose. None of the Scriptures are so limited in purpose as to give us only moral instruction or lifestyle correction. Paul says that even the law itself functions as our "schoolmaster to bring us unto Christ" (Gal. 3:24 KJV). Jesus also says that the law and all the prophets testify about him (see Luke 24:27; John 5:39).

We will call into question the accuracy of these sweeping claims of Paul and Jesus if we think of messianic revelation only in terms of direct statements about the person of Christ. Vast portions of both the Old and New Testaments make no explicit mention of Christ. Even the prophetic books that predict the coming Messiah contain much material that does not have Jesus as the direct subject. Christ surely knew this; Luke records the Savior's postresurrection teaching about himself: "And beginning with Moses and all the Prophets, he explained to them what was said in all the Scriptures concerning himself" (Luke 24:27 NIV). How can Jesus offer such exposition, and by corollary require such exposition from us, if the text does not make direct reference to him?[4]

The apostle Paul helps us answer that question in his discussions of how the law of God reveals dimensions of the Bible's redemptive hope. Though Paul never denies the importance, rightness, or necessity of obedience, he explains that through the law he died to the law. That is to say, the righteous requirements of the holiness of God that were always beyond his grasp signaled the death of hope in human

---

4. See CCP, 275–76.

achievement for spiritual life. The moral instruction of a holy God revealed that no one was capable of holiness by his or her own efforts. Our best works are judged but filthy rags in the Old Testament (Isa. 64:6), and the Savior echoes, "So you also, when you have done everything you were told to do, should say, 'We are unworthy servants; we have only done our duty'" (Luke 17:10 NIV).

The same law that reveals the requirements of God's holiness also reveals the inescapable reality of our unholiness. Because of "the great disproportion" between our best works and God's righteousness, we are always and forever incapable of the righteousness that would reconcile us to a holy God.[5] This hardly seems a redemptive message. And it would not be were it not for the alternative it demands.

By exposing the holy nature of the God who provides redemption and by exposing the finite nature of humanity that requires redemption, the law points to the necessity of a Redeemer and prepares the human heart to seek him. The law, however, is only one aspect of Scripture that helps reveal the person and work of Christ without making explicit mention of him.

Christ-centered exposition of Scripture does not require us to unveil depictions of Jesus by mysterious alchemies of allegory or typology; rather, it identifies how every text functions in furthering our understanding of who Christ is, what the Father sent him to do, and why. The goal is not to make a specific reference to Jesus magically appear from every camel track of Hebrew narrative or every metaphor of Hebrew poetry (leading to allegorical errors) but rather to show how every text contributes to the unfolding revolution of the grace of God that culminates in the person and work of Christ.

Such an interpretive approach will always take the preacher to the heart of the Redeemer by requiring discernment of the progressive and ever-present revelation of God's sovereign grace throughout Scripture. Discerning the gracious character of God in his revelation also rescues our theology from abstraction. By consistently preaching about the God who traverses the universe he created in order to redeem his creatures by his blood, we become relationally bound to the reality of a living and loving Lord.[6] Our listeners become so bound as well—truly linked to God in heart rather than being proud of thoughts or practices that they feel distinguish them from others who are less informed or less good.

5. WCF, XVI.5.
6. Sidney Greidanus, *Preaching Christ from the Old Testament: A Contemporary Hermeneutical Method* (Grand Rapids: Eerdmans, 1999), 54.

Discerning the Redemptive Context

A primary approach to discerning the redemptive nature of a biblical text is identifying how the passage *predicts*, *prepares* for, *reflects*, or *results* from the person and work of Christ.[7] Part Two of this book provides examples of sermons that take one or more of these approaches to a biblical text. Each of these approaches is a version of biblical theology, employing redemptive-historical methods of interpretation.

Redemptive-historical methods seek to identify how a passage from any portion of Scripture furthers our understanding of what Christ has done or will do in redemptive history. Prophecies obviously *predict* Christ and explain much of what he will do. The temple sacrifices predict what Christ will do but also typologically *prepare* the people of God to understand the nature of the atoning work of the Savior. The relationship of Hosea and Gomer not only prepares the covenant people to understand how God will love Israel despite her sin but also *reflects* the need for and nature of God's pardoning mercy in all ages. Our ability to seek that pardoning mercy at the throne of grace is a *result* of our great High Priest going before us to prepare the way and to make petitions in our behalf.

Dead Ends and Bridges

The preceding four categories of redemptive-historical explanation are not—and should not be—rigidly segregated. Our goal is not to make every passage fit neatly into a human category of interpretation. Instead, preachers bear the greatest expository fruit when they understand that what they are seeking to expose are gospel truths that signal and apply God's work of redemption in Christ.

Entire epochs and genres of Scripture are designed by the Holy Spirit to reveal dimensions of grace that will ultimately be accomplished and applied in Christ.[8] These broad aspects of Scripture may contain multiple expressions of redemptive revelation, including information about paths that do not lead to spiritual safety. For example, the period of the judges not only reveals the power of divine aid; it also demonstrates the folly of seeking to do what each person finds acceptable in his own eyes to maintain a covenant people. The kingship

---

7. See *CCP*, 282–88.

8. Sidney Greidanus, *The Modern Preacher and the Ancient Text: Interpreting and Preaching Biblical Literature* (Grand Rapids: Eerdmans, 1988), 166.

of Israel similarly demonstrates the folly of depending on human leaders to establish a righteous rule for the covenant people. The Old Testament takes us down many such redemptive *dead ends* for the purpose of turning us from human to divine dependence.[9]

By way of contrast, some aspects of Scripture function as redemptive *bridges* that allow the covenant people to progress in their understanding of redeeming grace. For example, the Lord's calling and preservation of the diminutive nation of Israel serves as a perpetual statement that God's mercy is extended not just to the strong, capable, and deserving (Deut. 7:7). The provision of the manna in the wilderness, as well as the provision of the prophets of the Word, helps all subsequent generations remain confident in God's provision of living bread—his Word (John 6:35; 1 Cor. 10:3, 16). No single account reveals all that needs to be known, but each account bridges chasms in human understanding until the highway of salvation leading to Christ is complete.

Again, these categories of dead ends and bridges should not be rigidly maintained. The temple sacrifices are, on one level, a dead end in that they demonstrate that the blood of bulls and goats could never fully atone for sin (Heb. 10:1–4). Yet, at another level, the sacrificial system is also a bridge to understanding what God did later for the nations through the Lamb of God (Heb. 10:5–9). The primary reasons to be aware of these differing categories are so that (1) we will *not* try to make every portion of Scripture a positive expression of grace; sometimes God saves by saying, "Don't go down this path!," and (2) we will *not* try to make a passage a final statement of God's salvation plan, if it is only a bridge.

Sermon examples in Part Two of this book will also show how biblical passages can function as redemptive dead ends and/or bridges in order to lead us to a fuller understanding of Christ's necessity and purpose. Highlighting these purposes is not meant to exclude other insights. Passages can be classified in numerous ways that help relate the many varieties of Scripture passages to the person and work of Christ.[10] The goal is not to determine a master metaphor that will provide a proper niche for all passages. Such pigeonholing of texts typically limits the implications of the Bible's own rich variety of metaphors that are used to relate redemptive truth (e.g., kingdom, family, Sabbath, tree). What we should not lose sight of among

9. See *CCP*, 305–6.
10. Edmund P. Clowney, *The Unfolding Mystery: Discovering Christ in the Old Testament* (Phillipsburg, NJ: P&R Publishing, 1988), 9–16.

the many legitimate possibilities for redemptive interpretation is the necessity of exposing the grace of God that all Scripture is designed to help us see.[11]

Macro- and Micro-Interpretations

We should always observe biblical texts through spectacles containing the lenses of these two questions: How is the Holy Spirit revealing in this text the nature of God that provides redemption? And how is the Holy Spirit revealing in this text the nature of humanity that requires redemption? As long as we use these lenses, we will interpret as Christ did when he showed his disciples how all Scripture spoke of him.

Asking these two questions (or using these two lenses) maintains faithful exposition and demonstrates that redemptive interpretation does not require the preacher to run from Genesis to Revelation in every sermon to expound a text's redemptive truths. While there is nothing wrong with such macro-interpretations, it is also possible—and often more fruitful—to identify the doctrinal statements or relational interactions in the immediate text that reveal some dimension of God's grace. The relational interactions in such micro-interpretations can include how God acts toward his people (e.g., providing strength for weakness, pardon for sin, provision in want, faithfulness in response to unfaithfulness) or how an individual representing God provides for others (e.g., David's care for Mephibosheth, Solomon's wisdom recorded for others less wise).[12] Examples of both macro- and micro-redemptive interpretation will be provided in Part Two of this book.

Fallen Condition (Divine Solution) Focus

In essence, redemptive exposition requires that we identify an aspect of our fallen condition that is addressed by the Holy Spirit in each passage, which he inspired for

---

11. Jonathan Edwards proposes such an approach in his "Letter to the Trustees of the College of New Jersey," saying, "The whole of it [Christian theology], in each part, stands in reference to the great work of redemption by Jesus Christ" as the "*summum* and *ultimum* of all the divine operations and decrees." See Clarence H. Faust and Thomas H. Johnson, eds., *Jonathan Edwards* (New York: American Book, 1935), 411–12.

12. See CCP, 306–8.

our edification, and then show God's way out of the human dilemma.[13] Identification of an appropriate fallen condition focus (FCF) will occur in each sermon of this book. Attention to such a pattern in Scripture not only exposes the human predicament that requires God's relief but also forces the preacher to focus on a divine solution. Our salvation rests in God's provision. God's glory is always the highest purpose of the sermon. The vaunting of human ability and puffing of human pride vanish in such preaching, not because imperatives of the law of God are minimized, but because God is always the hero of the text.[14] He enables our righteousness, pardons our unrighteousness, and provides our strength rescuing us from our human dilemma.

Preaching the Grace of Holiness

This consistent preaching of the dimensions of God's grace does not render superfluous the commands of the law but honors their authority by providing the biblical motivation and enablement necessary for our obedience. However, the fear that the regular preaching of grace will lead to antinomianism is sometimes justified. The human heart is more than capable of abusing grace as a means of excusing sin. Those who come from a legalistic background often overcompensate for their gospel-weak past by launching into law-deaf pastimes. Still, despite this danger, there is no legitimate alternative to preaching the grace that underlies all biblical testimony. Such preaching defines grace not as the world does (a license to do as I please) but as the Bible teaches (a mercy so overwhelming that it compels me to do what pleases God).[15]

Grace-based preaching does not eliminate the moral obligations of the law. In the example sermons of this book, both the explanation and the application of texts will include appropriate use of the imperatives of Scripture. We need to remember that the Bible's standards for our attitudes and behaviors reflect the character of God and are provided for our good and his glory. The preaching of grace should not negate the law but provide an antidote for pride in its performance and an incentive for conscientiousness in its observance.[16]

13. See *CCP*, 48–52 and 299–305.
14. See *CCP*, 289–95.
15. J. I. Packer, *Rediscovering Holiness* (Ann Arbor, MI: Vine Books, 1992), 75.
16. *Westminster Shorter Catechism*, question 1; *Westminster Larger Catechism*, questions 32, 97, 168, 174, 178; *Heidelberg Catechism*, questions 1, 2, 32, 86; WCF, XVI.2; XIX.6, 7; XX.1; XXII.6.

Motivating Holiness by Grace

The motivating power of grace becomes evident in Christ's words, "If you love me, you will keep my commandments" (John 14:15). Because the redemptive interpretation of Scripture leads to sermons marked by consistent adulation of the mercy of God in Christ, people who hear such preaching are continually stoked with more fuel to love God.[17] Such inflamed love becomes the primary motivation for Christian obedience, ethics, and compassion as hearts respond with fervor for the purposes of the Savior they love.[18]

For the believer, there is no greater spiritual motivation than grace-stimulated love—not fear or guilt or gain (though each of these can have secondary roles in God's motivation hierarchy if they are not separated from love).[19] As our love results in discipleship that demonstrates the beauty and blessing of walking with God, greater love for God grows and stimulates even more desire for loving him, his purposes, his creation, and his people.

The Bible recognizes no definition of grace that excuses sin, encourages moral license, or creates disregard for the needs of others. The burning love for God ignited by the consistent preaching of grace makes those in whom the Spirit dwells want to walk with God and follow the commands that please him. This is why the apostle Paul could say that the grace of God "teaches us to say 'No' to ungodliness and worldly passions" (Titus 2:12 NIV). When grace is properly perceived, the law is not trashed; it is treasured.

In grace-based preaching, the rules do not change; the reasons do.[20] We serve God *because* we love him, not *in order* to make him love us. After all, how could production or presentation of filthy rags—which is the status of our best works before a holy God (Isa. 64:6)—make him love us? The grace of Christ releases us from the performance treadmill that (falsely) promises to provide holiness through human effort. The effect on the heart is love that compels us to please him (2 Cor. 5:14). For this reason all of the sermon examples in this book will

17. See the author's *Holiness by Grace: Delighting in the Joy That Is Our Strength* (Wheaton: Crossway, 2001), 154; and *CCP*, 321.

18. Thomas Chalmers, "The Expulsive Power of a New Affection," in *History and Repository of Pulpit Eloquence*, ed. Henry C. Fish, vol. 2 (New York: Dodd, Mead, 1856), 326. See also Walter Marshall, *The Gospel Mystery of Sanctification* (1692; repr., Grand Rapids: Reformation Heritage, 1999).

19. Chapell, *Holiness by Grace*, 29–31; *CCP*, 320–23.

20. *CCP*, 312.

attempt to expose grace in a way that stimulates greater love for God and, as a consequence, greater obedience to him.

Consistent focus on the grace of God does not automatically create disdain or disregard for God's standards. Rather, his overwhelming and unconditional mercy that ensures "there is now no condemnation for those who are in Christ Jesus" (Rom. 8:1 NIV) is the kindness that leads to repentance (Rom. 2:4). When we are deeply touched with the greatness of this kindness through consistent preaching of the grace that is throughout Scripture, then we love God more. As a consequence, we *want* to turn from the sin that grieves the One we love (Eph. 4:30). Our affections, though still flawed and still capable of wandering, are transformed (Rom. 8:5–15). The heart that once found pleasure in sin now only finds peace, satisfaction, and joy in the presence and purposes of the Savior.

Motivating Holiness by the Cross

The primary message that stimulates such compelling love is the cross of Christ. Contemporary theologians may wince at such statements about Christ's atoning sacrifice because they may seem to slight the resurrection, second coming, and other key redemptive events. It is certainly true that without the resurrection the cross would have signaled nothing but a gory death on a distant hill. The victory over sin accomplished by the resurrection and the vindication of righteousness promised in the consummation are vital truths for perseverance in Christian faithfulness. Still, when Paul wrote to the Corinthians that he resolved to preach nothing among them but Christ crucified (1 Cor. 2:2), he reflected a profound understanding of humanity. The Father's matchless gift of the life of his Son and Jesus's selfless offering of himself stir the human heart at its deepest levels to make it tender toward God, receptive of his Word, and responsive to the Spirit.

The old preaching imperative "make much of the blood" reflects great wisdom about human motivation. The cross stimulates love for God, the resurrection zeal for his purposes, and the second coming perseverance in his cause. All are necessary, but God's mercy toward the undeserving—as it unfolds through Scripture and culminates in the cross—is still the message that programs the heart to receive and employ all the other truths of the gospel.

The primary reason we must preach the grace of God from all the Scriptures is not so that we will master an interpretive skill or even produce correct exegesis. Biblical theology practiced merely as a science of interpretation encourages theological debate and spiritual pride as we strive to find and exhibit the golden thread that will unite all Scripture under a dominant theme (e.g., kingdom, covenant, creation-fall-redemption-consummation, family). Such themes undeniably aid our perceptions of the structure of Scripture, but the true goal of redemptive preaching is to expound the ways in which God progressively and consistently shows dimensions of his mercy in all ages so that we will understand Christ's sacrifice more fully and, consequently, love him more.[21] Any practice of biblical theology that does not have this relational aim is misdirected.[22] Thus, all of the example sermons in the pages that follow seek to reveal dimensions of God's provision that will stimulate greater love for him.

If stimulation of love for God seems inappropriate as a primary goal for preaching, then we have not fully considered the primary goal of our lives. Our "chief end," said the great leaders of the Reformation, is "to glorify God, and to enjoy him."[23] Without a profound love for him, we can do neither. Love for him leads us to seek him, serve him, repent to him, and return to him. All the requirements of love for God find their impulse at the cross. From there radiate many implications and imperatives, but still the cross is the center for the heart seeking God.

Enabling Holiness by Union with Christ

Christ's victory on the cross provides freedom from both the guilt and power of sin. The apostle Paul reminds us that, because Jesus resides in us, we possess the resurrection power that raised Jesus from the dead (Gal. 2:20; Eph. 1:18–23). John adds, "He who is in you is greater than he who is in the world" (1 John 4:4). This is more than a promise that Jesus will add to our strength or aid our resolve. Because we are in union with Christ, all of the merits of his righteousness have become ours, and his Spirit now enables us to resist the sin that he reveals to us.[24] In the terms of classic theology, once we were not able not to sin (*non posse non*

---

21. Geerhardus Vos, "The Idea of Biblical Theology," a pamphlet form of Vos's inaugural address upon assuming the new chair of biblical theology at Princeton Seminary (a copy in the Covenant Theological Seminary Library, n.d., ca. 1895), 16. This address in elaborated form became the introduction of Vos's *Biblical Theology* (1948; repr., Grand Rapids: Eerdmans, 1975).

22. Graeme Goldsworthy, *Preaching the Whole Bible as Christian Scripture: The Application of Biblical Theology to Expository Preaching* (Grand Rapids: Eerdmans, 2000), 92–96.

23. *Westminster Shorter Catechism*, question 1.

24. Chapell, *Holiness by Grace*, 52–63, 140–43.

peccare), but now we are able not to sin (*posse non peccare*).[25] Enough of the influence of our sin nature persists that we will not perfectly perform his will until we are with Jesus in eternal glory when we will be not able to sin (*non posse peccare*), but even now we are freed from Satan's lie that we cannot change. Sin has no more dominion over us (Rom. 6:14–18). We can make progress against the besetting sins of our lives because we are alive in Christ—whose resurrection power indwells us.

The release of sin's guilt *and* the reception of Christ's benefits are required content for messages that preach a complete gospel of grace. Sometimes preachers preach only a partial gospel, indicating that the debt of our sin has been paid by the suffering of Christ (i.e., his passive righteousness). This is a glorious and precious truth for all Christians who know their need of forgiveness. Yet even if our debt has been paid, it is still possible to live with a sense of inadequacy and humiliation because of our sin. It is as though we recognize that our debt has been paid, but though we are grateful, our spiritual math still indicates that we have only a zero-sum balance: Christ's death on our behalf makes us feel guilty and small, rather than free of debt.

To counter such feelings, we need to understand the full benefits of the gospel, which are ours by virtue of our union with Christ. Yes, we have been freed of our debt, but we also have been supplied with Christ's righteousness (resulting from his active and passive righteousness). Before God, we are already accounted as heirs of heaven, coheirs with Christ, and children of God (Rom. 8:16–17). This adoption signals our worth and preciousness to God prior to our entry into heaven. So sure is our status and so rich is our righteousness that our heavenly Father already considers us holy and pleasing to him (Rom. 12:1) and has already seated us in heavenly places (Eph. 2:6). Because we are in union with Christ, his status is ours (1 Cor. 1:30; 2 Cor. 5:21; Gal. 2:20). Though we are striving with the power of Christ's Spirit to overcome sinful thoughts and acts in our lives, God has already reckoned us holy by his grace embraced through our faith. This positional sanctification gives us the foundation for our progressive sanctification (Heb. 10:14).[26] The security we have in heaven provides the foundation we need to resist the assaults of Satan on earth. These concepts are so key, and so often missing in evangelical preaching, that they are a special focus of the messages in Part Three of this book.

---

25. John Murray, *Principles of Conduct: Aspects of Biblical Ethics* (Grand Rapids: Eerdmans, 1957), 216–21.

26. See the author's *In the Grip of Grace: When You Can't Hang On: The Promises of Romans 8* (Grand Rapids: Baker, 1992), 54–58; and Jerry Bridges, *The Discipline of Grace: God's Role and Our Role in the Pursuit of Holiness* (Colorado Springs: NavPress, 1994), 108.

Preaching the Indicatives of the Gospel

Part Three will also focus on the relationship between the indicatives of our relationship with Christ (*who we are* as redeemed persons) and the imperatives for
the Christian life (*what we are to do* as those called from darkness into his marvelous light). The indicatives of the gospel assure us of God's love and strengthen us
for his purposes despite our present weaknesses. The imperatives identify God's
purposes and the standards we must follow in order to fulfill them.

The power of the indicatives of the gospel results when believers understand
that we are not waiting to enter heaven to claim the benefits of God's grace. The
future reality of sinless perfection awaits us in glory, but we already possess its
status through the certainty of the promises of God and the guarantee of the
Spirit in us (2 Cor. 5:5). We are already dearly loved children (Eph. 5:1), robed
in Christ's righteousness (2 Cor. 5:21), by faith counted holy before God (1 Pet.
2:9), and indwelled by his Spirit (Rom. 8:11).

The mark of that Spirit in us is not the absence of sin in our lives but the presence
of new desires and new power to overcome temptation (Rom. 8:5–15). When
we weep over our sin, we may question if the power of the Spirit is real in us. But
in a wonderful confirmation of our status as new creatures in Christ, the grief we
feel for sin is the assurance of our ability.[27] Before the Spirit filled us, our hearts
were—and could only be—hostile to God. But now when we sin, we hate it. The
hatred of sin and godly sorrow for its expression are the evidence of the Spirit in
us and of heaven before us. Were not the Spirit in us, there could be no sorrow
for sin (other than the sorrow of consequences). But when we truly grieve that
our sin has grieved the Spirit, trampled on the blood of our Savior, and offended
our heavenly Father, then we evidence a heart renewed by the Spirit and made
able by him to resist sin.

Preaching the Imperatives of the Gospel

Hatred of sin, freedom from past guilt, possession of Christ's righteousness and
power, and assurance of future grace combine to equip Christians for the holy
race God calls us to run (Heb. 12:1). However, it is important to remember that

27. Chapell, *In the Grip of Grace*, 32–37.

all of these truths rest on the person and work of Jesus Christ. There will be no progress in the Christian life without the past, present, and future grace of our Lord. Jesus said, "Apart from me you can do nothing" (John 15:5). No sentence in Scripture better underscores the need for Christ-centered preaching. The grace of God that is ultimately revealed in Christ frees us from our guilt and enables us to obey. Preaching that seeks to issue imperatives (what to do) from a biblical text without identifying the indicatives of the gospel (who we are by grace alone) to which the text points robs listeners of their only source of power to do what God requires.[28]

No one can serve God apart from Christ. A message full of imperatives (e.g., "be like [a commendable Bible character]"; "be good [by adopting these moral behaviors]"; "be disciplined [by diligence in these practices]") but devoid of grace is antithetical to the gospel. These "be messages" are not wrong *in* themselves; but *by* themselves they are spiritually deadly because they imply that we make or break our relationship with God by our works.[29]

When we preach a biblical imperative in isolation from grace, we take what should be a blessing and make it deadly for the soul. The imperatives of the law are good and nourishing for the Christian life only to the extent that grace motivates and empowers their fulfillment.[30] Without a foundation of grace, sermons on holiness will only sink hearers' souls into the quagmires that surround human inadequacy.

We must remember that even our best works deserve God's reproof unless they are sanctified by Christ.[31] God delights in our good works only when they are presented to him in Christ.[32] This means that even if we do not mention Jesus by name in the explanation of a text, we must show how the text reveals aspects of his grace in order to provide hope that the obligations of the text can be fulfilled.[33] Just as the necessity of a Christ-focus in all preaching is indicated by Jesus's words, "Apart from me you can do nothing," so also the power of such a focus is indicated in Paul's words, "I can do all things through him who strengthens me" (Phil. 4:13).

28. Herman Ridderbos, *Paul: An Outline of His Theology*, trans. John Richard de Witt (Grand Rapids: Eerdmans, 1975), 253.

29. *CCP*, 289–95.

30. John Calvin, *Institutes of the Christian Religion*, II.7.i–iii and ix.

31. *WCF*, XVI.5.

32. *WCF*, XVI.6.

33. *CCP*, 303.

The necessity and sufficiency of grace for power to obey God are dominant themes in the example sermons of Part Three of this book.

Keys to Enabling Power

Christian preaching must consistently proclaim the grace of God because in helping God's people to love him we also enable them to serve him. The final emphasis of Part Three is exploration of the relationship between the motivations and the enabling power of application. In *Christ-Centered Preaching* I indicate that sermons should help listeners to answer four questions about a biblical text's application to their lives:

1. What am I to do?
2. Where am I to do it?
3. Why am I to do it?
4. How am I to do it?

Preachers often focus only on questions 1 and 2. Christ-centered preaching gives equal importance to questions 3 and 4. Question 3 is important because doing the right things for the wrong reasons is wrong. If I practice spiritual disciplines to bribe God for his favor, the disciplines are good but my motive makes my practice of them abhorrent to God. Question 4 is important because telling people what to do without telling them how is cruel. If my sermon admonishes people to correct bad behavior but gives no means or tools for such correction, then I have left people in a hopeless quandary.

Already I have discussed how love for God motivates Christian obedience. Expressing our love for God in response to his grace is the greatest motivation for the Christian.[34] But it is possible to love another and still not be able to express it adequately. Virtually all Christians want to serve God better. We want to withdraw from our addictions, overcome our fears, become more compassionate, offer forgiveness more readily, defeat our weaknesses, and find fresh courage. Our problem is not that we do not want to change but that we do not know how. Key

34. As discussed in *CCP* (322–23) and *Holiness by Grace* (195–97), there are other motivations for obedience, but love for God must remain the motivation of highest priority in order for Christian obedience truly to honor God above all else.

to our enabling with the power of the gospel is understanding that the *why* is the *how*; motivation and enablement unite in the victory of holiness.[35]

Great love for God is also great power for obedience. This is not only because love is necessary for true faith but also because love is power. In order to understand the power of love, we must ask ourselves a critical question: What is the primary reason that sin has power in our lives? Sin's power has already been defeated; we are no longer its slaves. So why do we yield to sin? The ultimate answer is that we love it. If sin had no attraction for us, then it would have no power over us.

We sin because, in the moment and for earthly benefits, we love the sin more than we love the Savior. People who sin but claim that they still love God may not think that they are lying, but in the moment that they sin, they love the sin more than they love God. Such people are no different than an adulterer who says to his wife, "The other woman meant nothing to me; I still love you." The man may still love his wife, but in the moment of the sin, he loved the other person—or at least the passion—more than he loved his wife.

The reality of love for sin, which provides sin's power, leads to a second critical question: What will drive love for sin from our hearts? The answer: a surpassing love. When love for Christ supersedes love for sin, then the attraction of sin is displaced by a desire to honor him.

This answer does not deny that Scripture clearly motivates us with *warnings* that the pleasures of sin are temporary, its consequences are ruinous, and the discipline of God is painful. Additionally, we are told that *rewards* of blessings and peace accompany obedience—although the full blessings may not be experienced in this life, and the peace may be beyond understanding (Rom. 8:18; Phil. 4:7). The warnings and rewards in Scripture are intended to direct us from sin, and we must preach the practical implications of such to be faithful expounders of the whole counsel of God.

We should recognize, however, that warnings and rewards are made effective by self-love; that is, we heed warnings to avoid personal loss, and we pursue rewards for personal gain. God stoops to his children to guide us by such self-affection, but these motivations—as important and right as they are for the saints—cannot be the most important for those whose "first" and "greatest" commandment is to

35. See *CCP*, 323–27.

"love the Lord your God with all your heart and with all your soul and with all your mind and with all your strength" (Mark 12:30 NIV).

There is a reason that love for God is the primary and foundational commandment. Though warnings and rewards dampen our desire for sin, they are not sin's most powerful deterrent. What will cut off love for sin at its source? The answer, again, is a surpassing love. Our love for sin—which provides its present power—is overcome when love for sin is displaced by a greater love. Thomas Chalmers's famous sermon "The Expulsive Power of a New Affection" yet rings true.[36] When love for Christ exceeds all other loves, then the desire to walk with him exceeds all other desires. Thus, Jesus said, "If you love me, you will keep my commandments" (John 14:15). These words of the Savior make it clear that when love for God is our primary motivation, then honoring him is our chief and most compelling desire.

Now we have a final critical question to answer in order to determine the full content of the applications we preach: If love for God is the Christian's primary motivation and power for honoring him, then what will fill our hearts with love for him? The answer: "Amazing grace . . . that saved a wretch like me." He loved me before I knew him. He died for me while I was yet his enemy. He keeps me when I fall. He holds me when I fail. He abides faithful though I am faithless. He forgives me when I am wrong and loves me, loves me still. Such grace fills our hearts with surpassing love for God, which is the power for Christian living because such love displaces love for sin and supersedes love for self with love for the Savior.

The power of grace to stimulate love for God is the ultimate reason we preach redemptive interpretations of Scripture. Sermons marked by consistent adulation of the mercy of God in Christ continually fill the Christian heart with more cause to love God. This love becomes the *primary* motivation and power for Christian obedience, as hearts in which the Spirit dwells respond with love for their Savior. This is why the apostle Paul wrote: "The love of Christ controls us, because we have concluded this: that one has died for all, . . . that those who live might no longer live for themselves but for him who for their sake died and was raised" (2 Cor. 5:14–15).

Our preaching should be designed to fuel a preeminent love for God that makes doing his will the believer's greatest joy (2 Cor. 5:9), knowing this joy is

---

36. Chalmers, *History and Repository of Pulpit Eloquence*.

the strength for fulfilling our responsibilities (Neh. 8:10). Preaching grace fans into flame zeal for the Savior. Thus, emphasizing the grace of all the Scriptures is not simply an interpretive scheme required by the Bible's overarching themes; it is regular exposure of the heart of God to ignite love for him in the heart of believers. We expound the gospel truths that pervade Scripture in order to fill the hearts of believers with delight in service to him, which is the strength of their living for him. Grace leads to godliness because it stimulates love that makes service to the Savior our greatest joy.[37]

Preaching the Power of Joy

The final sermon examples in this book explore the themes of empowering joy. Preaching remains a joy when pastors discern that their task is not to harangue or guilt parishioners into servile duty but rather to fill them up with love for God by extolling the wonders of his grace. Too many preachers leave ministry or become ineffective in it because they perceive their lot in life to be whipping recalcitrant parishioners into more diligent service. Of course, preaching must condemn sin and challenge the slothful, but without the context of love such ministry becomes a burden to all—including the minister. There is a better way to preach.

The better way always connects Scripture's commands with the motivation and enablement of grace. Imperatives do not disappear from such preaching because the commands of God are an expression of his nature and of his care for us. Still, the imperatives are always founded on the redemptive indicatives that give people confidence in God's faithfulness even in the face of their failures. We discourage people from basing their justification on their sanctification (i.e., determining if they are right with God based on the quality or quantity of their religious performance), and instead encourage them to live in the assurance of the completed work of Christ in their behalf.[38]

When our people perceive the present value of the blood of Christ, which unites them to him, then they serve God with growing confidence in his blessing and power rather than with increasing dread of, or callousness to, his frown. Those who know that their forgiven status and family position are not jeopardized by the

---

37. Chapell, *Holiness by Grace*, 107–9; and *CCP*, 326.
38. Richard F. Lovelace, *Dynamics of Spiritual Life: An Evangelical Theology of Renewal* (Downers Grove, IL: InterVarsity, 1979), 101.

xxviii   Introduction

weaknesses of their present humanity live in loving service to Christ rather than in self-justifying competition and judgment of others.[39]

Consistent preaching of the gospel's assurances drives despair and pride from the Christian life. As a consequence, congregations find that spiritual fatigue, competitiveness, and insensitivity wane; in their place flow new joy in Christ, desire to make him Lord over the whole of life, understanding of the weak, care for the hurting, forgiveness for those who offend, and even love for the lost. In short, the Christian community becomes an instrument of grace because God's love becomes the substance of the church's soul. In such contexts, ministers thrive and their ministries become a blessing to all (including themselves and their families) rather than a burden. Without question, there will also be challenges and disappointments, but even these will not destroy the joy that God builds on a foundation of grace.

The necessity of grace for preaching that is true to the gospel leads to a basic question that all must answer in order to affirm that they are preaching the Christianity of the Bible: "Do I preach grace?" Would your sermons be perfectly acceptable in a synagogue or mosque because you are only encouraging better moral behavior that any major religion would find acceptable?[40] If this is so, the path to a better, more Christian message is not through preaching any less of Scripture but through preaching more. Do not stop preaching until Christ has found his place in your sermon and his grace has found its way into the heart of your message. In this way, the people to whom you preach Christ-centered sermons will walk with him, and his joy will be their strength to do his will.

---

39. Francis Schaeffer, *True Spirituality* in *The Complete Works of Francis A. Schaeffer*, vol. 3 (Westchester, IL: Crossway, 1982), 200; and *The God Who Is There* (Downers Grove, IL: InterVarsity Press, 1968), 134.

40. Jay Adams, *Preaching with Purpose: A Comprehensive Textbook on Biblical Preaching* (Grand Rapids: Baker, 1982), 152.

Part One

Structure

꙳꙳꙳꙳꙳꙳꙳꙳꙳꙳꙳꙳꙳꙳꙳꙳꙳꙳꙳꙳꙳꙳꙳꙳꙳꙳꙳꙳꙳꙳꙳꙳꙳꙳

Organizational tools that help communicate biblical truths predominate the early chapters of my book *Christ-Centered Preaching*, and the sermon examples in Part One of this companion volume highlight these tools. These examples feature both formal and informal structures, along with comments about techniques that will help listeners understand and remember messages.

Expository Sermon in Formal Structure Format

This first example sermon introduces the formal wording and structure of sermons constructed according to classical standards as described in chapter 6 of *Christ-Centered Preaching*.[1] The example contains many notations, format identifiers, and footnotes that function as instructional commentary. This "extra" commentary makes the sermon appear unusually long, but the actual preaching content is that of a traditional thirty- to thirty-five-minute sermon.[2]

The principles and suggestions introduced in this sermon are meant to serve as instructive examples. No one should employ all of these standards all of the time, but informed preachers will have enough knowledge of them to use those most appropriate for the text and task at hand. Just as a musician practices scales to develop the skills for more nuanced compositions, preachers who have knowledge and mastery of these basic components of sermon structure are best prepared to alter, adapt, mix, or reject them in order to take the approach most appropriate for their particular text, congregation, and circumstance.

1. Bryan Chapell, *Christ-Centered Preaching: Redeeming the Expository Sermon*, 2nd ed. (Grand Rapids: Baker Academic, 2005); hereinafter *CCP*.
2. For the typical length of components of a traditional thirty-minute message, see *CCP*, 350–51.

These structural components are the working tools of experienced preachers. My goal in presenting them is to outfit the tool bag of starting preachers. In later examples we will alter the use of these tools and explore new techniques, but for now the goal is to create familiarity with the "hammer and nails" of traditional sermon construction. The reason for starting with the basics is simple: it is very unusual to find a skilled preacher who does not have a working knowledge of standard sermon components such as introductions, propositions, main points, illustrations, applications, and conclusions.

Natural talent and instinct are certainly sufficient for some preachers of special gifting. But for most of us, slowing down long enough to learn these tools of our trade is the wisest approach, though it may seem constraining at first. The finest craft usually will come from those who best know their materials, tools, and options, even though they will not expect to use them all in every project.

This first sermon is *expository*, meaning that it explains a particular passage of Scripture by clarifying the main and subordinate ideas of the author in the context of the biblical passage and by applying these spiritual truths to our contemporary situations. The approach is *deductive*, meaning that it moves from the development of general principles to the statement of particular applications (*inductive* sermons move in the opposite direction). The text itself is from a *didactic* (i.e., teaching through thought development) portion of a New Testament epistle. Later we will explore other approaches to other types of biblical literature (e.g., historical narrative, prophecy, poetry).

Proclaim His Word

2 Timothy 4:1–5

[Note: Words in brackets below are *not* said out loud but are shown here to indicate how various sermon components are used as a traditional sermon progresses.]

[**Announce text**] Please look with me in Scripture at 2 Timothy 4:1–5.[1]

[**Scripture introduction**][2] Paul's second letter to Timothy was written near the end of the apostle's life. Realizing that he must pass the baton of his ministry, Paul gives this charge to Timothy, a young minister who is facing many of the same questions and fears we will face as ministers today.[3]

[**Reannounce and read text**] Read with me these words of equipping from 2 Timothy 4:1–5. [The preacher reads the Scripture passage out loud.]

[**Prayer for illumination**] Pray with me as we ask God to guide us in the study of his Word. [The minister offers a brief prayer asking the Holy Spirit to bless the understanding of the preacher and hearers as God's Word is proclaimed.]

---

1. I wish to express my thanks to former students Rev. John Gullet and Rev. Norm Reed for their initial writing and formatting of this example sermon in their seminary days. In years following their graduation from Covenant Seminary, I have continued to edit and modify this work to demonstrate various aspects of formal sermon structure.

2. The nature and aspects of the Scripture introduction are discussed in *CCP*, 249–51.

3. Note that the Scripture introduction includes a brief explanation of the *context* of the text and a brief tie of the themes of the text to our situation in order to *create longing* in the listener for the message that follows. Note that most of the listeners are those training or considering training to become preachers (or their spouses).

[**Introduction**]⁴ As she listened to her neighbor's brazen confession, my mother's worst fears about her friend and neighbor were sadly confirmed. My mother had witnessed a growing relationship with another man that seemed dangerous and inappropriate for this married friend that I will only identify as "Betty." So, to protect her friend and to try, if possible, to correct her, my mother decided she had to say something. Tentative questions of concern were met with surprising candor from Betty. "It's all right," she said. "You don't need to be worried. God has graciously led me to this new relationship. I'll be so much happier with a new husband."

My mother left the conversation shaken by Betty's callous disregard for her marriage. She was sad about Betty's choices but also afraid for her. My mother knew that if Betty continued on her present course, God would not ignore her abandonment of her marriage vows and her abuse of his grace. Ultimately he would **judge**⁵ the **sin**. Betty needed to hear the correction of God's **Word**, as well as the grace he offers to those who repent. The hard question with which my mother wrestled was this: "How can I warn my friend that God **judges sin** and yet provide her with hope in the help he offers?" As that wrestling continued internally, my mother confessed later that she struggled to say anything externally.

How would you respond in such a situation? My mother's account reminds us that an opportunity to proclaim the truths of God's **Word** can arise at any time. For his **purposes**, God continually places us in situations in which we can help others by carefully and faithfully applying the **Word** of God. But *most of us struggle to speak up with clarity and conviction when God calls us to this **purpose** despite our knowledge that God will **judge*** [**FCF**].⁶ Questions about what to say and how to say it silence us. But we can overcome our hesitations by learning from Paul's charge to proclaim God's Word in 2 Timothy chapter 4 [**Scripture bond**].⁷ Instead of making God's **judgment** a cause for question, Paul makes it a source for motivation, indicating that . . . [the preacher now states the following proposition]

4. The content and structure of a formal sermon introduction are discussed in *CCP*, chap. 9.
5. The boldface indicates how key words of both phrases of the sermon's proposition appear in the introduction to ready the ear of the listener for the concepts and terms that will capture the major themes of the message.
6. The fallen condition focus (FCF) is a negative aspect of the human condition that the truths of the passage will address with biblical instruction and the hope of the gospel. The preacher typically states the FCF (or burden of the text) in the introduction so the listeners know the specific struggle the sermon will address (and will long for corresponding application). See *CCP*, 48–54 and 240–43.
7. For description of the Scripture bond component of the sermon introduction, see *CCP*, 244.

[**Proposition**][8] Because God will **judge sin**, we must **proclaim** his **Word** for the **purposes** he intends.

Paul first gives a solemn context for the purposes of proclaiming God's Word. He writes to Timothy in verse 1, "I charge you therefore before God and the Lord Jesus Christ, who will judge the living and the dead at His appearing and His kingdom."[9] Everything we do is "before God and the Lord Jesus Christ, who will judge."[10] In light of the divine oversight of the One who will hold everyone accountable, Paul urges the proclamation of God's Word for these purposes: <u>to rescue the needy</u>, <u>to defend the truth</u>, and <u>to fulfill our duty</u>.[11] First Paul tells us that . . .

[**Main point 1**] Because God will judge sin,[12] we must proclaim his Word to rescue the needy.[13]

People's needs vary, so Paul's instruction for the proclamation of God's Word varies accordingly as the apostle addresses the needs of those <u>who do not believe</u> God's Word, those <u>who do not obey</u> God's Word, and those <u>who have lost confidence</u> in God's Word.[14]

[**Subpoint 1**] How should we approach those who do not believe God's Word? We should convince them.[15]

8. For discussion of the reasons for and content of a formal sermon proposition, see *CCP*, 143–49.

9. Unless otherwise indicated, Scripture quotations in this sermon are from the New King James Version.

10. With this contextualization, the preacher is also establishing the proof or truth of the "anchor clause" of the proposition and main points. Such establishment typically happens just before or after the proposition; in this case it occurs both before and after (see *CCP*, 150).

11. Key phrases from all of the sermon's main points are used here as a "billboard" to indicate the major thought divisions that are coming in the remainder of the message. For a further explanation of "billboards," see *CCP*, 264–65.

12. In this formally worded main point, the anchor clause remains consistent (unchanging) with the anchor clause of the proposition to signal the ear of the listener that the proposition's main theme will now be developed. For discussion of the structural components (e.g., anchor and magnet clauses) of formal main points, see *CCP*, 135–43 and 149–51.

13. The magnet clause of the main point changes the *key terms* of the parallel clause in the proposition to indicate specifically how the theme of the proposition will develop in this main point. These key-term changes draw the attention of the listener to the new thought development they indicate and thus also are the focus of the subpoints. The subpoints support and/or develop the thought of the magnet clause. For discussion of the types (e.g., analytical-question responses, interrogatives, bullets) of subpoints, see *CCP*, 156–61.

14. Note the billboard that also occurs after the statement of the main point to prepare the listener for the coming subpoints. Billboards are *not* needed in every main point (and always using them would be tedious for the listener), but they are frequently helpful (see *CCP*, 264–65).

15. The subpoints under this main point are worded as interrogatives. Each successive question sets up an answer containing the key words and concepts that will be proven or supported from the biblical text.

Paul says to Timothy in verse 2, "Preach the word! Be ready in season and out of season. Convince, rebuke, exhort, with all longsuffering and teaching." The first task listed that those proclaiming God's Word should "be ready" to do is "convince." Paul has just reminded Timothy in verse 16 of chapter 3 that "all Scripture is given by inspiration of God, and is profitable for doctrine, for reproof, for correction, for instruction in righteousness." Scripture has this divine and authoritative character because it is God's means to rescue sinful people from the judgment to come. The God who will judge sin also mercifully provides the gospel whose truths redeem those who believe it. Therefore, Paul gives the highest priority to using Scripture—the Word inspired by God—to convince others of its truths.

Such convincing may require us to explain the meaning or defend the credibility of God's Word. These matters almost always require great patience and careful teaching, so Paul further reminds Timothy that he must be prepared to convince others, "with all longsuffering and teaching." In other words, convincing others requires our reflecting to them the same patience and care God exhibited in redeeming us. Those who do not believe God's Word must be convinced by those of us to whom he has revealed his truth and in whom his truth now lives.

But not only the unconvinced need the proclamation of the gospel.

> [**Subpoint 2**] How should we approach those who do not obey God's Word? We should **rebuke** them.

There are those who know but do not obey. Those who believe the right things can still fall into error. In verse 2 Paul also tells us how to respond to these people. There he instructs, "rebuke" with "longsuffering and teaching." Rebuking involves identifying wrongdoing as being wrong. There are times when we must confront others and tell them directly to stop disobeying or distorting or even denying God's Word. As Jesus says in Luke 17:3, "If your brother sins against you, rebuke him; and if he repents, forgive him."

Not every wrong needs rebuke all the time—"love will cover a multitude of sins" (1 Pet. 4:8)—but rebuke must be in the arsenal of faithful proclaimers of God's Word. When people ignore the clear teaching of the Word, we must be

---

The answer comes immediately after the interrogative and then is proven and developed in the explanation of the text that follows. The answer also holds the key word(s) of the subpoint that will be the focus of this main point's illustration and application.

willing to warn them of the consequences of continuing down the wrong path. If God did not love his children, he would not warn them of the dangers of their sin. Yet because he does love, God does warn, and he uses faithful proclaimers of his Word to warn others through rebuke that is intended to rescue them from the horrible consequences of unrepented sin.

[*Transition*] Some are unconvinced, some do not obey—Paul has addressed how to deal with each of these—but some also wander because they have lost confidence in the truths of God's Word.

> [**Subpoint 3**] How should we approach those who have lost confidence in God's Word? We should **exhort** them.

Paul continues in verse 2 by commanding Timothy to "exhort, with all long-suffering and teaching." People need to understand the importance, as well as the content, of what God's Word requires. To "exhort" them means to urge them with the counsel of God's Word to act upon the hope and strength that Christ offers. Our exhortation should direct God's people to the assurances and "teaching" they need in order to do what he requires, even if it seems difficult. Paul tells us in 2 Corinthians 12:9 that God himself exhorted the apostle in a time of trial by saying, "My grace is sufficient for you, for My strength is made perfect in weakness."

Because Jesus will judge humankind, we must proclaim God's Word to those who need to be **convinced**, to those who need to be **rebuked**, and to those who need to be **exhorted**.[16]

[*Illustration*] The Cuban Resettlement Camp in Key Largo, Florida, was abuzz one morning. There were almost eight hundred Cuban refugees in the camp, and they all seemed to be anticipating someone's imminent arrival. As the next busload of refugees from the Key West site arrived, seven older gentlemen in wheelchairs at last departed from the buses. The crowd, which normally was loud and exuberant at the arrivals' newfound freedom, was silent and reverent, while at the same time extremely attentive to the needs of these seven. These were the seven prisoners of conscience who never denied their faith in Jesus Christ. The first three were arrested for street preaching in the main park of Havana in the early 1960s, and

---

16. The summary of the explanation prior to the illustration uses the key terms of *all* the preceding subpoints, since the illustration illustrates them *all*. If the illustration were only for one of the subpoints, then the summary would include the key terms of only that particular subpoint. The use of illustrations is discussed in chap. 7 of *CCP* (esp. 194 and 197).

the others were arrested for openly carrying their Bibles across that same park as a signal to others of an underground church meeting.

For their faith these seven endured decades of imprisonment and brutal torture, which had left them crippled and disfigured. Despite multiple broken bones, they refused to renounce their Savior and to swear allegiance to the atheistic communist regime. In the following weeks, the camp officials noticed that these seven would hold religious services every morning, afternoon, and evening in which many would be **convinced**[17] of their sins upon hearing the gospel message for the first time. The seven also openly **rebuked** the sins of individuals with firmness, confidence, and love as they gave instruction on the keys of the Christian life through the study of the Word. But the most impressive acts of these seven involved the **exhortation** they provided in others' times of weakness and despair. The seven had learned such faithful ministry in their Cuban prison. There, through both silent suffering and open rejoicing in God's grace, these men of faith had **exhorted** many who had lost hope. They also **exhorted** each other with reminders of God's promises when anyone felt weak, as well as rejoiced when anyone felt the strength of God coursing through them.

These seven, who had every right to be bitter, were rejoicing that they had been counted among the body of Christ in a Christless land and that they were now free again to proclaim the Word of God to a searching people through words and actions that **convinced, rebuked**, and **exhorted**. The devotion of these men to one another and their commitment to helping others understand God's Word display well the faithfulness that God desires of us to rescue the needy.

[Application] We who would proclaim God's Word to needy persons must also become able handlers of the tools of **convincing, rebuking**, and **exhorting**.[18]

If we really want to **convince** others to honor God's Word, then we must faithfully encourage one another to remember that we live in the presence and sight of God and that, as his children, we are to live by the standards of his Word. Such proclamation does not only have to be the responsibility of professional ministers—in

17. Key terms of the subpoint statements "rain" down into the illustration. This term consistency makes it obvious that the illustration focuses on the concepts of the subpoints. For the nature and importance of "expositional rain," see *CCP*, 197 and 224–25.

18. Key terms of the subpoint statements also "rain" down into the application (application is discussed in chap. 8 of *CCP*). This term consistency makes it obvious that the preacher is applying what the message proved the text was about (and not extraneous ideas), thus giving the application relevance to the text and authority from the text.

fact, it should not only be the responsibility of pastors. Those of you who still are in secular college settings may already have a great opportunity to be involved in a ministry of proclaiming God's Word. Not only are the opposition and temptations you face daily on a college campus much easier to overcome when you become involved in Christian fellowship, but by being so involved you also help **convince** others that faithfulness is possible in such a challenging environment.

Such **convincing** may not result simply from the life you live. You do not have to be on a secular campus long to know that Christianity is often openly opposed by professors and students. When the truth of God is challenged in your classes, God may call you to **convince** those challengers of their error. If you find yourself puzzled and doubting, seek out fellow believers who can **convincingly** help you answer the false ideas with which you are being bombarded. Sometimes you may feel isolated and strange because of your beliefs. It is times like these when you may need to find those who can also **exhort** or even **rebuke** you. I don't say this to be harsh, but rather to acknowledge that all of us can be tempted to despair or apathy in the face of opposition to God's Word. We need God's Word, and we need each other to be faithful proclaimers of its truth.

But college students aren't the only ones who are called to faithful proclamation of God's Word.[19] All of us, whether we are at home, at church, or at work, are called to the same concern—because we are called to care for others who need God's Word. When a friend in your small group falls into sin that he or she will not acknowledge, you must be willing lovingly to **rebuke**. Husbands and wives, when your spouse is discouraged and weighed down with children's tasks or distasteful work or a crazy schedule, you must be there lovingly to **exhort** and encourage with God's Word. When the coworker with whom you have been sharing the gospel expresses doubts about the Christian faith, you must be ready, with the Holy Spirit's help, to **convince** them of the reasons for the hope that you have. We have many opportunities to proclaim God's Word to needy people, and knowing that we live before God and the Lord Jesus Christ, who will judge them and us, will motivate us strongly to proclaim God's Word in accord with God's purposes.

[**Transition**] Just as there are situations in which we must be prepared to **convince**, **rebuke**, and **exhort** for the sake of those who need the truth, the apostle

---

19. The college student example provided a concrete application for the truths previously explained. Now the preacher "unrolls" other application examples more briefly to indicate that the truths of this main point also apply to other people and situations. For a discussion of unrolling application, see *CCP*, 224–27.

Paul also challenges us to be prepared to defend God's Word for those who have embraced falsehood.[20]

[**Main point 2**] Because God will judge sin, we must proclaim his Word to defend the truth.[21]

 [**Analytical question**] When must we defend the truth?[22]

[**Subpoint 1**] When others **abandon sound doctrine**.

At the beginning of verse 3, Paul warns Timothy about a reaction some people will have to the proclamation of God's Word: "For the time will come when men will not put up with sound doctrine." Paul addressed the core problem of turning away from truth in Romans chapter 1 while writing about the nature of the ungodly. Paul says, "They exchanged the truth about God for a lie" (v. 25 NIV). The prophet Isaiah wrote similarly concerning those who abandon the truth in chapter 30, verse 10, saying, "They say to the seers, 'See no more visions!' and to the prophets, 'Give us no more visions of what is right!' Tell us pleasant things, prophesy illusions" (NIV). This consistent theme across the Scriptures should alert us that in all ages there is great temptation to turn from truth to lies that temporarily seem more satisfying. Our day is no different, and because God wants to prepare us to proclaim his Word, he has warned us in advance that many people will not respond faithfully. We, therefore, must be prepared for people to abandon sound doctrine.

Being prepared for people to abandon what is sound requires us to anticipate others teaching what is false. Therefore, we must also defend the truth . . .[23] [With this transition that echoes the analytical question before subpoint 1, continue to the statement of the next subpoint.]

[**Subpoint 2**] When others **honor false teachers**.

20. These few lines of transition *review* what has been said previously and *preview* what comes next. For a further explanation of transitions, see *CCP*, 262–65.

21. In this formally worded outline, the second main point maintains the wording of the proposition's anchor clause and indicates new focus by the changes in key terms in the magnet clause.

22. The following subpoints are set up by a single analytical question that each will answer in turn.

23. The essential wording of the opening analytical question reappears as transition, setting up each subsequent subpoint and conceptually tying the whole main point together.

Paul continues in verse 3 by saying, "Instead, to suit their own desires, they will gather around them a great number of teachers to say what their itching ears want to hear" (2 Tim. 4:3 NIV). In Matthew 24:5, Jesus also indicates this can happen by saying, "For many will come in my name, claiming, 'I am the Messiah,' and will deceive many" (NIV). We all love teachers who tell us what we want to hear and who make us feel good about ourselves by not requiring us to question beliefs or practices with which we have grown comfortable. Many people flock to one type of teacher or another because that person makes them feel happy or satisfied with themselves. Because people are apt to listen to such things, there is never a lack of false teachers.

Not only must we defend the truth when others abandon sound doctrine and when others honor false teachers, but also . . .

[**Subpoint 3**] When others **will not even listen**.

Paul tells Timothy in verse 4, "They will turn their ears away from the truth" (NIV). In the midst of this passage where Timothy is being encouraged to preach the Word in every situation, Paul writes to him honestly of those who will not listen at all. Yet, though they may not even listen, Paul still commands Timothy to preach the Word.

Luke describes such a situation in Acts chapter 17 where a mob forms against Paul in Thessalonica and then follows him to Berea. Those in Berea were willing to search the Scriptures to see if what Paul was saying about the Christ was true. But the mob from Thessalonica and those in Berea who were influenced by them were unwilling to listen, regardless of what Scripture said and regardless of Paul's proclamation. The circumstances were challenging but not so hard as to dissuade Paul from going on to proclaim God's Word at his next stop, Athens—where, again, some would listen and some would not.

Such accounts remind us that though others may **abandon what is sound**, **honor what is false**, and "turn their ears away from the truth" so as **not even to listen**, we still have an obligation to "preach the Word."[24]

[*Illustration*] As he stood before the church court on the afternoon of April 18, 1521, Martin Luther was asked one question: "Will you recant of your writings

---

24. Note again the summary of key terms of all the subpoints, preparing for the illustration that uses them all.

and the errors which they contain?" After spending the night in prayer, searching for the right thing to say, he answered, "Unless I am convicted by Scripture and plain reason—I do not accept the authority of popes and councils, for they have contradicted each other—my conscience is captive to the Word of God. I cannot and I will not recant anything, for to go against conscience is neither right nor safe. Here I stand, I cannot do otherwise. God help me. Amen." Martin Luther believed the Word of God required him to stand for the truth even in such a difficult situation. He knew that though others might **abandon sound doctrine,**[25] he must stand firm. While his human judges had the power to excommunicate, exile, or even execute him, he knew the Judge in heaven would declare the most important verdict. Thus, Luther said, "My conscience is captive to the Word of God." Luther believed that the church had succumbed to honoring **false teachers,** and knowing that they very probably would **not even listen,** he still answered his accusers by saying, "Here I stand." He viewed himself as ultimately responsible only to a divine Judge, and it motivated him to remain faithful to proclaim God's Word in the most challenging of situations. You and I have a very similar calling in this day and age when truth is "relative" to most people and "tolerance" for so many kinds of evils is encouraged. Defending the truth in our day can be dangerous to our friendships, reputations, and careers, but we too should stand in our day, knowing that one day we will stand before the One who judges the living and the dead.

[*Application*] Paul wrote this letter to a young pastor in Ephesus, a major city of Greco-Roman culture that was filled with many false religions and philosophies. But the words still apply as directly to us as they did to Timothy. Every day we are faced with spiritual challenges, and we must regularly decide whether we will defend the truth. Certainly Paul's warnings apply to the challenges we face from false religions around us and doctrinal battles in the church. But the challenges to spiritual truth are not limited to the "religious" realms of our world.

In the business world there can be pressure from every side to **abandon doctrinally sound ethics** because they are supposedly the "old-fashioned" way of doing things. Numerous well-publicized examples of scandals among corporations with formerly solid reputations make it clear that "whatever it takes to succeed" was recently the ethic guiding entire companies—even entire industries. Whether dealing with the need to show a profit, the hiring and firing of employees, or simply gaining

---

25. Key terms of the subpoints "rain" into the illustration for term and concept consistency.

the approval of peers, believers in the workplace often find themselves in situations in which unethical behavior is not only overlooked but expected. Christians may find themselves working for supervisors who **will not even listen** to alternatives. In these situations we must not succumb to the herd mentality that **honors false teachers** with their vain assurances of easy success because "Everyone is doing it" or "It's necessary." The battle for faithfulness to God's Word is not as often fought in grand church councils as it is in daily work decisions.

In a culture of pervasive ethical compromise, rising above the current tide of **abandoned truth** has become difficult in every avenue of life. From the corporate executive who is offered a handsome bonus if she will look the other way on a shady deal, to the student who is encouraged by his peers to cheat on the big exam. From the church official asked to fudge on enrollment numbers, to the fifth grader urged by friends to download bootlegged music. How many heads would turn and mouths hang wide open if in those situations Christians were to say, "I can't do this because to do so would violate the Word of God"? I will not tell you that such a proclamation of God's Word will meet with everyone's approval. I cannot promise you that others **will even listen**. But I can promise you that God will be honored by those who stand for him, and there will be souls safe in eternity because they have witnessed sacrificial faithfulness that is a beacon of truth. Knowing this, may you and I be motivated to say with Martin Luther, "'My conscience is captive to the Word of God,' and I will stand for the truth **even when others do not listen**."

[**Transition**] The Lord has definitely given us a challenge in the words of Paul by calling us to defend the truth. But the apostle doesn't stop there. He goes on to tell us *how* to do this task. Paul reinforces his commands by reminding us that . . .[26]

[**Main point 3**] Because God will judge sin, we must proclaim his Word to fulfill our duty.[27]

And how does the apostle Paul say that we are to fulfill our duty? By **being watchful**, by **enduring affliction**, and by **doing the work of an evangelist**.[28]

---

26. This transition between main points does not use the classic "not only . . . but also . . ." language, but the conceptual progression is the same—i.e., reviewing past concepts and setting up those that will follow.

27. In this formally worded outline, the third main point maintains the wording of the proposition's anchor clause and indicates new focus by the changes in key terms in the magnet clause.

28. Here an analytical question sets up a billboard of the following subpoints that will be presented as bullet statements in the development of the third main point.

[**Subpoint 1**] We must be **watchful**.

In verse 5 Paul commands Timothy to be watchful. The apostle writes, "But you, keep your head in all situations" (NIV). The literal meaning is to "be sober" or to "be clearheaded." Paul commands us not to lose our focus or composure but rather always to be watchful for both opposition and opportunities that would affect our fulfillment of Christ's purposes. In his letter to the Colossians, Paul similarly writes,

> Devote yourselves to prayer, being watchful and thankful. And pray for us, too, that God may open a door for our message, so that we may proclaim the mystery of Christ. . . . Be wise in the way you act toward outsiders; make the most of every opportunity. Let your conversations be always full of grace, seasoned with salt, so that you may know how to answer everyone. (Col. 4:2–6 NIV)

So be clear in your thinking, not distracted or overly distressed by your circumstances, so that you may be watchful for the gospel opportunities God is providing. God gives his people many different kinds of opportunities to make his truth known. People may ask you questions such as, "How can you be so joyful? How can you have such hope in the midst of such difficulty? Why don't you take the shortcuts that others do? Why do your children obey you? Why do you so honor your spouse?" If you walk with Jesus, there are many ways that you will stand out in this fallen world. So if you are watchful, God will use the questions others have about you to tell them about him.

[*Illustration*] About three years ago, God allowed me the opportunity to get to know someone who was indeed always **watchful**—a man who wonderfully fulfilled his duty of proclaiming God's Word to the lost.[29] His name was Chuck. He was an older gentleman in my church who began Bible studies in his home. He would teach anyone who would listen. He taught me many things about God's Word in those studies, but probably the greatest thing he taught me was the importance of **watching** for opportunities to share Jesus Christ with others. He was always **watching** for someone who did not know about God's grace so that he could tell them about it.

About a year ago Chuck was diagnosed with cancer. It spread quickly, and within a few short months he found himself lying in a hospital, waiting to die. But even

---

29. In this third main point, the illustration is moved higher to separate it from the conclusion's illustration (as discussed in *CCP*, 258). Note also that the illustration is only about the first subpoint, so the only key terms that "rain" into the illustration are from that subpoint alone.

in that difficult situation, even in the midst of his pain and this terrible physical challenge, he was sober-minded about the opportunities God was providing. He remained **watchful** for gospel opportunities. He discovered that some of the nurses who continually came to check on him were not believers. So he patiently and lovingly shared God's Word with them. Chuck died just a few weeks later. But two of the nurses who had cared for Chuck and had heard him talk so openly about his faith came to a saving faith in Jesus Christ. Just as Chuck was always **watchful** to see how he might meet challenges to the gospel and how he might make the most of opportunities for the gospel, so we too must also be **watchful**. But God may require more than watchfulness of us, even as he required more of my friend, Chuck.

Not only must we be watchful, but also like Chuck . . .

[**Subpoint 2**] We must be willing to **endure hardship**.

Continuing in verse 5, Paul writes, "Endure afflictions." This must be one of Paul's most personally challenging commands. Remember the setting of this letter: the apostle is in prison, bound in chains, and waiting to be executed. Paul knew all about afflictions. In 2 Corinthians 11, Paul writes, "Five times I received from the Jews forty lashes minus one. Three times I was beaten with rods, once I was pelted with stones, three times I was shipwrecked. . . . I have been in danger from rivers, in danger from bandits, in danger from my fellow Jews, in danger from Gentiles. . . . I have known hunger and thirst and have often gone without food" (2 Cor. 11:24–27 NIV). All for the sake of the gospel!

Now, you may think, "I really don't plan on being stoned or shipwrecked." Yet in 2 Timothy 3:12 Paul writes, "In fact, everyone who wants to live a godly life in Christ Jesus will be persecuted" (NIV). It's a guarantee and a promise. You will suffer hardships and afflictions if you live for Christ. But recall verse 2 in our passage. God has given us his Word—the very words he breathed out. The same breath of wisdom and love that breathed life into the original man also provided and pervades God's Word, so that we might always have the wisdom and love of God to encourage us. We are able to endure in ministering God's Word not only because it represents his truth but also because it reflects his character. God ministers to us the reality of who he is as we minister his Word to others. Thus, by proclaiming God's Word, the power of his Spirit and the realities of his Son invade our circumstances, embrace our hearts, and strengthen our wills for the work that must be done. This shouldn't surprise us because the spiritual reality is that when we proclaim the Word of God, the living Word—Christ himself—is present ministering to us by his Spirit and truth.

When my friend Chuck was dying of cancer, he felt that he was best able to proclaim God's Word to the nurses at the hospital. This wasn't just because he knew heaven was near for him. Rather, through Chuck's ministering the truths of Christ, the Lord also became more powerful and present to him. Chuck's afflictions had stripped away the temporary comforts of this world, so the truths of the Word became even more dear to him. And as he proclaimed those truths with greater love, they also became more real to him, making his witness to others even more powerful. Perhaps this is why Paul waits until after telling us to endure hardship to let us know the last duty of faithful proclaimers of God's Word: doing the work of an evangelist.

[**Subpoint 3**] We must **work as evangelists**.

In the remainder of verse 5 Paul writes, "Do the work of an evangelist, discharge all the duties of your ministry" (NIV). You may not think of yourself as an evangelist. But when you share with a lost friend the way Jesus encourages you and comforts you in times of trouble, you are indeed engaged in evangelism. When you talk to a coworker while playing racquetball at the gym about how God has radically changed your life and your marriage, you are engaged in evangelism. When you tell your child, "Jesus loves you," you are engaged in evangelism. Such engagements are in God's plan and purpose. He calls us to make the most of every opportunity. People's souls are at stake. Jesus will judge all people, but he extends his mercy through us to others. God's Word has the amazing power to change eternity for those who believe its truths. We must proclaim these truths so that Christ's message may be heard and believed. This is more than our duty; it is the privilege of being colaborers with Jesus in the eternal salvation of those who are in danger of hell apart from him.

[*Application*] The application of these verses is probably obvious for those in church ministry occupations. I hope that there are other implications that are now becoming clear for every believer. For example, some of you are stay-at-home moms, and your days often seem completely chaotic: chasing children around the house, running endless errands, and doing all sorts of other things that may seem far removed from proclaiming God's Word. But consider the duties you are fulfilling in the apostle Paul's terms. By all the hard work you do to serve your family, friends, and neighbors, you **endure hardship** in service to Christ. By being concerned for their spiritual welfare and taking opportunities to speak of Jesus to friends and to your own children, you **work as an evangelist**. By monitoring the hearts and actions of every person around you to see when a word of testimony, encouragement, or correction should be given, you remain **watchful** for God's opportunities. By ministering in these ways to your family, your children, and your neighbors, you fulfill your duty of proclaiming God's Word in every situation.

In so ministering, you also teach others to do the same. By showing children that God's Word is real and exciting and that it comforts us in the midst of afflictions, you teach them to be **watchful**. By thinking of ways to model Christ's servant heart and to show love to those around you—neighbors, the woman who works at the deli counter, or the person who cuts your family's hair—your children learn the **work of evangelism**, and they may also learn what it means to **endure hardship** while you are there to help them through it.

Such opportunities to fulfill God's purposes exist for us in the myriad situations of life, if we will only remain **watchful**. Moms at home, students at college, those in professional careers—all have the opportunities to **work** and to **endure** for Christ's name. God does not isolate us from others, and we should always be considering the evangelistic opportunities given to us. Who admires you and looks to you for guidance? Who rubs elbows with you? Who enjoys your company? Who does business with you? These people are your responsibility—your duty—because God has put them in your life. Consider how you can share Christ with them. By God's grace and by the power of his Holy Spirit that dwells in you, others will know of him through you!

[Conclusion][30] The just God who judges sin, through Paul, has laid before us a high and holy charge that will require serious commitment from all of us. In his grace, God has called us, motivated us, and enabled us to overcome our fears so that we may proclaim his Word to fulfill his purposes.[31] God has called you to fulfill your duty to speak of him by putting in your heart the concern to proclaim

---

30. For discussion of the nature and content of a conclusion, see *CCP*, chap. 9.

31. Note the terms of this sentence and others in the conclusion echo the terms of the proposition, giving the entire sermon a sense of unity and clear purpose.

the truth to <u>rescue the needy</u> and to <u>defend the truth</u> against those who would deny it to the spiritually needy.[32]

The enabling presence of Jesus has been clearly seen in the difficult situation that my mother faced with her friend Betty.[33] Although my mother is not a naturally gifted evangelist, the Lord has used her to speak the truth faithfully and lovingly to seek to convince Betty to turn from her sin. Over many months, my mother has patiently but firmly exhorted Betty from God's Word. My mother was even bold enough to detail the consequences of Betty's unfaithfulness in the hope that such loving rebuke would turn Betty from her sin. There were times when it was obvious Betty was determined to abandon the truth, and there were times when she would not even listen, but my mother continued to <u>fulfill her duty</u> and to <u>defend God's truth</u> in order to <u>rescue the person in need</u>.

We don't yet know what the final chapter of Betty's story will be. But for now Betty is still with her family, still in her marriage, and still talking to my mother. Though only the Lord knows the full story of Betty's life, another story has already unfolded in the life of my mother. By fulfilling her gospel duties with courage and care, my mother possesses the joy and blessing of a clear conscience toward Betty. In addition, by doing the work of an evangelist, my mother has been strengthened and encouraged to speak God's Word with more confidence than ever before. The gospel has become more real and precious to my mother because the reality of God's judgment has motivated her to share the message of God's grace with her neighbor.

You and I can also know this reality more deeply as we faithfully proclaim God's Word to those in our lives. As we rehearse what God has done for us by sending his Son to rescue us from judgment, his grace becomes fresh motivation to obey him and to speak of him. May this grace now motivate you to be his instrument of salvation in every context in which he places you. Proclaim his Word to fulfill his purposes for your life.

---

32. Key terms of the magnet clauses of the main points reappear in the conclusion to act as a concise summary of the entire message (see *CCP*, 254–55).

33. This sermon concludes with a "wraparound" illustration, finishing the account that began the sermon in order to provide a sense of intended direction, clear purpose, and definite closure (see *CCP*, 259).

Expository Sermon
in Fundamental Reduction Format

This second sermon shows how the formal wording of the proposition and main points in the first sermon of this book can be easily reduced to make them reflect more natural speech. The first step in this fundamental reduction is to make the formal outline's anchor clause (with the "because" or "if/since" term removed) serve as the sermon's proposition.[1] Next, the preacher interrogates this proposition by following it with an analytical question, and then the preacher answers the question with the magnet clause of the first main point, which serves as the entire main point. Successive main points are introduced by repeating this or a similar analytical question that serves as the transition between main points.

If the description of the fundamental reduction sounds too complex in the technical terms of the paragraph above, think of the process in these more basic terms. After the introduction, the preacher makes a strong, succinct statement of the sermon's theme (something like, "God calls his people to serve him in tough times"). This serves as the proposition. Next, the preacher asks a question about that thematic statement that listeners might ask, if they thought they could

---

1. For further discussion of how and why to do fundamental reductions, see the author's *Christ-Centered Preaching: Redeeming the Expository Sermon*, 2nd ed. (Grand Rapids: Baker Academic, 2005), 136–39, 148–49, and 151–55; hereinafter CCP.

(something like, "What kind of tough times will we face?"). Then the preacher answers that question with a series of statements that are the main points (e.g., "God calls us to serve him in times of suffering; . . . in times of loneliness; and . . . in times of attack").

The preacher may re-ask the first question to transition into each of the main points later in the sermon or may, at those later points, ask similar questions that still naturally unfold from the original proposition (such as, "What are the tough times God calls us to face?" and "Why does God call us to face tough times?"). Interrogating the proposition in this way is probably the most natural and common form of sermon progression. Even without formal training, preachers naturally follow this pattern because it reflects natural patterns of conversation.

Since it is simply a rewording of the first sermon, the example sermon that follows is also *expository*. The approach remains *deductive*, and the text is *didactic*.[2]

---

2. For explanations of these terms, see the page at the beginning of the first example sermon in this book.

Proclaim His Word

2 Timothy 4:1–5

[Note: Words in brackets below are *not* said out loud but are shown here to indicate how various sermon components are used as a traditional sermon progresses.][1]

[**Announce text**] Please look with me in Scripture at 2 Timothy 4:1–5.

[**Scripture introduction**] Paul's second letter to Timothy was written near the end of the apostle's life. Realizing that he must pass the baton of his ministry, Paul gives this charge to Timothy, a young minister who is facing many of same questions and fears we will face as ministers today.

[**Reannounce and read text**] Read with me these words of equipping from 2 Timothy 4:1–5. [The preacher reads the Scripture passage out loud.]

[**Prayer for illumination**] Pray with me as we ask God to guide us in the study of his Word. [The minister offers a brief prayer asking the Holy Spirit to bless the understanding of the preacher and hearers as God's Word is proclaimed.]

[**Introduction**] As she listened to Betty's brazen confession, my mother's worst fears about her friend and neighbor were sadly confirmed. My mother had

---

1. This sermon differs from the first example sermon in the changed wording of the proposition and main points. These have been reduced to demonstrate how their wording may be made more natural and colloquial while retaining many of the advantages of formal structure. For explanation of other commentary or notations, please return to the notes for the first example sermon.

witnessed a growing relationship with another man that seemed dangerous and inappropriate for this married friend that I will only identify as "Betty." So, to protect her friend and to try, if possible, to correct her, my mother decided she had to say something. Tentative questions of concern were met with surprising candor from Betty. "It's all right," she said. "You don't need to be worried. God has graciously led me to this new relationship. I'll be so much happier with a new husband."

My mother left the conversation shaken by Betty's callous disregard for her marriage. She was sad about Betty's choices but also afraid for her. My mother knew that if Betty continued on her present course, God would not ignore her abandonment of her marriage vows and her abuse of his grace. Ultimately he would **judge** the **sin**. Betty needed to hear the correction of God's Word, as well as the grace he offers to those who repent. The hard question with which my mother wrestled was this: "How can I warn my friend that God **judges sin** and yet provide her with hope in the help he offers?" As that wrestling continued internally, my mother confessed later that she struggled to say anything externally.

How would you respond in such a situation? My mother's account reminds us that an opportunity to proclaim the truths of God's Word can arise at any time. For his purposes, God continually places us in situations in which we can help others by carefully and faithfully applying the Word of God. But *most of us struggle to speak up with clarity and conviction when God calls us to this **purpose** despite our knowledge that God will **judge*** [**FCF**]. Questions about what to say and how to say it silence us. But we must overcome our hesitations to proclaim God's Word because of the simple point Paul forcefully drives home in 2 Timothy chapter 4 [**Scripture bond**]. Here Paul says . . . [the preacher now states the following proposition]

[**Proposition**] God will **judge sin**.[2]

Paul says this plainly to Timothy in verse 1: "I charge you therefore before God and the Lord Jesus Christ, who will judge the living and the dead at His appearing and His kingdom."[3]

---

2. In this fundamental reduction, the anchor clause (only) of the formally worded proposition and main points becomes the proposition. The magnet clauses of main points become the main point statements and are set up in presentation by transitional questions or statements that include key words/concepts from the anchor clause (which is now the proposition).

3. Unless otherwise indicated, Scripture quotations in this sermon are from the New King James Version.

[**Analytical question**] In light of the certainty of this divine judgment, how should we respond?

[**Billboard**] This passage answers by saying we should proclaim the Word of God. And the apostle also says why: <u>to rescue the needy</u>, <u>to defend the truth</u>, and <u>to fulfill our duty</u>. Let's now consider the first of these obligations that are ours in light of God's judgment.

[**Main point 1**] We must proclaim the Word of God to rescue the needy.

People's needs vary, so Paul's instruction for our proclamation varies accordingly as he addresses the needs of those <u>who do not believe</u> God's Word, those <u>who do not obey</u> God's Word, and those <u>who have lost confidence</u> in God's Word.[4]

[**Subpoint 1**] How should we approach those who do not believe God's Word? We should **convince** them.[5]

Paul says to Timothy in verse 2, "Preach the word! Be ready in season and out of season. Convince, rebuke, exhort, with all longsuffering and teaching." The first task listed that those proclaiming God's Word should "be ready" to do is "convince." Paul has just reminded Timothy in verse 16 of chapter 3 that "all Scripture is given by inspiration of God, and is profitable for doctrine, for reproof, for correction, for instruction in righteousness." Scripture has this divine and authoritative character because it is God's means to rescue sinful people from the judgment to come. The God who will judge sin also mercifully provides the gospel whose truths redeem those who believe it. Therefore, Paul gives the highest priority to using Scripture—the Word inspired by God—to convince others of its truths.

Such convincing may require us to explain the meaning or defend the credibility of God's Word. These matters almost always require great patience and careful teaching, so Paul further reminds Timothy that he must be prepared to convince others "with all longsuffering and teaching." In other words, convincing

4. Note this internal "billboard" serving within a main point to indicate the subpoints that will follow. Such billboarding is not always necessary but can help listeners navigate a complex message.

5. The subpoints under this main point deal only with the wording and concept of the magnet clause that has become the main point in this fundamental reduction. As in the formally worded sermon example, these subpoints are worded as interrogatives. Fundamental reduction of the main points does not change the nature or variety of subpoints that may be used. Also, key words that hold the central idea of the subpoint and that will "rain" into wording of the illustration and application are bold.

others requires our reflecting to them the same patience and care God exhibited in redeeming us. Those who do not believe God's Word must be convinced by those of us to whom he has revealed his truth and in whom his truth now lives.

But not only the unconvinced will face the judgment of God.

> [**Subpoint 2**] How should we approach those who do not obey God's Word? We should **rebuke** them.

There are those who know but do not obey. Those who believe the right things can still fall into error. In verse 2 Paul also tells us how to respond in these situations. There he instructs, "rebuke" with "longsuffering and teaching." Rebuking involves identifying wrongdoing as being wrong. There are times when we must confront others and tell them directly to stop disobeying or distorting or even denying God's Word. As Jesus says in Luke 17:3, "If your brother sins against you, rebuke him; and if he repents, forgive him."

Not every wrong needs rebuke all the time—"love will cover a multitude of sins" (1 Pet. 4:8)—but rebuke must be in the arsenal of faithful proclaimers of God's Word. When people ignore the clear teaching of the Word, we must be willing to warn them of the consequences of continuing along the wrong path. If God did not love his children, he would not warn them of the dangers of their sin. Yet because he does love, God does warn, and he uses faithful proclaimers of his Word to warn others through rebuke that is intended to rescue them from the horrible consequences of unrepented sin.

> [**Subpoint 3**] How should we approach those who have lost confidence in God's Word? We should **exhort** them.

Paul continues in verse 2 by commanding Timothy to "exhort, with all longsuffering and teaching." People need to understand the importance, as well as the content, of what God's Word requires. To "exhort" them means to urge them with the counsel of God's Word to act on the hope and strength that Christ offers. Our exhortation should direct God's people to the assurances and "teaching" they need in order to do what he requires, even if it seems difficult. Paul tells us in 2 Corinthians 12:9 that God himself exhorted the apostle in a time of trial by saying, "My grace is sufficient for you, for My strength is made perfect in weakness."

Because Jesus will judge humankind, we must proclaim God's Word to those who need to be **convinced**, to those who need to be **rebuked**, and to those who need to be **exhorted**.

[Illustration] The Cuban Resettlement Camp in Key Largo, Florida, was abuzz one morning. There were almost eight hundred Cuban refugees in the camp, and they all seemed to be anticipating someone's imminent arrival. As the next busload of refugees from the Key West site arrived, seven older gentlemen in wheelchairs at last departed from the buses. The crowd, which normally was loud and exuberant at the arrivals' newfound freedom, was silent and reverent, while at the same time extremely attentive to the needs of these seven. These were the seven prisoners of conscience who never denied their faith in Jesus Christ. The first three were arrested for street preaching in the main park of Havana in the early 1960s, and the others were arrested for openly carrying their Bibles across that same park as a signal to others of an underground church meeting.

For their faith these seven endured decades of imprisonment and brutal torture, which left them crippled and disfigured. Despite multiple broken bones, they refused to renounce their Savior and to swear allegiance to the atheistic communist regime. In the following weeks, the camp officials noticed that these seven would hold religious services every morning, afternoon, and evening in which many would be **convinced** of their sins upon hearing the gospel message for the first time. The seven also openly **rebuked** the sins of individuals with firmness, confidence, and love as they gave instruction on the keys of the Christian life through the study of the Word. But the most impressive acts of these seven involved the **exhortation** they provided in others' times of weakness and despair. The seven had learned such faithful ministry in their Cuban prison. There, through both silent suffering and open rejoicing in God's grace, these men of faith had **exhorted** many who had lost hope. They also **exhorted** each other with reminders of God's promises when anyone felt weak, as well as rejoiced when anyone felt the strength of God coursing through them.

These seven, who had every right to be bitter, were rejoicing that they had been counted among the body of Christ in a Christless land and that they were now free again to proclaim the Word of God to a searching people through words and actions that **convinced**, **rebuked**, and **exhorted**. The devotion of these men to one another and their commitment to helping others understand God's Word display well the faithfulness that God desires in order to rescue the needy.

[Application] We who would proclaim God's Word to needy persons also must become able handlers of the tools of **convincing**, **rebuking**, and **exhorting**.

If we really want to **convince** others to honor God's Word, then we must faithfully encourage one another to remember that we live in the presence and sight of God and that as his children we are to live by the standards of his Word. Such proclamation does not only have to be the responsibility of professional ministers—in fact, it should not only be the responsibility of pastors. Those of you who still are in secular college settings may already have a great opportunity to be involved in a ministry of proclaiming God's Word. Not only are the opposition and temptations you face daily on a college campus much easier to overcome when you become involved in Christian fellowship, but by being so involved you also help **convince** others that faithfulness is possible in such a challenging environment.

Such **convincing** may not simply result from the life you live. You do not have to be on a secular campus long to know that Christianity is often openly opposed by professors and students. When the truth of God is challenged in your classes, God may call you to **convince** those challengers of their error. If you find yourself puzzled and doubting, seek out fellow believers who can **convincingly** help you answer the false ideas with which you are being bombarded. Sometimes you may feel isolated and strange because of your beliefs. It is times like these when you may need to find those who can also **exhort** or even **rebuke** you. I don't say this to be harsh, but rather to acknowledge that all of us can be tempted to despair or apathy in the face of opposition to God's Word. We need God's Word, and we need each other to be faithful proclaimers of its truth.

But college students aren't the only ones who are called to faithful proclamation of God's Word. All of us, whether we are at home, at church, or at work, are called to the same concern—because we are called to care for others who need God's Word. When a friend in your small group falls into sin that he or she will not acknowledge, you must be willing lovingly to **rebuke**. Husbands and wives, when your spouse is discouraged and weighed down with children's tasks or distasteful work or a crazy schedule, you must be there lovingly to **exhort** and encourage with God's Word. When the coworker with whom you have been sharing the gospel expresses doubts about the Christian faith, you must be ready, with the Holy Spirit's help, to **convince** them of the reasons for the hope that you have. We have many opportunities to proclaim God's Word to needy people, and knowing that we live before God and the Lord Jesus Christ, who will judge them and us, will strongly motivate us to proclaim God's Word in accord with God's purposes.

There are situations in which we must be prepared to **rebuke, convince,** and **exhort** for the sake of **those who need the truth**.

[Analytical question transition] What other obligations are ours in light of the certainty of God's judgment?[6]

[**Main point 2**] We must proclaim the Word of God to defend the truth.

[**Analytical question**] When must we defend the truth?[7]

[Subpoint 1] When others **abandon sound doctrine**.

At the beginning of verse 3, Paul warns Timothy about a reaction some people will have to the proclamation of God's Word: "For the time will come when they will not endure sound doctrine." Paul addressed the core problem of turning away from truth in Romans chapter 1 while writing about the nature of the ungodly. Paul says, "They exchanged the truth about God for a lie" (v. 25). The prophet Isaiah wrote similarly concerning those who abandon the truth in chapter 30, verse 10, saying, "They say to seers, 'See no more visions!' and to the prophets, 'Give us no more visions of what is right!' Tell us of pleasant things, prophesy illusions" (NIV). This consistent theme across the Scriptures should alert us that in all ages there is great temptation to turn from truth to lies that temporarily seem more satisfying. Our day is no different, and because God wants to prepare us to proclaim his Word, he has warned us in advance that many people will not respond faithfully. We, therefore, must be prepared for people to abandon sound doctrine.

Being prepared for people to abandon what is sound requires us to anticipate others teaching what is false. Therefore, we must also defend the truth . . . [With this transition that echoes the analytical question before subpoint 1, continue to the statement of the next subpoint.]

[Subpoint 2] When others **honor false teachers**.

6. Again, the transition returns to the key thought of the proposition to set up the next main point. In this case, the transition is again an analytical question.

7. The following subpoints are set up by a single analytical question that each will answer in turn. Again, since the main point only has the words of the magnet clause, the subpoints are only about that clause.

Paul continues in verse 3 by saying, "Instead, to suit their own desires, they will gather around them a great number of teachers to say what their itching ears want to hear" (2 Tim. 4:3 NIV). In Matthew 24:5, Jesus also indicates this can happen by saying, "For many will come in my name, claiming, 'I am the Messiah,' and will deceive many" (NIV). We all love teachers who tell us what we want to hear and who make us feel good about ourselves by not requiring us to question beliefs or practices with which we have grown comfortable. Many people flock to one type of teacher or another because that person makes them feel happy or satisfied with themselves. Because people are apt to listen to such things, there is never a lack of false teachers.

Not only must we defend the truth when others abandon sound doctrine and when others honor false teachers, but also . . .

[Subpoint 3] When others **will not even listen.**

Paul tells Timothy in verse 4, "They will turn their ears away from the truth." In the midst of this passage where Timothy is being encouraged to preach the Word in every situation, Paul writes to him honestly of those who will not listen at all. Yet, though they may not even listen, Paul still commands Timothy to preach the Word.

Luke describes such a situation in Acts chapter 17 where a mob forms against Paul in Thessalonica and then follows him to Berea. Those in Berea were willing to search the Scriptures to see if what Paul was saying about the Christ was true. But the mob from Thessalonica and those in Berea who were influenced by them were unwilling to listen, regardless of what Scripture said and regardless of Paul's proclamation. The circumstances were challenging but not so hard as to dissuade Paul from going on to proclaim God's Word at his next stop—Athens—where, again, some would listen and some would not.

Such accounts remind us that though others may **abandon what is sound, honor what is false,** and "turn their ears away from the truth" so as **not even to listen,** we still have an obligation to "preach the Word."

[Illustration] As he stood before the church court on the afternoon of April 18, 1521, Martin Luther was asked one question: "Will you recant of your writings and the errors which they contain?" After spending the night in prayer, searching for the right thing to say, he answered, "Unless I am convicted by Scripture and plain reason—I do not accept the authority of popes and councils, for they have contradicted each other—my conscience is captive to the Word of God. I cannot and I will not recant anything, for to go against conscience is neither right nor safe. Here I stand, I cannot do otherwise. God help me. Amen." Martin Luther believed the Word of God required him to stand for the truth even in such a difficult situation. He knew that though others might **abandon sound doctrine**, he must stand firm. While his human judges had the power to excommunicate, exile, or even execute him, he knew the Judge in heaven would declare the most important verdict. Thus, Luther said, "My conscience is captive to the Word of God." Luther believed that the church had succumbed to honoring **false teachers**, and knowing that they very probably would **not even listen**, he still answered his accusers by saying, "Here I stand." He viewed himself as ultimately responsible only to a divine Judge, and it motivated him to remain faithful to proclaim God's Word in the most challenging of situations. You and I have a very similar calling in this day and age when truth is "relative" to most people and "tolerance" for so many kinds of evils is encouraged. Defending the truth in our day can be dangerous to our friendships, reputations, and careers, but we too should stand in our day, knowing that one day we will stand before the One who judges the living and the dead.

[*Application*] Paul wrote this letter to a young pastor in Ephesus, a major city of Greco-Roman culture that was filled with many false religions and philosophies. But the words still apply as directly to us as they did to Timothy. Every day we are faced with spiritual challenges, and we must regularly decide whether we will defend the truth. Certainly Paul's warnings apply to the challenges we face from false religions around us and doctrinal battles in the church. But the challenges to spiritual truth are not limited to the "religious" realms of our world.

In the business world there can be pressure from every side to **abandon doctrinally sound** ethics because they are supposedly the "old-fashioned" way of doing things. Numerous well-publicized examples of scandals among corporations with formerly solid reputations make it clear that "whatever it takes to succeed" was recently the ethic guiding entire companies—even entire industries. Whether dealing with the need to show a profit, the hiring and firing of employees, or simply gaining the approval of peers, believers in the workplace often find themselves in situations in which unethical behavior is not only overlooked but expected. Christians may find themselves working for supervisors who **will not even listen** to alternatives. In these situations we must not succumb to the herd mentality that **honors false teachers** with their vain assurances of easy success because "Everyone is doing it" or "It's necessary." The battle for faithfulness to God's Word is not as often fought in grand church councils as it is in daily work decisions.

In a culture of pervasive ethical compromise, rising above the current tide of **abandoned truth** has become difficult in every avenue of life. From the corporate executive who is offered a handsome bonus if she will look the other way on a shady deal, to the student who is encouraged by his peers to cheat on the big exam. From the church official asked to fudge on enrollment numbers, to the fifth grader urged by friends to download bootlegged music. How many heads would turn and mouths hang wide open if in those situations Christians were to say, "I can't do this because to do so would violate the Word of God"? I will not tell you that such a proclamation of God's Word will meet with everyone's approval. I cannot promise you that others **will even listen**. But I can promise you that God will be honored by those who stand for him, and there will be souls safe in eternity because they have witnessed sacrificial faithfulness that is a beacon of truth. Knowing this, may you and I be motivated to say with Martin Luther, "'My conscience is captive to the Word of God,' and I will stand for the truth **even when others do not listen**."

The Lord has definitely given us a challenge in the words of Paul by calling us to rescue the needy and to defend the truth.

[Analytical question transition] But how does the apostle tell us to do this task in light of God's judgment?[8] The apostle reinforces his previous instructions by reminding us that . . .

[**Main point 3**] We must proclaim God's Word to fulfill our duty.

And how does Paul say that we are to fulfill our duty? By **being watchful**, by **enduring affliction**, and by **doing the work of an evangelist**.

[**Subpoint 1**] We must be **watchful**.

In verse 5 Paul commands Timothy to be watchful. The apostle writes, "But you, keep your head in all situations" (2 Tim. 4:5 NIV). The literal meaning is to "be sober" or to "be clearheaded." Paul commands us not to lose our focus or composure but rather always to be watchful for both opposition and opportunities

---

8. Again, the transition returns to key words and concepts of the proposition to prepare listeners for the final main point. By continuing to tie each main point to the proposition, the preacher unifies the entire message around its central theme.

that would affect our fulfillment of Christ's purposes. In his letter to the Colossians, Paul similarly writes,

> Devote yourselves to prayer, being watchful and thankful. And pray for us, too, that God may open a door for our message, so that we may proclaim the mystery of Christ. . . . Be wise in the way you act toward outsiders; make the most of every opportunity. Let your conversations be full of grace, seasoned with salt, so that you may know how to answer everyone. (Col. 4:2–6 NIV)

So be clear in your thinking, not distracted or overly distressed by your circumstances, so that you may be watchful for the gospel opportunities God is providing. God gives his people many different kinds of opportunities to make his truth known. People may ask you questions such as, "How can you be so joyful? How can you have such hope in the midst of such difficulty? Why don't you take the shortcuts that others do? Why do your children obey you? Why do you so honor your spouse?" If you walk with Jesus, there are many ways that you will stand out in this fallen world. So, if you are watchful, God will use the questions others have about you to tell them about him.

[*Illustration*] About three years ago, God allowed me the opportunity to get to know someone who was indeed always **watchful**—a man who wonderfully fulfilled his duty of proclaiming God's Word to the lost. His name was Chuck. He was an older gentleman in my church who began Bible studies in his home. He would teach anyone who would listen. He taught me many things about God's Word in those studies, but probably the greatest thing he taught me was the importance of **watching** for opportunities to share Jesus Christ with others. He was always **watching** for someone who did not know about God's grace so that he could tell them about it.

About a year ago Chuck was diagnosed with cancer. It spread quickly, and within a few short months he found himself lying in a hospital, waiting to die. But even in that difficult situation, even in the midst of his pain and this terrible physical challenge, he was sober minded about the opportunities God was providing. He remained **watchful** for gospel opportunities. He discovered that some of the nurses who continually came to check on him were not believers. So he patiently and lovingly shared God's Word with them. Chuck died just a few weeks later. But two of the nurses who had cared for Chuck and had heard him talk so openly about his faith came to a saving faith in Jesus Christ. Just as Chuck was always **watchful** to see how he might meet challenges to the gospel and how he might make the most of opportunities for the gospel, so we too must also be **watchful**. But God may require more than watchfulness of us, even as he required more of my friend Chuck.

Not only must we be watchful, but also like Chuck . . .

[**Subpoint 2**] We must be willing to **endure hardship**.

Continuing in verse 5, Paul writes, "Endure afflictions." This must be one of Paul's most personally challenging commands. Remember the setting of this letter: the apostle is in prison, bound in chains, and waiting to be executed. Paul knew all about afflictions. In 2 Corinthians 11, Paul writes, "Five times I received from the Jews forty lashes minus one. Three times I was beaten with rods, once I was pelted with stones, three times I was shipwrecked. . . . I have been in danger from rivers, in danger from bandits, in danger from my fellow Jews, in danger from Gentiles. . . . I have known hunger and thirst and have often gone without food" (2 Cor. 11:24–27 NIV). All for the sake of the gospel!

Now, you may think, "I really don't plan on being stoned or shipwrecked." Yet in 2 Timothy 3:12 Paul writes, "In fact, everyone who wants to live a godly life in Christ Jesus will be persecuted" (NIV). It's a guarantee and a promise. You will suffer hardships and afflictions if you live for Christ. But recall verse 2 in our passage. God has given us his Word—the very words he breathed out. The same breath of wisdom and love that breathed life into the original man also provided and pervades God's Word so that we might always have the wisdom and love of God to encourage us. We are able to endure in ministering God's Word not only because it represents his truth but also because it reflects his character. God ministers to us the reality of who he is as we minister his Word to others. Thus, by proclaiming God's Word, the power of his Spirit and the realities of his Son invade our circumstances, embrace our hearts, and strengthen our wills for the work that must be done. This shouldn't surprise us because the spiritual reality is that when we proclaim the Word of God, the living Word—Christ himself—is present ministering to us by his Spirit and truth.

When my friend Chuck was dying of cancer, he felt that he was best able to proclaim God's Word to the nurses at the hospital. This wasn't just because he knew heaven was near for him. Rather, through Chuck's ministering the truths of Christ, the Lord also became more powerful and present to him. Chuck's afflictions had stripped away the temporary comforts of this world, so the truths of the Word became even more dear to him. And as he proclaimed those truths with greater love, they also became more real to him, making his witness to others even more powerful. Perhaps this is why Paul waits until after telling us to endure hardship to let us know the last duty of faithful proclaimers of God's Word: doing the work of an evangelist.

[**Subpoint 3**] We must **work as evangelists**.

In the remainder of verse 5 Paul writes, "Do the work of an evangelist, discharge all the duties of your ministry" (NIV). You may not think of yourself as an evangelist. But when you share with a lost friend the way Jesus encourages you and comforts you in times of trouble, you are indeed engaged in evangelism. When you talk to a coworker while playing racquetball at the gym about how God has radically changed your life and your marriage, you are engaged in evangelism. When you tell your child, "Jesus loves you," you are engaged in evangelism. Such engagements are in God's plan and purpose. He calls us to make the most of every opportunity. People's souls are at stake. Jesus will judge all people, but he extends his mercy through us to others. God's Word has the amazing power to change eternity for those who believe its truths. We must proclaim it so that Christ's message may be heard and believed. This is more than our duty; it is the privilege of being colaborers with Jesus in the eternal salvation of those who are in danger of hell apart from him.

[*Application*] The application of these verses is probably obvious for those in church ministry occupations. I hope that there are other implications that are now becoming more clear for every believer. For example, some of you are stay-at-home moms, and your days often seem completely chaotic: chasing children around the house, running endless errands, and doing all sorts of other things that may seem far removed from proclaiming God's Word. But consider the duties you are fulfilling in the apostle Paul's terms. By all the hard work you do to serve your family, friends, and neighbors, you **endure hardship** in service to Christ. By being concerned for their spiritual welfare and taking opportunities to speak of Jesus to friends and to your own children, you **work as an evangelist**. By monitoring the hearts and actions of every person around you to see when a word of testimony, encouragement, or correction should be given, you remain **watchful** for God's opportunities. By ministering in these ways to your family, your children, and your neighbors, you fulfill your duty of proclaiming God's Word in every situation.

In so ministering, you also teach others to do the same. By showing children that God's Word is real and exciting and that it comforts us in the midst of afflictions, you teach them to be **watchful**. By thinking of ways to model Christ's servant heart and to show love to those around you—neighbors, the woman who works at the deli counter, or the person who cuts your family's hair—your children learn the **work of evangelism**, and they may also learn what it means to **endure hardship** while you are there to help them through it.

Such opportunities to fulfill God's purposes exist for us in the myriad situations of life, if we will only remain **watchful**. Moms at home, students at college, those in professional careers—all have the opportunities to *work* and to **endure** for Christ's name. God does not isolate us from others, and we should always be considering the evangelistic opportunities given to us. Who admires you and looks to you for guidance? Who rubs elbows with you? Who enjoys your company? Who does business with you? These people are your responsibility—your duty—because God has put them in your life. Consider how you can share Christ with them. By God's grace and by the power of his Holy Spirit that dwells in you, others will know of him through you!

[*Conclusion*] The Lord, through Paul, has laid before us a high and holy charge that will require serious commitment from all of us. In his grace, God has called us, motivated us, and enabled us to overcome our fears so that we may proclaim his Word to fulfill his purposes. God has called you to <u>fulfill your duty</u> to speak of him by putting in your heart the concern to proclaim the truth to <u>rescue the needy</u> and to <u>defend the truth</u> against those who would deny it to the spiritually needy.[9]

The enabling presence of Jesus has been clearly seen in the difficult situation that my mother faced with her friend Betty. Although my mother is not a naturally gifted evangelist, the Lord has used her to speak the truth faithfully and lovingly to seek to convince Betty to turn from her sin. Over many months, my mother has patiently but firmly exhorted Betty from God's Word. My mother was even bold enough to detail the consequences of Betty's unfaithfulness in the hope that such

---

9. Key terms of the fundamentally reduced main points reappear in the conclusion to act as a concise summary of the entire message.

loving rebuke would turn Betty from her sin. There were times when it was obvious Betty was determined to abandon the truth, and there were times when she would not even listen, but my mother continued to <u>fulfill her duty</u> and to <u>defend God's truth</u> in order to <u>rescue this person in need</u>.

We don't yet know what the final chapter of Betty's story will be. But for now Betty is still with her family, still in her marriage, and still talking to my mother. Though only the Lord knows the full story of Betty's life, another story has already unfolded in the life of my mother. By fulfilling her gospel duties with courage and care, my mother possesses the joy and blessing of a clear conscience toward Betty. In addition, by doing the work of an evangelist, my mother has been strengthened and encouraged to speak God's Word with more confidence than ever before. The gospel has become more real and precious to my mother because the reality of God's judgment has motivated her to share the message of God's grace with her neighbor.

You and I can also know this reality more deeply as we faithfully proclaim God's Word to those in our lives. As we rehearse what God has done for us by sending his Son to rescue us from judgment, his grace becomes fresh motivation to obey him and to speak of him. May this grace now motivate you to be his instrument of salvation in every context he places you. Proclaim his Word to fulfill his purposes for your life.

Expository Sermon
in Inductive (Narrative) Format

Deductive sermons approach listeners through the front door, declaring the main truth of the biblical text "up front" in proposition and main points. Inductive and narrative sermons go through the side door, letting listeners discover the truth alongside the preacher through their mutual experience of biblical truth.[1] Inductive and narrative sermons also occasionally approach listeners through the back door, veiling a truth until an ending revelation or ironic twist that gives listeners an "aha!" of self-discovery.

Narrative and inductive sermons remain expository so long as the truths the sermon develops are provable in the biblical text, are developed from the text, and cover the scope of the text. A narrative sermon often parallels the structure of the biblical narrative as the preacher frames each stage (or move) of the message with observations or questions that allow listeners to reflect upon the implications of the text's development (e.g., situation, complication, resolution). Instead of propositions and main points preannouncing the truths of the text, inductive

1. Note that while narrative sermons most often have inductive characteristics, not all inductive sermons are narrative in structure or source. See discussion of inductive and narrative forms in the author's *Christ-Centered Preaching: Redeeming the Expository Sermon*, 2nd ed. (Grand Rapids: Baker Academic, 2005), 162–68; hereinafter *CCP*.

approaches use the elements of experience to help listeners identify with the truths of the text—often through reflecting upon or asking questions about an aspect of the "story" or "experience" the biblical author unfolds.

Rather than developing general principles and deducing particular applications, an inductive sermon begins with the particulars of the text (or the particulars of listeners' similar experience) and leads to general implications. Preachers who have never tried inductive sermons have probably already practiced its techniques in the introductions to their traditional sermons. There the particulars of a story typically lead to the general truths of the proposition. Not only is this approach common to sermon introductions, it echoes ordinary conversation, where we often give examples before making a point. This is Jesus's approach with parables, as distinct from Paul's deductive propositional development. Inductive approaches often help application, while deductive approaches are stronger in argumentation. Each has its place, not only in different sermons, but sometimes in different parts of a single sermon.

The inductive sermon that follows is based on a biblical narrative and also begins our consideration of how we should preach the "exemplars" (i.e., the heroes) of the Bible.[2] A common approach is to identify a hero in the Bible and urge listeners to similar good deeds. The problem with this approach is that there are few real heroes in the Bible. The greatest figures remain terribly flawed, except for One. The Bible does not blush to present the warts of all humanity in all of Scripture because the God of grace does not wait to appear in the New Testament. Throughout the Bible, God demonstrates his saving nature by using people as messed up as David, Abraham, and, in this text, Gideon to bring the message of unmerited grace to equally messed up people such as us.

---

2. See discussion of preaching the heroes of the Bible in *CCP*, 273–80 and 289–91.

Use for the Useless

Judges 6, 7, and 8

[Note: Words in brackets below are *not* said out loud but are shown here to indicate how various sermon components are used as an inductive sermon progresses.]

[**Announce text**] Today we are going to begin our study of Scripture in Judges 7.

[**Scripture introduction**][1] An old *Peanuts* cartoon shows Lucy, Linus, and Charlie Brown lying on the grass and looking at the clouds. "What do you think you see, Linus?" asks Lucy. Linus points at the clouds and answers, "Well, those clouds up there look to me like the map of the British Honduras on the Caribbean. That cloud up there looks a little like the profile of Thomas Eakins, the famous painter and sculptor. And that group of clouds over there gives me the impression of the stoning of Stephen, I can see the apostle Paul standing there to one side." Then Lucy asks, "What do you see in the clouds, Charlie Brown?" Says Charlie, "Well, I was going to say I saw a duckie and a horsie, but I changed my mind."

When we estimate the worth of our ideas or accomplishments by comparing ourselves to others, we can often feel pretty inadequate. That's true not just in a *Peanuts* cartoon; that can be true in the Bible too. We read the great exploits of Bible heroes and wonder if our contributions will amount to anything. The accounts we think were written to make us do big things, instead make us feel small—useless.

---

1. The nature and aspects of the Scripture introduction are discussed in *CCP*, 249–51.

If Bible heroes ever made you feel that way, then today's Scripture is for you. It's the account of Gideon. He's a hero, but don't let that worry you. He may be a lot more like you than you ever imagined.[2]

[**Reannounce and read text**] Read with me Judges 7:1–7, and then we will continue in verses 16–22 to remind ourselves of the great victory the Lord gave Gideon. Later we will also look at some surrounding passages to get the full picture of the *real* nature of this "hero" and the grace he *really* needed. [The preacher reads the Scripture passage out loud.]

[**Prayer for illumination**] Pray with me as we ask God to guide us in the study of his Word. [The minister offers a brief prayer asking the Holy Spirit to bless the understanding of the preacher and hearers as God's Word is proclaimed.]

[**Sermon introduction**][3] In his book *Mourning into Dancing*, Walter Wangerin tells the story of a woman named Gloria who mourns the death of an uncle who is the closest thing to a father she has ever known. When Gloria was a little girl, her uncle went away to war. But before he left, he gave her an Indian Head nickel and told her that if she tucked it in her purse and never lost it, he would come back for it. She did and he did. But now, after he has died, the mature Gloria dreams a childlike dream in which the uncle appears and promises her that he will yet again return for the nickel. He doesn't. And as the months pass, the reality of his permanent departure drives Gloria into a depression of useless passivity. She lets life go by without her.

Her son is affected. He begins to stay out late, sleep in, and skip school. One day he punches out a back window on the house for reasons that he can't explain. The pastor comes over, talks to the boy, and helps him fix the window. Then the minister tries to lift Gloria from her listlessness with conversation and care. She keeps her head down, looking like a delinquent in the principal's office. She won't talk. She won't respond. She knows she's useless—useless in the conversation, useless to her family, useless to herself.

---

2. I would not normally use this long a Scripture introduction, but the length of the Scripture reading and the unexpected turn the sermon will take justify the extra attention given to preparing hearers for the passage's themes.

3. The content and structure of a formal sermon introduction are discussed in *CCP*, chap. 9. The introduction of a deductive and an inductive sermon vary little since both are setting up the theme of the sermon. However, a deductive sermon introduction typically leads to a propositional statement, whereas an inductive sermon introduction often leads to an analytical question.

The pastor senses the uselessness that shames her, and knowing her background, he leans forward and touches her forearm, then speaks of the gospel. "Gloria," he says in essence, "I wish my words were an Indian Head nickel and your heart were a purse, so I could tuck this into you and you would never lose it: God loves you, Gloria. God loves you."

Why would God love her? She's useless. And why say such sappy words to her? They seem useless too. But if you have ever felt useless, you know the assurance of God's love can mean everything to you. That's actually the message in this account of Gideon. He's useless too. But understanding how God uses the useless is really the key to gaining the assurance of God's love that we all need. For those of us who know what it means to feel as useless as Gloria, the story of Gideon is in the Bible.

[**Analytical question instead of a formal proposition**] How does the Bible use Gideon to assure us that God can use the useless?[4]

You won't get the answer if you just focus on the "hero" passage we just read. You have to go back a little in the story to understand what Gideon and God are really dealing with. Gideon is useless. And we begin to understand the dimensions of his uselessness in chapter 6. Look with me there in your Bibles.

Chapter 6 of Judges is really an exposé of the nature of Gideon's nerve.

I. [**Analytical question setting up inductive discussion of first main point**] What do we learn about our "hero's" nerve in this earlier account?[5]

The answer begins to unfold as we get our first glimpse of Gideon. He is threshing wheat in a winepress, when an angel of the Lord appears to Gideon and says, "The LORD is with you, mighty warrior" (6:11–12).[6] Now, you have to get the irony. Normally you thresh wheat in an open area so the wind will blow chaff away. Wine is pressed in an enclosed or sheltered area to keep the dust away. Why is Gideon threshing wheat in a winepress? He's afraid. He's hiding from his enemies. The Midianites have invaded the territory, and Gideon is scared. For the angel to

---

4. An analytical question serves instead of a proposition to indicate the main subject the message will address.

5. The main point statement is substituted by a question, indicating the subject that will be addressed, but not yet declaring a biblical principle until the story unfolds enough to disclose that idea. Thus, this portion of the sermon leads to a main point statement rather than declaring it up front.

6. Unless otherwise indicated, Scripture quotations in this sermon are from the New International Version.

call this cowering wheat thresher "mighty warrior" is roughly akin to going to a teenage cook at McDonalds and saying, "Greetings, great chef." The situation belies the title. Gideon is no mighty warrior. *Gideon's fears are obvious.*[7]

What else do we learn about Gideon's nerve in this account?

Despite Gideon's obvious unsuitability for service, the angel says, "The LORD is with you, mighty warrior." Gideon answers, "Pardon me, my lord . . . but if the LORD is with us, why has all this happened to us?" Gideon reacts to God's assurance by questioning its truth. And he is going to ask more questions: "Where are all his wonders that our ancestors told us about when they said, 'Did not the LORD bring us up out of Egypt?'" But the questions are not the worst sign of his fear. The questions are followed by an accusation: "But now the Lord has abandoned us and given us into the hand of Midian" (v. 13).

Showing patience and restraint, the one whom Scripture now describes as the Lord himself tries a second time to put some iron into Gideon's backbone: "Go in the strength you have and save Israel. . . . Am I not sending you?" (v. 14). Gideon's response: "Pardon me, my lord . . . but how can I save Israel? My clan is the weakest . . . and I am the least in my family" (v. 15). Translation: "Here am I. Send somebody else!" Gideon's responses to God's assurances are first questions, then accusations, and finally, evasion. Gideon's fears are not just obvious; *Gideon's fears are offensive.*[8]

And that's not the end of what we will learn about Gideon's usefulness as a warrior. *What else do we learn in this account about Gideon's nerve?*

The Lord responds to Gideon's offensive fear by promising, "I will be with you, and you will strike down all the Midianites" (v. 16). And how does "mighty warrior" respond to this? He says in essence, "Prove it" (v. 17). Remarkably, God does so. The angel of the Lord brings fire from a rock to consume an offering of Gideon's and then disappears (v. 21). Pretty good sign!

Then the angel of the Lord appears to Gideon again and, as a warm-up for greater battles ahead, tells Gideon to stand for the Lord among his own family. God tells Gideon to destroy his father's idols (v. 25). And "mighty warrior" does

---

7. Note that the first subpoint appears at the end of a portion of the story's exposition; then another question—still related to the analytical question that began this main point—introduces the exposition that will lead to the next subpoint.

8. This second subpoint appears at the end of the story exposition that was set up by the question two paragraphs earlier. Again, because the structure is inductive, the experience of the story leads to the sermonic point being made, rather than the point being pre-declared.

go . . . *at night* because he is *afraid* and wants no one to see him (v. 27). And the next morning when people ask, "Who did this?," does Gideon say, "It was I standing for the Lord Almighty"? No. He lies low and is saved by the smooth defense of his daddy, who doesn't honor God, but rather says in effect, "Baal can take care of himself against the likes of my son" (v. 31).

Only after his "noble" passing of this battle test amidst his own family does Gideon consider God's call to face the Midianites. And how does Gideon begin his campaign against Midian? He again asks God to prove himself. Gideon builds his courage by testing God. Gideon says to his Lord, "I'm going to put this wool fleece on a threshing floor, and in the morning I want you to make it wet and the surroundings dry" (paraphrase of vv. 36–37). And the Lord does it! So how does "mighty warrior" respond to this supernatural answer to his petition? "Uh, Lord, would you do it again, but this time make the fleece dry and the ground wet" (paraphrase of v. 39). He tests God, again. The angel of the Lord has appeared to him, spoken to him, given him a mighty name, repeatedly performed miracles for him, and still Gideon is afraid. This "mighty warrior's" fears are not just obvious, and they are not just offensive. *Gideon's fears come over and over again.*[9]

Would you pick this guy to be on your team? He seems so useless; his fears make him such an unlikely leader of God's people.

Why do we need such a timid "hero" in Scripture? Because I identify with his fears so well—as I suspect you do. Some time ago, I received a call from a pastor who was concerned about a difficult matter with which our denomination was wrestling. In the call, he not only told me what conclusion he thought I should reach, but added that I needed to decide in this way so that I and my family and the seminary I serve would "not get hurt." When he first uttered that not-so-subtle threat, I silently scoffed and thought to myself, *Who does he think he's threatening? I have faced bigger adversaries than this man.* But then I got on a plane. And in the seclusion of that long flight, I began to do the *obvious*—worry. Could his threat be real? Could he hurt me or my family or the seminary? God has protected us in other controversies, given us remarkable growth as a seminary, multiplied our resources, provided us with wonderful support inside and outside our church, but in the quiet isolation of my own reflection I became afraid. I know that sounds **offensive** in the light of God preserving us **over and over** again, but I really did get scared.

9. The third subpoint also follows the story exposition rather than coming before it.

Some of you now are frightened about things as *obvious*[10] as whether you can handle the academics that are ahead.[11] You wonder if you have made the right choice in leaving behind security and family, and question if God will continue to preserve you in this place. Present finances are likely to frighten many of you. And most of you also have questions about future positions, placements, and your aptitude for handling the demands and criticisms and controversies of ministry.

Sometimes such fears can be as **offensive** as Gideon's. We also think, *If the Lord is with us, then why has all this happened to us? Where is the God who delivered Israel from Egypt?* In moments of trial, when finances are short, or your family is suffering, you can also accuse: "God has brought us here and abandoned us." And you know as well as I do that these fears can take hold of us **over and over** again.

For the moment, I am not going to excuse these fears, nor promise you a quick remedy for them, nor even talk to you about God's forgiveness of them. I simply want you to note this: such fears, expressed even **over and over** again, do not disqualify you from God's service. Fear of the present, fear of the future, fear of people, fear of God, fear of the dark, fear of the enemy, fear of your neighbor, fear of a test, fear of failure, fear of pink bushy-tailed elephants—all of these may characterize you without disqualifying you. God can use the fearful for his purposes. [Note: This is the first main point statement at which we have arrived inductively.] After all, God used the useless "mighty warrior" Gideon for the glory of heaven, and God can use you for his purposes despite your fears.

From my earliest years in Vacation Bible School, one of the images that has stayed with me is Miss Kinley helping us memorize Psalm 91:4: "He will cover you with his feathers, and under his wings you will find refuge." "Children," Miss Kinley said, "when a friend of mine was confronted by a robber, she was so afraid that she almost fainted. All she could think of in that moment of danger was that God had promised that he would keep her 'under his wings.' So without being able to think or do anything else, those words just burst out of her. Over and over again in a voice of panic, she said, 'Under his wings, under his wings, under his wings.' Well, the robber thought she must be a crazy lady, and not knowing what she would do next, he got afraid and ran away." Then Miss Kinley said, "See, children, even when

10. Note that the key words of each of the preceding subpoints still "rain" into this interwoven illustration/application to give the message term consistency.

11. This sermon was first preached in a seminary setting with those preparing for ministry as the primary audience.

we are afraid, God is with us." That is my message to you too, though Miss Kinley may have taught it better: *Even when you are afraid, God is with you, and that is why he can use the fearful for his purposes.*[12] Being afraid doesn't make God go away.

Eventually Gideon's fears seem to go away, but his problems are not over with. There is much more that challenges his usefulness. While Judges chapter 6 tells us a great deal about the limitations of Gideon's nerve, chapter 7—despite telling us about his military victory—also tells us much about the limitations of Gideon's qualifications.[13]

> II. [**Analytical question setting up inductive discussion of second main point**] What do we learn about Gideon's qualifications in this account?

Did Gideon have a great victory over 135,000 Midianites because of his army's great qualifications?

Now you know well enough the **count** of Gideon's army—whittled down to three hundred—to answer no. There was nothing in his army's might that qualified Gideon for Israel's victory.

But I want you also to think about the **character** of Gideon's men as you consider the qualifications of those God used to accomplish his purposes. From where did this army of Gideon come? From the nation of Israel, which we have already been told at the beginning of the Gideon account "did evil in the eyes of the LORD" (6:1 NIV). The evidence of that evil is that Gideon's own father has a Baal altar, and when Gideon tears it down the people are *not* happy; they want Gideon's blood. That's what you know about **the character of the people** from whom this army comes. And what do you know about their leader? You already know what a "mighty warrior" he is. If Israel is going to have great victory, it will not be because of **the character of their leadership**. Well, then, perhaps the reason for the victory is **the character of the men** who fight—"the noble three hundred."

I was delighted to hear thoughts about the character of these three hundred warriors from our Israeli guide when my family visited the actual Spring of Gideon a few years ago. From my childhood days in Sunday school, I had been taught that

---

12. It is worth noting here that illustrations and applications often meld when the preacher's goal is to illustrate the application (not only the explanation). Illustrating the application is often a powerful means of connecting the message to the lives of listeners.

13. Note that these transition sentences return to the overall theme of "uselessness" while also setting up the next major idea (main point in question form) of the sermon.

God arranged for Gideon to get the choicest three hundred men from Gideon's original army of thirty-two thousand, through the whittling down process this passage describes. First, Gideon sent home the scaredy cats, the twenty-two thousand who said they were afraid. Then, he chose from the remaining ten thousand those who knelt to drink and lapped water with their hands to their mouths rather than those who fell down on their bellies to drink (Judg. 7:5–7). Always, I'd heard that those who lapped were the ones of better **character**,[14] the more vigilant ones, who kept their eyes peeled for the enemy as they knelt beside the spring. However, our guide asked an interesting question: "Which were likely to be the better soldiers: those who hardly seemed to need water, so they lapped it up with their hands, or those who had worked so hard in battle preparations that they fell on their faces in desperate need?" His contention was that the good soldiers would have been the ones whose hard work had made them thirstier. The ones who lapped the water would be those who had been "dogging it" through the day and, thus, were not so thirsty. Our guide was contending that the soldiers of worse *character* were the ones that God picked. This would really make it clear that the victory that came was by God's hand and not the soldiers' ability.

Now to be honest, I don't think that you can prove which group of soldiers (those who knelt or those who fell to the ground) was of better **character**, but what you can prove conclusively is that a **count** of three hundred was a **frail** force to send against 135,000 Midianites—especially three hundred from this nation and with this leader. Whether you consider the **character** or the **count** of Gideon's army, you know this was a **frail** force spiritually and physically to fight for God. Yet by using such as these, God clearly shows that he can use those without adequate ability for his purposes. Just as God can use those whose fears should disqualify them for his purposes, so also God can use the frail for his purposes. [Note: This is the second main point statement at which we have arrived inductively.][15]

On March 1, 1998, a group of evangelical leaders met with Jiang Zemin, then the president of China. The Chinese president spoke movingly of the care that a single Christian nurse gave him when he was a child—and of his appreciation for Christianity as a result. The head of the Christian delegation used the comment

14. Note that the illustration is only of the second subpoint; thus, the key word *character* is the only one that "rains" into the storytelling.

15. In a traditional deductive sermon, this main point (*God can use the frail for his purposes*) would have had the preceding material in two traditionally worded subpoints (*God can use those frail in count*, and *God can use those frail in character*).

as an opportunity to present Jiang Zemin with a Bible and said, "Perhaps you could begin with the Gospel of John." Then the president of more than a billion people in China, the president who had recently increased religious repression, the president of sixty million persecuted Christians, responded with these words: "I should begin with John."

And in that book these words appear:

> Remember what I told you: "A servant is not greater than his master." If they perse-
> cuted me, they will persecute you also. If they obeyed my teaching, they will obey
> yours also. They will treat you this way because of my name, for they do not know
> the one who sent me. If I had not come and spoken to them, they would not be
> guilty of sin; but now they have no excuse for their sin. (John 15:20–22)

And these words appear:

> I am the resurrection and the life. He who believes in me will live, even though
> he dies; and whoever lives and believes in me will never die. Do you believe this?
> (John 11:25–26)

And these words appear:

> God so loved the world that he gave his only begotten Son, that whosoever believeth
> in him should not perish, but have everlasting life. (John 3:16 KJV)

Only in heaven will we know the true effects of that meeting of Christian leaders and Jiang Zemin. We do know that the intense repression of Chinese Christians eased soon after that meeting during the tenure of Jiang Zemin. We do know that now there are as many as one hundred million Christians in China. We also know that no one physically or militarily overpowered the Chinese leadership to make the governmental changes that both sparked and allowed such growth. But in heaven we may see that much of this happened because, without notice or fanfare, God used the **character** of a single nurse caring for a little child in the name of Jesus. The world would say that she didn't **count**, but we know that God uses such **frail** means for such powerful purposes, so that the glory will be all his.

The simple message of Gideon (and all Scripture) is that the Lord uses the **frail** for his glory. We should not **count** ourselves out because we do not measure up according to human estimations. Inadequate character or resources—these mean nothing where God is at work.

If you have not yet known them, you will soon come to know those people who all their lives are jockeying for position in the church—maneuvering and moving about, looking always for what is bigger and more prestigious and more rewarding. But only God determines who and what will be truly influential. While I do believe it should always be our concern to use our gifts (as best we can discern them) in the most effective ways that we can, our goal should be to seek how best we can be used rather than how high we can rise. No one this side of heaven can know what work will truly make the biggest difference for heaven's purposes. God seems regularly to use those whose **count** and **character** are **frail** to accomplish his greatest purposes, so that the glory for what is accomplished will all go to him. When you know this is how God works, you will be more willing to consider the obscure places of mission, the insignificant pulpits with precious people who need your care, the small ministries that go unnoticed by the world but are measured by heaven as the greatest of the gifts that you can give to the King.

I don't always like thinking this way. I want to **count** noses too. I want to brag that now we are a big seminary, that we are more important and that we can influence more. But only God knows what is truly influential for kingdom purposes, and the more we trust our numbers and our **character**, the less likely will be true moving of the Spirit of God through us. God works in those who embrace their **frailty**, who know that apart from him we can do nothing, and who are constantly seeking to become more dependent on him.

Toward the end of *Pilgrim's Progress*, the traveler who has journeyed so far is allowed into the Celestial City. There he is shown the storehouse of weapons for those who inhabit that city of God's glory. Can you guess what weapons are displayed there? The weapons are trumpets and broken pots, the tools by which God used the **frailty** of a totally inadequate Gideon to bring divine victory. So even when we recognize our **frailty**, we need not **count** ourselves out of being useful to God.

Perhaps your conclusion, as we have progressed this far in Gideon's story, is that such victories come to such frail people because they are spiritually superior to ordinary people like you and me. If they faced their fears and frailties by turning to God, then it would make sense for God to use ones of great spiritual character for great spiritual victories.[16] If you think this way, you may be ready to disqualify yourself from seeking God's purposes because you know your life does not reflect all the spiritual priorities that it should. If this is the case, then once more you need Gideon—and the portion of the story that describes the spiritual priorities of his life.

III. [**Analytical question setting up inductive discussion of third main point**] What do we learn about Gideon's heart in the final account?

In the chapter following Gideon's great victory, success goes to his head. The people want to make him a king (8:22). He refuses, saying only God should rule the covenant people (v. 23). In addition, "mighty warrior" doesn't want to make anybody mad (remember the lesson of chaps. 6 and 8:1–3, where Gideon avoids confrontation with his father, the townspeople, and the Ephraimites).

But though Gideon refuses the royal office, he grabs for the privileges that accompany kingly status. He consolidates power (8:29), multiplies wives (v. 30), names a son "My father is the King" (v. 31), and also uses the gold taken in his victory over the Midianites to make an idolatrous priestly vestment (called an ephod) to divine the will of God. In this way he makes all Israel dependent on him and his family (vv. 23–27). Scripture records, "All Israel prostituted themselves by worshiping [the ephod] . . . , and it became a snare to Gideon and his family" (v. 27). So the same Gideon who God used to defeat the 135,000 Midianites with three hundred men—this same "mighty warrior"—also made an idol from the spoils of the victory God provided.

Now, what would you do to Gideon if you were God? You expect God to send lightning bolts and plagues, don't you? But the Bible says, "During Gideon's lifetime, the land had peace forty years" (v. 28). "How can this be?" you ask. The answer is that God can use rotten eggs to make a wonderful omelet. I am not denying that there were consequences for sin in Gideon's life. The Bible says that the ephod became a snare to Gideon's family, and tragedy followed the family as they vied for power in Israel. But the nation itself was still blessed by God's use of Gideon. The Lord displayed his wonderful grace in Old Testament clothes by demonstrating that he could and would use those with flaws as great as Gideon's for divine purposes.

---

16. Note the recapitulation of the key words of previous main points in this transition that prepares for the analytical question setting up the third main point.

There is no question that Gideon was a terribly flawed hero, but blessing flowed from him. Blessing flowing from flawed leaders is not that unusual. Perhaps you have already discovered it, or you soon will. Even in the church today, great leaders often have great flaws. You may have been longing to meet or even work for someone for years, and when you finally do, it is not unusual to find out that such leaders have **fears**, **frailties**, and **flaws** that you could scarcely imagine would be in a person of such stature.[17] You wonder how this could be, that a person could have such stature in the kingdom and be so fallible. The answer is that <u>God can use the flawed for his purposes.</u>[18]

Why make the point that God can use greatly flawed people for the greatest of heaven's purposes? Because of what can happen to us in ministry training. We can become so facile with the Word that we can develop the ability to excuse almost any sin. In this way, we become the flawed leaders who, like Gideon, take advantage of God's provision and must rely on his grace to be of any continuing use to him.

Rather than hiding our flaws with our knowledge of Scripture, others of us may expect the seminary experience to sanctify us so much that if any flaws remain, we believe they will disqualify us from being used by God. For this reason, our flaws get magnified to the point of devastating us. A difficulty with your spouse, an embarrassing blunder that you have made in statement or action, a hidden wrestling with a moral demon, a repeated battle with anger or depression, a lapse in integrity, a failure to care—one or more of these may get exposed to your conscience by the Holy Spirit, and as a result, you may be ready to disqualify yourself from kingdom service. Please remember that God uses flawed people for his purposes.

Here I have to be careful: unchecked and unrepentant repetition of serious sin should make you question your aptitude for full-time ministry and will come under the judgment of God (Gideon's family suffered for his sin), but at the same time you must remember that God uses broken vessels to pour out his glory. No one is really worthy of ministering the gospel, until they recognize their unworthiness. We minister grace best when we know we need it. Thus, there is a real sense in which we are not ready to administer God's victories until we recognize that we are the broken pitchers and blown trumpets that he will use to make his glory and grace most clear. We are broken and we have blown it—apart from

17. Note that the use of key words from two preceding main points and the present main point are united in this sentence to form an internal summary of the message.
18. This is the third main point statement at which we have arrived inductively.

God there is no blessing we deserve or victory we can win. Yet despite our flaws, God still can use us.

God's use of the fallible Gideon is the message of grace in Old Testament clothes. *God pours out his love on the fearful, frail, and flawed.* Recognition of such love is the blessing that empowers us to serve God, the mercy that keeps us from being devastated by our sin, and the grace that motivates us to keep serving him. When we know that God uses the fearful, frail, and fallible, then we begin to believe that he could even use someone like you and me. We become fearless, resilient, righteous—or willing to confess our failings and try again—by knowing that **God uses the useless for his glory.** [Note: This last statement—repeated in various forms earlier—is the point to which the sermon has inductively led. This could have been the proposition in a traditional sermon. But in an inductive sermon it is the central concept to which the listeners have been led.]

I have heard my friend and radio preacher Steve Brown say that the only people who ever get any better spiritually are those who know that if they never get any better, God will love them anyway. Steve's clever but wise words apply not only to what makes our hearts glad but also to what makes our lives useful. The only people that ever really serve God well are those who know that if they never entirely get over their *fears, frailties,* and *flaws,* God can use them anyway.[19]

[**Conclusion**] In 1947, six weeks after their first child was born, Cameron Townsend and his wife left Peru to visit a missionary training camp in southern Mexico. The Townsends had labored many years in Mexico before going to Peru, and they were returning with great joy to show off their firstborn child. A crowd of friends gathered to watch them leave from the rough Peruvian jungle airfield. The little family squeezed into a small chartered plane and took off. They bounced down the runway, lifted off, and the inexperienced pilot then banked the plane for a turn, but too soon. With insufficient speed and altitude, the tail of the plane hit the top of a tree on the edge of a small ravine beyond the end of the runway. The plane, with all aboard and all the crowd watching, crashed. Months of recuperation followed for the family. Though the baby was safe, the parents had suffered serious trauma, with their bodies and spirits broken in many ways.

Their experience may be a metaphor for your own in this place. You come to seminary to do ministry, but with friends and family looking on, there has been

---

19. Key word summary of the main points summarizes the entire message in preparation for the conclusion.

a crash of some sort—some revelation of a **fear**, a **frailty**, or a **flaw** that is now evident to others or to you. Such things can and do happen here.

The good news regarding the Townsends is that they did not let their brokenness keep them from seeking to be useful to God. In the months of the family's recuperation, the need for dependable aviation for jungle missions seared into Cameron Townsend's mind. From his hospital bed, he conceptualized and began the ministry of JAARS, Jungle Aviation and Radio Service, the missionary ministry that has become the life-support system for thousands of missionaries for more than half a century in jungle regions around the world.

The simple message of the Townsends and of Gideon is that crashes do not have to signify an end. Though **fears**, **frailties**, and **flaws** may characterize where you have been, they need not characterize where you are going. Be a vessel, though broken, in God's hand so that he may pour his glory from you. Be willing, though having blown it, to be a trumpet of his grace. Broken pots and blown trumpets are yet mighty weapons in the hands of our <u>God who uses the useless for his glory</u>.

Topical Sermon
for a Special Occasion

This is an example of a topical sermon prepared for a special occasion.[1] A topical sermon bases its topic (i.e., theme or main subject) on some aspect of a biblical passage. Unlike an expository sermon that follows the development of the passage by taking its main points and subpoints from the biblical text, a topical sermon is organized according to the subject's nature rather than the text's distinctions or divisions. Only the main idea is from the text. This main idea may not be the main thought of the text but may only be referenced in the text or suggested by the text. Topical sermons may well serve to bring biblical ideas to occasions (weddings, funerals, holiday observances, special services, etc.) in which the detailed study of Scripture would be inappropriate.

Aspects of the development of the main idea of a topical sermon may come from how the subject has been addressed in history or present culture. Other aspects of the sermon's development may come from other biblical passages. None of these topical sermon characteristics mean that it is necessarily unbiblical or inferior to an expository message. There can be many legitimate reasons to explore a subject along lines other than those formed by a specific passage of Scripture. If

---

1. For a further description of topical sermons, see the author's *Christ-Centered Preaching: Redeeming the Expository Sermon*, 2nd ed. (Grand Rapids: Baker Academic, 2005), 129–30; hereinafter *CCP*.

for a portion of the sermon we wanted to explore present thinking about racism, elder care, or consumerism, there is nothing wrong with examining how attitudes have developed in our culture, even if those issues are not specifically mentioned in the biblical text. There is often great pastoral wisdom in proving why a subject needs to be addressed before showing how Scripture speaks to it.

Topical sermons can be very biblical, even if they do not follow the structure of a biblical passage. The key to remaining biblical is making sure that the subject is ultimately addressed according to principles drawn from Scripture. Even in a topical message, it is often important to develop key ideas expositionally. A sermon on what it means to be a biblical father may come from several passages and may also reflect on society's present views, but the message will be weak if there is no place where the preacher says, "The Bible specifically teaches in this passage that godly fathering requires . . ."

The danger of a topical sermon is that it may drift into expressing personal or popular opinion. Because the message is not anchored to a biblical text, the preacher may float free from biblical truths. This is *not* inherently true. A topical sermon can be very biblical, but this is more a consequence of the commitments of the speaker rather than the structure of the sermon.

The following example of a topical sermon was delivered on the occasion of a special service in an African American church that ministers to a large segment of our city's population. I wrote and delivered the message in a dialogical style typical of the African American tradition, with strong emphasis on alliteration, repetition of key phrases, occasional rhyme, opportunity for response from listeners, and a culminating crescendo of phrasing and emotion in the conclusion.

The Glory of the Lord

Psalm 126

Scripture Reading

Read with me Psalm 126:

> *When the LORD brought back the captives to Zion,*
>   *we were like men who dreamed.*
> *Our mouths were filled with laughter,*
>   *our tongues with songs of joy.*
> *Then it was said among the nations,*
>   *"The LORD has done great things for them."*
> *The LORD has done great things for us,*
>   *and we are filled with joy.*
>
> *Restore our fortunes, O LORD,*
>   *like streams in the Negev.*
> *Those who sow in tears*
>   *will reap with songs of joy.*
> *He who goes out weeping,*
>   *carrying seed to sow,*
> *will return with songs of joy,*
>   *carrying sheaves with him.*[1]

1. Scripture quotations in this sermon are from the New International Version.

I want first to offer my thanks to Pastor Michael Jones and to the people of
Friendly Temple Missionary Baptist Church for the privilege of addressing this
great congregation in honor of a great man on this day of special remembrance
and anticipation.[2] I do not take the privilege lightly. There may not be a greater
week of commemoration and celebration in the African American community for
generations. To be invited here, as a white man, to address you, to rejoice with your
rejoicing, to share in your hope on the day we honor Dr. Martin Luther King Jr.,
during the week in which we will inaugurate the first African American president
of these United States—this is an honor I have no right to expect will be repeated
in my lifetime. It is also a mark of your love, graciousness, and forgiveness that
is both a model and inspiration for me and for the entire church of Jesus Christ.

I begin this sermon with the observation that the people of God are never
more blessed than *when God's prophecy becomes their history*[3]—when what has
been long anticipated is suddenly here and, then, behind us: prophecy becoming
history. The prophecy of the psalmist in the passage just read is that the people of
God will reap his blessings with songs of joy. But the prophecy itself has a history.
Those who reap with songs of joy must sow the seeds of their blessings with tears.
Tears come before songs.[4]

The tears of this people's history are plain. The people of God have been in
slavery in Babylon for generations. They are in a foreign nation under a reign of
cruelty and deprivation. They have been led from their homeland in chains, their
families have been divided, their livelihood used for the privilege of others. They
have been denied freedom, stripped of dignity, enslaved to poverty, and denied
life itself if they objected to such treatment. This was the history that brought the
tears. The Scriptures record that when the Israelites were deported, their captors
demanded songs of joy, but instead the psalmist states, "By the rivers of Babylon
we sat and wept when we remembered Zion" (Ps. 137:1). No one understands

2. This sermon was originally delivered on January 18, 2009, at Friendly Temple Missionary Baptist
Church in St. Louis, Missouri. The service commemorated the national holiday honoring Dr. Martin
Luther King Jr. and was two days prior to the inauguration of Barack Obama, the first African American
president of the United States.

3. This phrase not only establishes the theme of the message but will be echoed many times in the
message both to aid memory and to give the sermon a unifying concept that will keep listeners oriented
to the main theme. Echoing a theme throughout the sermon is a common practice in African American
preaching that will increasingly serve our wider culture as it becomes more oral, rather than literary, in
its communication practices.

4. This sentence not only summarizes the biblical truth; it also provides the key terms of the structure
to follow: a discussion of "tears" and "songs."

these tears of history better than the people gathered in this church. I confess to you (what you already know) that I have not fully experienced what you or the generations before you have experienced. But I have seen the tears of your history more closely than you may imagine.[5]

I grew up in Memphis, Tennessee—land of King Cotton; the home of Elvis; the city of the Mason Temple Church of God in Christ, the last place where Martin Luther King Jr. preached; and the Lorraine Hotel, the last place he breathed. The tears that were shed on that awful day of Memphis history were not the first shed for the racial cruelty that thrived there.

In 1962 James Meredith sought to be the first African American to attend the University of Mississippi. He was denied entry until a federal court order required his admission. Violent riots sought to prevent his attendance, resulting in the wounding of scores of federal marshals (twenty-eight by gunfire) and two deaths.

On June 5, 1966, James Meredith began the "March Against Fear," intending to march from Memphis to Jackson, Mississippi, to protest the continuing denial of rights to African Americans. I know. I was there. My mother, in sympathy and support, lined up on Highway 51 with her six children at the state line of Tennessee and Mississippi to have us see history. We watched James Meredith walk past. I was only eleven. I would not remember except for the report hours later that the man I had just seen walking down Highway 51 had been shot in Hernando, Mississippi—the place where I used to play in the town swimming pool. I still might not remember except that the news made my mother, who was watching the reports on our little television, sit on the sofa and weep—as she had a few years before when President John F. Kennedy was shot, and as she would again two years later when Martin Luther King Jr. was shot in Memphis.

That violence and those tears made me dream of this day. I do not fail to recognize its significance. We are days from the one hundredth anniversary of the founding of the NAACP. The founding of that organization was intentionally set to coincide with the one hundredth birthday of Abraham Lincoln. And now as we mark the two hundredth birthday of Lincoln, the one hundredth birthday of the

---

5. Kenneth Burke, the great speech theorist of the twentieth century, taught the importance of speakers identifying with listeners by writing, "You persuade a man only insofar as you can talk his language . . . identifying your ways with his." See *A Rhetoric of Motives* (Berkeley: University of California Press, 1969), 55, 57. I sought to identify with my listeners and close the obvious distance between me, a white academic, and my urban, African American audience by citing a key event in my past that gave me insight into their experience and gave them reciprocal insight into our shared values.

NAACP, the birthday of Martin Luther King Jr., and the inauguration of the first
African American president of the United States, I know of the joy that follows
after long years of tears.

The birthdays of all those who led to this day were the birthdays of those who
only dreamed of such a day. And the songs of joy they *wished to* sing and we *do* sing
now ring with greater ecstasy because they were composed in the context of tears.
There is greater joy in the morning when we have known the tears of the night and
feared that the dawn would never come. So long and bitter have been our tears over
dispossession and oppression that we can well identify with the emotions of the
one who wrote the opening words to this Psalm: "When the LORD brought back
the captives to Zion, we were like men who dreamed" (NIV 1984).

The reality of deprivation has been so deep and so long that the reality of new
privilege and promise seems unreal: What do you mean a black man is president?
Am I dreaming? What do you mean that he is the son of a single mother? *Are you
dreaming?* What do you mean that his name is Barack Obama? *Is this a dream?*[6]

No. This is reality. This is the dream come true. Martin Luther King Jr.'s dream
that a man could be judged for the content of his character instead of the color of his
skin is no longer future. It is *today*. It is *our* today. The prophecy is about to become
history. The seeds of hope sown in tears are about to become songs of thanksgiving sung in joy. By this time next week, we will be able to say with the psalmist:

> *Our mouths were filled with laughter,*
> *our tongues with songs of joy. . . .*
> *The LORD has done great things for us,*
> *and we are filled with joy.*[7]

So dear to my heart are the songs of joy now being sung that I want to guard
them, to conduct them with care, to teach others to love them, so that nothing
and no one shall keep us from singing them to nations and generations. Because

6. The echoes of Martin Luther King Jr.'s "I Have a Dream" speech are an example of "synecdochic
reference," i.e., the use of a phrase or image familiar in the culture of the listeners that will bring to their
minds larger concepts relevant to the purposes of the speaker. Numerous reference to phrases or images
made significant by the civil rights movement of the 1960s occur throughout this message.

7. In many African American settings, the preacher often pauses after emphatic statements of key
phrases or verses such as these in order to allow for listeners to say, "Amen." This "pulpit dialogue" between
preacher and congregation, which is common in the experience of many African Americans, is highly
energizing and encouraging for preachers not distracted by the comments or desperate to elicit them.

I love the songs of liberty and equality and grace toward all, I speak to you now of *the joys we must claim, the fears we must face,* and *the hope we must keep alive*[8]—so that no one shall keep us from singing.[9] First consider the songs that come from . . . [Note to reader: The following first main point is now stated; such ellipses throughout this message indicate transition statements that flow into the statement of following points and subpoints.]

I. The Joys We Must Claim

All of Our Children Have Proof of the Truth of Their Potential[10]

No one I know has spoken more eloquently than your own Pastor Michael Jones of what the election of Barack Obama means to African American children. Until this election, no black mother or father could look her or his child in the eye and say with sincerity, "In this country, you can be anything you want to be." Who really thought before now that a person of color could be the president of this nation? Now who can deny it?

And the effect is not simply that young men and women of *every* neighborhood can grow up believing that it is possible for them to be president. They now also know that it really is possible for them to be doctors and attorneys and teachers and business leaders. If a person of color can be president, the walls of prejudice in every avenue of society will come tumbling down.[11]

So also tumbling down are the excuses of the young. I have heard Pastor Jones articulately preach these words: "There are young men around here who claim that

8. Even in a topical message such "billboarding" of main ideas is a helpful means of alerting listeners to the key themes and structure of the sermon (see *CCP*, 264–65).

9. This echo of the 1860s hymn "How Can I Keep from Singing," which became one of the "freedom songs" of the civil rights movement in the 1960s through the influence of folksinger Peter Seeger, is another example of synecdochic reference.

10. Rhyme and repetition (exhibited in the repeated use of the phrase "proof of the truth") are important tools for oral communication (see *CCP*, 122). These tools have a rich history in African American preaching and are used in significant ways throughout this message both to communicate with listeners and to enable me to identify with them through the use of a preaching style African Americans would find familiar but would not expect me to honor if I did not respect their traditions.

11. Here the synecdochic reference is to the biblical account retold in the Negro spiritual "Joshua Fit the Battle of Jericho," with its familiar refrain "And the walls came a tumblin' down"—an example of how powerful evil is overcome with God's aid of his less powerful people. Two generations ago, biblical allusions were the most commonly recognized literary references in Western culture. Now advertising slogans, pop music lyrics, and famous movie lines are the most commonly recognized literary references of our society and may well serve preaching purposes when judiciously used.

because of the doors our society has closed in their faces, the only opportunities open to them involve bouncing a ball or dealing on the corner." Barack Obama proves their claim a lie.

There are young women who believe that their only opportunity for a better future lies in selling their bodies or producing babies that will love them when no one else will. Michelle Obama proves that there is a better course for those who will not lose hope and will continue to take pride in themselves and in the dignity of family.

Why should young men and women believe in the truth of their own potential? Because in the election of Barack Obama, not only do *all our children have proof of the truth of their potential*, but also . . .

All of Our Nation Gave Proof of the Truth of Our National Creeds

Barack Obama was not elected by a minority. Barack Obama was not elected by a party. Barack Obama was elected by a *nation*. He is *our* president. He was not elected just *for* black people. He was not elected just *by* black people. He was elected by the nation—a nation that wanted change and now seems ready for it.

Are there still challenges ahead of us? Of course. Will there be setbacks? Of course. Will there be opposition? Yes. But never again can anyone say, "It is *not* possible for a person of color to reach the highest positions of power and privilege in this nation." Our national creeds declare that "all men are created equal," and when we elected Barack Obama, we said clearly that it is our determination to live by those convictions. We sing songs of joy this day because we are *not* dreaming. We have undeniable proof, perhaps for the first time in our nation's history, that most of the people of these United States are determined to live the truth of our national creeds.

I said "most of the people" are so determined to live. I did not say everyone. And so that we will keep on singing our songs of joy with proper understanding and necessary courage, we must face our fears. Here are some of . . .

II. The Fears We Must Face

Our President Is Not Safe

The extraordinary security measures being taken for this inauguration are not extreme. Because racism is alive, Barack Obama is at risk. What happened to

Martin Luther King Jr. proves it. Because Barack Obama is now a historic figure in our nation, lunatics wanting a footnote in history will try to write their names with his blood. Because Barack Obama seems to embody such hope for our nation, enemies of our nation will try to destroy him to demoralize us.

Our president is at risk not only physically but also politically. By this I do not mean that he should be above contradiction or debate.[12] Our nation will not be healthy if any person rises above legitimate challenge. But what I fear is that the challenges will not always be legitimate. While racial stereotyping is currently out of vogue in polite company and media discussion, I have little doubt that even a few missteps on Mr. Obama's part (which are inevitable with any merely human leader) will again surface racial hatreds and caricatures. False caricatures of race will be used to try to discredit legitimate ideas of our president, and false accusations of racism will be used to try to back down legitimate opposition to our president. All sides will be tempted to use the race card for political gain.

If such racial stereotyping and racial baiting gains traction, then that means not only that our president is not safe; it also means that . . .

Our Hope Is Not Secure

Any hope that rests on political solutions, party advantage, or popular approval will blow away in the next wind of change. And if our hope ultimately resides in this one man—or any other person—then our hope is truly vain. Dr. King would have just said, "Amen." If the hope of the civil rights movement had rested entirely on Dr. King, then justice would have died with him. It did not, because our hope did not rest entirely on him, and he did not want it to.

When he spoke of the Promised Land at Mason Temple in Memphis the day before his assassination, Dr. King said, "I may not get there with you. But I want you to know tonight, that we, *as a people*, will get to the Promised Land." The hope cannot lie with any one person, or it may die with that one person—and hope must not die. Today we must also remember . . .

12. The tightrope that I frequently walk in this message is celebrating the nation's triumph over racism through the election of Barack Obama and wanting to be clear that not all of his values are above the need for biblical correction.

III. The Hope We Must Keep Alive[13]

But what will it take to keep hope alive? What will it take for us "as a people" to get to the Promised Land where the light that shines brighter than the fears and prejudices of humanity is the glory of the Lord? What will it take for us truly to experience the glory of the coming of the Lord?[14]

The Lord!

When the chosen people of God returned to the Promised Land and began to live as history what had only before been prophecy, they rejoiced in their great blessing. They also clearly identified the source of their blessing: "The LORD has done great things for us."[15] Focus on the Lord must also be *our* hope. And our history should make clear the necessity of a hope founded on faith. We must first understand that such hope is . . .

Not Merely a Political Solution

From the 1940s through the 1970s, the hope of the nation was in *political solutions*. We hoped that by legislative changes governing schooling, housing, employment, and government assistance, the effects of racism would die. Much good *was* accomplished! But we were deindustrializing as a nation. And without jobs in the urban centers, the new laws enabled and encouraged an unintended migration of whites and blacks to segregated suburbs. We emptied our cities, leaving the poor and fatherless among boarded-up storefronts of once-thriving shopping centers, buying false hope from brightly lit liquor stores and from peddlers of dope, coke, and bodies on street corners.

The political solution was not enough to bring the glory of the coming of the Lord. Neither a "Great Society" nor a separate society fulfills God's purposes. As a consequence of the inadequacies of the political solution, from the 1980s to the

---

13. Note that this topical sermon has main points that follow the wording of the billboard given toward the beginning of the message. The speakers' maxim, "Tell them what you will say, say it, and then remind them what you said," is being followed in this message.

14. Synecdochic reference here is an echoing of the "Battle Hymn of the Republic." The echo not only helps explain the third main point but also sets up the wording and climax of the conclusion.

15. As is typical of topical messages, this sermon has spent much time developing concepts from the societal context. Still, to fulfill its biblical obligations, the message must deal with spiritual themes that are rooted in biblical contexts. To pursue these spiritual and biblical priorities, this message now begins to focus on themes derived from the biblical text presented at the outset of the sermon.

present moment, the nation has also tried the *psychological solution*. But we also discovered that hope is . . .

Not Merely a Psychological Solution

Cries for racial pride and black capitalism and even black nationalism reflected the powerful insight that no people can rise above their tragedies if they only believe themselves to be victims with someone else to blame and no responsibility for their future. In the minority community children rightly learned to believe "I am somebody," and in the majority community we did "diversity training" so that everyone would learn to feel good about themselves and others. I do *not* criticize these efforts. They have been noble and were done out of good hearts. Real strides have been made, but the psychological solution alone will not bring the glory of the coming of the Lord.[16]

The reality is that raising someone's self-esteem will not in itself feed a family. And if it makes you feel good to father children you will not raise, then self-esteem is a *sin*. If you feel good because you have education and wealth that your neighbor does not share, then self-esteem is *selfishness*. If you feel good because you have escaped the 'hood but do not care for the children without families, the elderly without homes, the sick without medicine, the young without purpose, the prisoner without hope—then your self-esteem may be in great shape, *but the glory of the Lord has not come.*

Neither the political solution nor the psychological solution is sufficient to bring the glory of the coming of the Lord. Neither the Great Society nor a separate society, neither victimhood nor self-image will fulfill the purposes of our God. Lives of hope do not fully flourish because of a political solution or a psychological solution . . .

But a Faith Solution

What remains necessary for our seeing the glory of the coming of the Lord? *You* know, Friendly Temple. I know of no church that knows it better. The ultimate solution is not a political solution or a psychological solution; it is a *faith*

16. This paragraph makes numerous references to social and political programs familiar to those who have engaged in civil rights efforts.

solution.[17] When the people of Israel were delivered from their slavery, they said to one another, "The LORD has done great things for us." Fundamentally, my self-esteem (and yours) must lie in understanding that "Jesus loves me." The greatest thing that God has done for us is to give us Jesus. And our future together lies in my understanding (and yours) that "Jesus loves you."

This is the hope to keep alive: the hope that the church of Jesus Christ will lead the way in providing the ultimate solution to racial hatred and discrimination because we have trusted in the Lord who does great things for us through his grace. The people of Israel were not deserving of God's love, but he gave it. They were not able to gain his love, but he gave it. They were not able to earn his love, but he gave it. This is the gospel—the message of a God who forgives sinners, who loves the unlovely, who saves the helpless, who promises eternity to those who have nothing earthly. This same God would send his Son from heaven's privilege to suffer our penalty for sin upon a cross. And this same God promises that all who believe in him will have his righteousness forever. *We could not gain heaven, so he gave it.*

When I understand the grace my God provides for me, I will love him. And I will love all those he loves *because I love him*—not because of what they have done *for* me and, perhaps, despite what they have done *to* me. In the ancient church of Ephesus, gentiles and Jews gathered to worship together. They were from different races, different nations, different classes—and they gathered in each others' homes, despite ancient antipathies and antagonisms. They had been transformed by Christ's love to love one another. Why did this happen?

The apostle Paul wrote that the intent of the Creator "was that now, through the church, the manifold wisdom of God should be made known to the rulers and authorities in the heavenly realms" (Eph. 3:10). Do you know what the word "manifold" means? It is the same word used in the Bible to describe Joseph's multicolored coat. And Paul says that when the multicolored wisdom of God is evident in the church, even the angels of heaven marvel at the greatness of the glory of God: "My, what a God, if he can get people so different to love one another and worship!"

When James Weldon Johnson penned the words of the anthem for racial justice, "Lift every voice and sing till earth and heaven ring," the words were not merely poetic imagery; they were spiritual reality.[18] The glory of the Lord comes

---

17. The goal is now to become explicitly spiritual in focus and priority.

18. This synecdochic reference occurs with quotation of this important "freedom song" of the civil rights movement.

to earth and rings in heaven when the church is the multicolored body of Christ that God intends. The faith solution requires the body of Christ to love one another despite our differences and to help one another despite our distance. I don't know how it will happen, but I do not believe that we, as the body of Christ, will have a more important time to express this love than during the next few years. I cannot imagine but that President Obama's racial background will be used by some to divide, deride, and suppress. If he makes a mistake, some will immediately blame his race. If he is challenged, some will immediately charge racism. If he is *not* challenged, some will immediately assume racial privilege. If he is hurt, the bonds that are the beauty and greatness of this nation may be challenged as never before.

There are debates ahead over how we as a nation will handle poverty, war, abortion, sexual preferences, immigration, employment, and issues not yet even known. Each has the ability to divide hearts, foster hate, and breed the ugliest commentary. But no matter what comes—even if we differ in the discussion[19]—if the people in the church of Jesus Christ will love one another as we have been loved by our Savior, then the glory of the Lord is coming. If we can love past disagreement, if we men can be brothers after the debate, if you women will be my sisters even though we differ, then we have begun to see the glory of the coming of the Lord. If we can link arms in common cause for all that the Bible says is just and right, despite past antipathies, failures, and sin, then we have begun to see the glory of the coming of the Lord. If we can forgive each other the failures of the past and the future, then we have begun to see the glory of the Lord. Even the angels will see the glory and say, "My, what a glorious God, who can make those people brothers and sisters!" Our mutual faith in Jesus Christ is the blessing of God that will ultimately usher in . . .

The Coming of the Glory of the Lord

It was said of Dr. King when he was introduced to speak the night before his assassination that he was "the moral leader of our nation." The words remind us that politics or psychology without the morality of faith is futile. The spiritual

---

19. It was important for my own integrity to maintain the right to differ with the newly elected president's policies while also celebrating the statement against racism and oppression that his election signified. Speakers who will take obvious risks for the sake of integrity gain respect from listeners that may allow consideration of ideas even when initial disagreement is present.

leadership the nation now needs is in the *church of Jesus Christ where we live as brothers and sisters in Christ.* So has it always been.

In the 1960s a wealthy woman in South Carolina named Rosalie Cassels was traveling with her black maid of many years named Bennie. Bennie got sick and needed a restroom, but Rosalie could not find a single service station or restaurant that would let her ailing maid and friend enter. No one would let a black woman even get sick in their restroom. The experience changed the perspective—and the world—of Rosalie Cassels. Despite her privilege and her race, she began to say, "This must change!" She became an activist for civil rights in her family, church, and community. For a time her family, church, and community shunned her. People would turn their backs in the country clubs and restaurants where Rosalie was once welcomed.

One of my favorite stories of these two women is about a time when an ice cream stand would not serve Bennie. Rosalie responded by inviting Bennie into the family Cadillac, drove to the ice cream stand, parked the Cadillac in front of the service windows, and refused to move until Bennie got served.[20]

No account of the bond of these two women was more moving than the weekly picture taken of the two of them on Rosalie's living room sofa studying the lesson that they would teach in their respective churches the following day. One of them, you see, was Presbyterian, and the other was Baptist—I won't tell you which was which. What is important is that the two considered each other sisters in Christ and modeled their lives and their teaching to reflect that profound gospel truth.

Knowledge of the commitment of these two women to each other in Christ's name made one aspect of Rosalie's passing even more sad for me when I attended her funeral service. I looked across the church sanctuary, and every face was white—not a black or brown face among them. *How sad,* I thought, *that here at Rosalie's passing there is no evidence of the gospel commitments that so motivated and cost her.* But then Rosalie's family came into the room—a procession led by her son, who walked arm in arm with Bennie. And behind them was Bennie's extended family with Rosalie's family—all entering the room as one family in Christ Jesus. They were declaring to their families, to the church, and to the community around them that by the blood of Jesus Christ we are all one family in Christ, *and that is the coming of the glory of the Lord.*

20. Humor may help preachers deal with sensitive subjects, if persons are mentioned respectfully and the emotional spirit is lifted not simply for entertainment but in order more powerfully to drive home a weighty concept.

When our lives make this prophecy our history, we make the glory of the Lord come down.[21] The glory of the Lord is *my* salvation. The glory of the Lord is *your* salvation. I believe that because we have been saved by the precious blood of Christ, we are one: one in heart, one in church, one in body—all one family. We are the family of the church of God in Christ Jesus. I will be your brother. Will you be my brothers and sisters? If your answer is yes, then let us praise God, make the prophecy our history, and *live the dream!*[22]

21. This concluding sentence begins with an echo of the theme that began the sermon, creating a "wraparound" (see *CCP*, 259). In music or literature this technique would be known as circular closure or an *inclusio*, a device that has the work end as it began, providing a sense of unity, purpose, and finality.

22. African American preachers are often particularly skilled at concluding sermons with a crescendo of key phrases that echo from the body of the sermon and climax with a telling phrase. Here I attempt to reflect such a pattern in a way that would be familiar to (and expected by) my African American listeners.

Biblical Theology

A primary approach to discerning the redemptive nature of a
biblical text is identifying how the passage *predicts, prepares*
for, *reflects,* or *results* from the person and work of Christ.
Part Two of this book provides examples of sermons that take
one or more of these approaches to a biblical text. Each of
these approaches is a version of biblical theology, employing
redemptive-historical methods of interpretation.

Sermon examples in Part Two of this book will also show
how biblical passages can function as redemptive dead ends or
bridges (or both) in order to lead us to a fuller understanding
of Christ's necessity and purpose. Examples will include both
macro- and micro-redemptive interpretations (spanning vast
epochs and focusing on specific events).

Example SERMON FIVE

Predictive Christ-Centered Interpretation

(A Bridge Example)

This is an example of an expository sermon on a prophetic passage of Scripture.[1] The prophets spoke about their time and about the future. As a consequence, the prophets address multiple concerns in their messages. A prophet may give ethical instruction to people of his time or may warn them of future consequences resulting from disobedience; he may announce judgment for rebellion or promise restoration through a Redeemer; he may speak of the future for God's people or outline God's purposes for the entire world; he may prophesy what will happen to one nation or to many nations or to the one Messiah. And these are only a few of the possible purposes of the prophets.

The goal of an expository message on a prophetic passage is to explain the particular purposes of the prophet in the passage and to indicate the implications of these purposes for God's people today. Ethical instruction may contain principles we yet must follow; a prophetic pronouncement already fulfilled may give us confidence in God's Word or character; and a fulfillment yet to be realized

---

1. For a further description of expository sermons, see the author's *Christ-Centered Preaching: Redeeming the Expository Sermon*, 2nd ed. (Grand Rapids: Baker Academic, 2005), 131–33; hereinafter *CCP*.

may give us hope in present trials. These implications do not exhaust the matters that a preacher may address in preaching from the prophets, but they are the most common.

The common mistakes made in preaching from the prophets result from missing the original purposes of the author and losing track of the time frame of the prophet's message. For example, a sermon of comfort based on Isaiah 40 may inspire with references to God's caring nature in the past, but if the preacher does not recognize that the passage promises care based on the ministry of the coming Messiah, then the sermon will fail to explain the prophet's real message.

Some prophetic passages unveil a single concept over many pages of Scripture; others cover centuries of world events in a single verse. This dynamic should remind us that one expository approach is to distill the essential truths of a lengthy text but another, equally legitimate, way to explain a text is to explode the implications of a small passage. If we choose the latter method, we should remember that "context is part of the text" so that our narrow focus does not miss the author's intention.

The sermon that follows explodes the implications of a short passage that speaks to the people of Jeremiah's time based on a prophecy that will be fulfilled in Christ's time. The fulfillment is future, but Jeremiah writes because of his people's sin in the past and present. He predicts future hope in the context of present failures and reveals principles of God's grace that still apply in our day. In this sense, Jeremiah's message becomes a bridge between our understanding of the gospel and the Old Testament people's anticipation of it.[2] Because Jeremiah's message predicts the coming Messiah, I chose it as the basis of a Christmas message, but the text also illustrates how an Old Testament passage may become Christ centered by its prediction of Christ's person and work.[3]

---

2. For a further description of how some passages become "bridges" to gospel understanding, see the introduction to this book and CCP, 305–6.

3. For a further description of how the "predictive" nature of some passages enables Christ-centered interpretation, see CCP, 282–83.

Tinsel for Twigs

Jeremiah 33:14–16

Scripture Introduction

When we decorated our Christmas tree this year, we discovered our old string of decorative lights no longer worked. So I went to the store to buy a new string but was unprepared for all the options: lights that bubble and blink and even sing with the help of little computer chips. Amazing is the array of ways we try to cheer ourselves. Long ago, God spoke to his people to cheer them with the message of Christmas too, but his message was not about a tree and its lights. Instead, he spoke of a *branch* and its *lineage*.[1] God presented this image through the prophet Jeremiah, whom he sent to Judah with the message that they would be cut down by Babylon because of their sin. Jeremiah wept to tell the people that message. Yet through his tears a hope still glistened in the image of this branch. When we understand this image, we can also know some of the special cheer and grace that this season holds for all the year and all our lives, even when our sin and failures make us weep.

---

1. This Scripture introduction is a bit lengthy as I labor to tie the disturbing aspects of Jeremiah's prophecy to the celebrations of our present Christmas season. The purposes of a Scripture introduction are to both contextualize the text and create longing in the hearts of congregants to hear it (see *CCP*, 249–51). Accomplishing both purposes briefly can be a challenge, and it is better to spend a little more time, if needed, to create longing rather than to leave listeners ho-hum about the text.

Scripture Reading

Read with me Jeremiah 33:14–16:

> Behold, the days are coming, declares the LORD, when I will fulfill the promise I
> made to the house of Israel and the house of Judah. In those days and at that time
> I will cause a righteous Branch to spring up for David, and he shall execute justice
> and righteousness in the land. In those days Judah will be saved, and Jerusalem will
> dwell securely. And this is the name by which it will be called: "The LORD is our
> righteousness."

Sermon Introduction

At a road intersection near us, a tree is growing. It is not a very grand tree. It really
is just a sprout growing out of the concrete. On the little triangular island of raised
concrete where they mount the yield sign, this twig has somehow taken root in a
crack. The baby tree is the most forlorn looking thing, particularly in the winter.
Surrounded by yards of barren asphalt, dwarfed by the traffic signs, and long de-
leafed by the winter cold, the little twig gets whipped by the winds of passing cars.
It is a most ignorable little stick. And yet I noticed it. As we drove home from a
shopping trip to the mall where lights blazed and music blared, the twig caught
my eye. A piece of tinsel had blown from some neighboring trash can or outdoor
display and had become entwined in the tiny branches of the twig. As the winter
wind lashed the sprout into a frenzied flutter, it seemed to wave the tinsel as a
banner that spoke to me more clearly of Christmas than any of the retail glitz we
had spent the day enjoying.

The tinsel was really just a castoff of the season, and yet its presence signaled that
it was Christmas again. The tinsel was a token of all that this time of year represents:
the promised Christ child is born, Jesus has come, and it's time to rejoice! Oh yeah,
it was just tinsel, but there was something special in recognizing that out of all the
magnificent objects in his creation God had chosen to decorate this insignificant,
ugly little sprout. Our Lord picked up that discarded sliver of silver and put it in
the hair of an ugly twig to make it beautiful to himself and to make a wonderful
beacon of grace for any who would notice. It is so typical of our God to act this
way—*to make the forlorn glorious.* Ultimately it's the message of Christmas, and the

message of this passage, that God provides tinsel for twigs: the ignored, the ugly, and the despised of this world receive his special care. We, too, need this message for all the seasons of life when we feel ignored, ugly, or despised. Our God loves to decorate.[2] He even provides tinsel for twigs like us.

This is how God decorates us:

He drapes us with his purpose,

he covers us with his love, and

he makes us shine with heaven's glory.[3]

I. God Drapes Us with His Purpose

How does God drape us with his purpose?[4] By using us. This passage well demonstrates that God can drape the despicable with divine purpose. At the end of verse 15 God promises that he will bring forth One who will "execute justice and righteousness in the land." God is promising the Messiah. But from where will the Messiah come? God says at the beginning of verse 15 that this Messiah, the one he calls "a righteous Branch," will spring up "for David"—a reference to God's promise of a Messiah through the lineage of David. The wording is important because it leads us to consider how God can use those made despicable by their *insignificance* and *failures*.

God Uses the Insignificant

With his "branch" image, Jeremiah makes it clear that *God uses the insignificant things* of this world for wonderful purposes. When Jeremiah speaks of the righteous branch, he is referring to an earlier prophecy of Isaiah:

2. This sentence becomes a refrain in the sermon (even more in its oral delivery than in this written form). Good essayists and English teachers may frown on redundancy, but preachers familiar with the dynamics of oral communication know that repetition is one of their most important tools for emphasis and organization.
3. This "billboard" establishes the main points of the message. Each is worded in parallel with the others to identify it as a main point, while at the same time distinguishing each.
4. A standard way of beginning a sermon is to "interrogate the proposition"; i.e., the preacher makes a strong statement of the sermon's proposition, next asks a question about that theme, and then answers the question with the main point statements (often repeating the question before each main point, as they appear later in the sermon). The same technique can be used within main points (see *CCP*, 108, 151–52, 159). Skilled preachers often follow the statement of the main point with a question that they then answer with the following exposition and/or subpoints.

There shall come forth a shoot from the stump of Jesse, and a branch from his roots shall bear fruit. (Is. 11:1)

Have you ever cut down a tree in your yard and then seen twigs start shooting up from the stump months later? That's the image Isaiah is calling to mind. For any Hebrew this image represents a shameful history.[5] The "Jesse" mentioned by Isaiah was the father of David, the hero king of Israel's glory days. God promised an eternal kingdom to David. And the nation of Israel expected greatness to follow. It did—at first. Under David and his son Solomon the kingdom grew and flourished. Then the people sinned. There was an ensuing division of the kingdom. Assyria wiped out the northern kingdom; and, now, Jeremiah prophesies that Babylon will also demolish Judah. The grand kingdom has been whittled away and now is to be cut down to a stump of its former self. Jeremiah looks forward to what the nation will be, and for all its present pride, all he sees is what Isaiah saw: a shoot coming up from a stump. The nation will be an insignificant nothing, a source of mockery for the enemies of God.

Yet from this shameful joke, Jeremiah sees something more than a shoot arising. The twig becomes a branch that will save Israel. David's rule will again be extended with righteousness and justice. What is this branch to which Jeremiah refers? The coming Messiah, Jesus Christ. The Savior of the world is going to come from this stump of a nation because God can drape the despised things of this world with his glory.[6] God is always doing this sort of thing. The apostle Paul says God uses the lowly things of this world—and the things that are not (significant)—to nullify the things that are (1 Cor. 1:28).

Use what you know of the nativity to consider how God drapes the insignificant with heaven's purposes: Jesus, the king of the universe, is born as a spitting baby, in a dirty stable, in an obscure village. Regardless of what we may know now, this was not an auspicious beginning. In his best seller, *All I Really Need to Know I Learned in Kindergarten*, Robert Fulghum speaks of his seasonal cynicism regarding Christmas this way: "Babies and reindeer both stink. I've been around them both, and I know. The little town of Bethlehem is a pit, according to those who have been there."

---

5. Instead of putting this historical context at the beginning of the message, which can have a deadening effect on listener interest, the historical information is woven into the body of the sermon and further explained with a strong image from everyday experience—a stump with twigs growing from it.

6. Here the prediction of Christ's coming is explicitly drawn from the prophetic message.

We may not like such disrespectful descriptions of our dearest Christmas images, but they're true—and we should be glad that they are. God did not pick the great things of this world to glorify his Son. He used his Son to bring glory to the insignificant things. With his Son, God brought beauty to Bethlehem and heaven to a stable. God made that which is insignificant and smelly so beautiful that we sing songs about it. In a later time, he would even make a despicable branch of thorns into a crown of glory and save souls by it. God consistently drapes the sparkling tinsel of holy purpose on the most insignificant things.[7] Our God loves to decorate.

God Uses the Failed

God also uses failures for his purposes. God's glorious design shines more brightly when we consider what made the once-great nation become insignificant. The nation's past division and coming ruin are signs of her failure. That the nation of Israel would be reduced to a sprout from the stump of so great a tree is a mark of terrible failure. Even Jeremiah's word "branch" became synonymous with Israel's failure. Another Hebrew word for "branch" (*netser*), used by Isaiah, is likely the root word behind Nazareth, the town where Jesus grew up. How clever of God to see to it that the Righteous Branch grows up in "branch town."[8] But far from this term being one of distinction, it was a mark of derision. To be from "branch town" (or "twig city") set you up for scorn because the name was reminiscent of Israel's shame. That is why, when Jesus said he was from Nazareth, the people snickered and said, "Can anything good come out of Nazareth?" (John 1:45–46). Yet by weaving his life into Nazareth, Jesus made that town special too.

It is important to remember that God can use failures to accomplish his glorious purposes because failure can come from so many directions in our lives. I once traveled to speak at a multiday conference for a well-known church. I stayed in the home of the pastor, who by all accounts is a godly and devoted man. One afternoon as I was preparing my message, I could not help hearing the pastor's

7. All of these specific aspects of Christ's life are not mentioned in the prophecy, but they are a consequence of the prophecy, exhibit the principles evident in the prophecy, and further explicate the nature of the prophecy.

8. The specific language note is not used merely to demonstrate the speaker's acquaintance with Hebrew or to educate listeners regarding an interesting concept. The Hebrew language discussion (being mentioned in the sermon itself) is justified only because it furthers understanding of the themes of the sermon.

children "playing" outside my window. One child, the nine-year-old son of the pastor, dominated the rest with cruelty and profanity. It was hard to listen to and even harder to study through. So after a while I took a break. The doorway to my room opened at the bottom of a stairway. As I walked past the stairs, a motion higher up caught my eye. I saw the mother of the boy watching him out the window at the top of the stairs. She was almost a silhouette against the window, making her drooped shoulders a poignant picture as she flinched at the latest profanity from her son. When she turned toward me, I could see that she was crying. She knew I also had heard her son. Through her tears she said, "I don't know what to do with him. His father doesn't know what to do either. All we know is that we have failed. He's only nine years old, and we have already failed."

Many of you also know the pain of such failure—with children, with a marriage, with a career, or with your walk of faith. More than once in my life I have heard the haunting lyrics of a '60s pop song, "I've had beautiful beginnings, but beautiful beginnings are all I've had." To have had beautiful beginnings and painful endings! To have been like Israel! To begin with great promise and then to face desolating failure! Many of us know such failure. But we worship the God whose Word promises he can use failures for glorious purposes. Most of us will need to remember these promises at some inevitable stage of life.

I have a friend who manages a retail store at a local shopping mall. A year ago the shopping center had extensive renovation, and the crowds flocked to his store. Though my friend was new in the business, his store was a huge success. But after the Christmas crowds diminished, local gangs moved in. Six months ago, there was a murder at the mall. As a result of fears about more gang violence, the shopping crowds have stayed away from the mall this year. Some of the store owners in the mall recently speculated that another murder would ruin them all. Two weeks ago, there was another murder. In one year, my friend's store has gone from being a phenomenal success to being a dismal failure.

Most of us also know, or will know, what it means to have begun well and, then, to have had things go wrong. I will not promise you that God will make all your problems melt away—this is a fallen world with its share of pain and failure for everyone. Still, I will assure you that God can use failures for his purposes. Nothing is more true of him. You may have given up on yourself, but as long as the God of Israel lives, so do his purposes. He has not given up on you. If he had no purpose for you, you would not be here today with the ability to learn from his Word. If you are here today, then he is preparing you for his purposes tomorrow. I do not know what they will be, but I do know this: in a new day is new hope. In a new day, there will be new responsibilities and new opportunities to serve him—and, perhaps, to address past failures. But even if past failures cannot be reclaimed, we are able to move from those negative experiences with greater wisdom or thicker skin for purposes God yet puts in our lives. Our God uses earth's failures for heaven's purposes. He loves to decorate.

Neither our insignificance nor our failures place us beyond usefulness to God. But Jeremiah will not end the message of hope there. In the following verses, he underscores God's willingness to drape with purpose those who were once despicable by showing how God uses those whose shame is their own fault.

II. God Covers the Unfaithful with Unfailing Love[9]

God's promise to provide the people of Israel with One who will execute justice and righteousness appears all the more gracious when you realize that their plight is a result of their own sin. God promises to cover a faithless people with unfailing love . . .

Though They Are Sinful

Why is the nation being cut down? The people have rebelled against God (Jer. 33:8). Their failure to live up to past glory and to future potential is not somebody else's fault. Pride, jealousy, and idolatry have turned God's people from him. Yet God promises to bring from this unfaithful people a branch who is Christ the Lord. Their failure, shame, and sin will not erase God's love or prevent the Savior from coming to them.

Perhaps even more surprising about this unfailing love is the fact that God promises it to these failed people . . .

9. Main point statements of this sermon contain alliteration; i.e., key words of the statements begin with the same consonant or vowel sound to catch the attention of the ear (see *CCP*, 138). Often separate main point statements are worded in parallel with alliteration reflective of other main points to signal the ear that another main division of the sermon is occurring (regarding parallel wording, see *CCP*, 137–38 and 151–59). Alliteration can be overused to the point that listeners either weary of the device or find it artificial. However, misuse should not rule out appropriate use. Alliteration is an important tool to give organization signals in an oral medium where people are not reading the text but listening for aural cues that indicate how it is being addressed.

Though They Are Being Punished

Jeremiah is called the weeping prophet because he weeps for the discipline that will come in the form of enemies who will chop Israel down (Jer. 33:5). But alongside the punishment, the prophet also sees God's continuing love and promise of future restoration (vv. 6–8). Through these divine actions, we learn a vital scriptural truth: the presence of divine discipline is never an indication of the absence of divine love. God yet promises to save his people despite their sin (v. 16a).[10] Even if our failure is the result of our sin, and even if we interpret a dire situation to be a revelation of God's punishment, we should never presume that God's love has departed from his children.

One of my great griefs in the pastorate was watching the slow ruin of a young woman as she moved through her teens. She was one of the glories of our church. In her adolescence, she was radiant, bright, fun to be around, and in love with the Lord. Then, slowly at first, something seemed to change about her. Her bright expressiveness became a dark evasiveness. A certain slyness crept into her eyes. Her warm, endearing smile hardened into a stony sneer about all she once held dear. Eventually the evasiveness became lies. The slyness became rebellion. Broken curfews turned into Saturday night drinking binges. Her stony silence erupted into angry curses. And a family once close seemed to go to war with itself in endless rounds of arguments, tears, and slammed doors.

After a four-year nightmare of drunkenness, drugs, and increasingly prolonged absences, this prodigal daughter returned to her parents' home one night with the announcement that she was expecting a child and needed their help. The help she had spurned she now begged for. Her parents took her in, knowing that she would probably take advantage of them again. And in many ways she did. She considered her pregnancy a punishment of God—a biologically-imposed grounding. But the necessary change of lifestyle slowed her down just enough for those who loved her to remind her of the God she had once loved and who still loved her. She had trouble accepting this love. She considered the sins she had committed deserving

---

10. One of the most difficult movements in homiletics is from the descriptive to the normative. How do we take description of actions or events and then derive from them principles by which we should live? A good answer is to "principle-ize" the text (a term many homileticians share but with various spellings). To principle-ize a text, first identify what truth principle is demonstrated by the text's details; next, state that principle; and then apply that principle to some aspect of our lives (see *CCP*, 153 and 164–65). This paragraph exhibits such "principle-izing."

of God's punishment and the infant she carried to be a clear indication of receiving it. So it was a blessing to be able to say to her, as I say to you from God's Word, "the Lord disciplines the one he loves" (Heb. 12:6). The presence of divine punishment does not indicate the absence of divine love. Our God is forever seeking to protect us from greater danger. He is always drawing his own back to his embrace and away from the brink of Satan's eternal hell.

Eventually, by God's grace, this young woman understood God's care and received it. And when that young mother brought her child for baptism, I'm sure some saw the child as a symbol of shame, perhaps even a symbol of punishment. But I did not see it that way, nor did her family, and nor did she. As the waters of the sacrament trickled down that infant's little head, we saw in the streams of water the tinsel of divine love covering shame and sin and saying to all, "God covers even the unfaithful with unfailing love."

I need to remind all of us of these gracious truths. There is as much to tempt the mature as the young. All of us are capable of sin that deserves God's rejection. The addictions and adulteries that tempt us and trip us can make us believe we have fallen away from God forever. You may consider your sin so serious as to have separated you from ever knowing God's love again. You may consider your difficulty to be the proof of God's punishment. But the message of Jeremiah is that even those people of God who are experiencing divine punishment for sin are loved no less by their God.

How can God act this way? How can he love those whose actions have made them shameful?

III. God Makes the Shameful Shine with Heaven's Glory

I have friends who recently got a new puppy. They gave it the name Josephine Chateaubolier Sofrier St. Vincent Marie. Must be some dog, right? Its breed is actually Heinz 57—it's a mix—a mutt. They gave a shameful mutt a wonderful name to proclaim that it is special to them regardless of what others may think. God does something very similar in this passage.

He Gives His People His Name

Because of our weaknesses, failures, or sin, we may feel ashamed before God, but we should recognize how special we are to him by the name he gives his people.

Do you see the name he gives his people in this passage? In verse 16 Jeremiah says that when the branch comes, the nation represented by Judah and Jerusalem will be saved, and "it" will be called "The LORD is our righteousness."

Sometimes great Scripture truths, like the best Christmas gifts, come in the smallest packages. The prophet makes a crucial point with the little pronoun "it." A few chapters earlier he applies the name "The LORD is our righteousness" to the coming Messiah (23:6). But now the despised and sinful nation is called "The LORD is our righteousness."[11] To emphasize the point, the prophet actually changes that little pronoun "it" to the feminine so that we cannot mistake his point: this despicable nation will be saved and *her* name will be "The LORD is our righteousness." God plans to give his name to his people. It sounds impossible that the nation that has been such a mix of sin and failure could be special to God, but to tell them that they are, he gives them a wonderful name.

But he gives them even more than a name. To make his people shine with his glory . . .

He Gives His People His Nature

Remember what the name means: "The LORD is our righteousness." The branch that is to come, the Messiah, is called the Lord Our Righteousness. His name indicates the nature of his ministry to us. He will provide the righteousness this sinful people could not provide for themselves.[12] The ancient people could not have known clearly what we now know so well. God would provide the righteousness he required through his own Son. He who knew no sin would become sin for us, so that in him we could become the righteousness of God (2 Cor. 5:21). By his work on the cross Jesus provides us with his righteous nature.

What a wonderful thought, that we have been granted the righteous nature of the Messiah. We cover our Christmas trees with tinsel that is supposed to look like silver, but it's really just tinfoil. The tinsel is not really what it is supposed

11. This insight reveals the importance of studying parallel texts to see how biblical concepts are developed within a book and over time.

12. Here the doctrinal aspects of grace are clearly on display though not fully developed. There is no full explanation of the atonement, but the prophet does let us know that the righteousness of the Messiah will become the righteousness of his people. This insight reminds us that redemptive truth may be evident in Old Testament texts by relational interaction (such as God's being faithful to failures) and also by doctrinal statement (such as God's giving his nature to those who do not have it). For discussion of how these various redemptive truths are communicated from Old Testament texts, see *CCP*, 306–8.

to represent. Yet God presents us to himself, not only by calling us by the name of his Son but also by making us what he calls us. We are named a righteous people and made a righteous people by the sacrifice of Christ. The Lord is our righteousness. He gives us the name and nature of his own Son and, thereby, makes us his own children. The glory he puts on us is not like tinfoil—it's the real thing! Despite our sin and shame, we have the righteous name and nature of God's own child.

Knowing that God grants us a new nature by the work of his Son can change the way we look at ourselves and others. I remember sitting in a worship service and listening to a lovely young woman sing. Hers is one of the most beautiful voices I believe I have ever heard. People listen to her and weep at the beauty of her voice. But I have heard her weep other times.

In the past, she was unfaithful to her husband, and now she feels terrible guilt. To escape her guilt, she drinks; and when she drinks, she loses control; and when she loses control, her children pay the price. Then the guilt of that sin presses on her conscience, and the cycle repeats itself again and again. Hers has been a horror story of modern family life.

Yet, as I listened to her sing during a worship service, she sang of the wonderful grace of Jesus. I confess that there was a part of me that winced at this incongruity. What a painful irony that one so flawed should sing so flawlessly. Then I realized that once again I was looking at the tinsel on a twig. That beautiful voice was the tinsel—the representation of the beauty of God—draped on a twisted twig. This woman's voice, like tinsel on a twig, was the Lord's banner of grace. By it he said, "My name and my nature are not reserved for the flawless. No one is holy enough for me, so I must give you my righteousness. I make the ugly beautiful. I make the destitute glorious. I make that which is dark with shame shine like gold because I love to decorate."

Yes, we can be tempted by cynicism and doubt when observing the terribly flawed creatures in the church who dare to call themselves Christian. We look at their foibles and flaws and think to ourselves, *How can they call themselves by that name?* But if we follow that line of questioning back toward our own sin and shame, we know the answer. They call themselves Christian not because of any righteousness in them but because the Lord is our righteousness. He has put his name upon us and his nature within us. His blood is the tinsel that covers us with the glory of his righteousness.

When we realize that it is not *our* goodness that makes us special to God, the real message of Christmas becomes clear. He who used stable straw for the King's bed can use a sinner's heart for the King's throne. God does not reject the despicable but makes them useful and glorious to him. Though we have been unfaithful, God's unfailing love gives us the courage to take our sins to him in open confession and humble repentance. God's provision of his own name and nature makes his righteousness ours to claim despite our shame. He can make the sinful shine with heaven's glory. It is his delight to do so, because he loves to decorate.

Has your sin made you flee from him, turn away in shame, or doubt that his power can again enter your life? Don't doubt him! He who decorates twigs with tinsel can renew his beauty in your life too.

Conclusion

When he was seven, my son Jordan became enamored with Christmas poinsettias. Something about the brilliant splash of red in the dead of winter fascinated him. He wanted a poinsettia so badly that we took him to buy one. Driving home from the store, he was the picture of entranced contentment. He nestled the little plant onto his lap to examine every detail. He smelled it, traced the edge of each leaf with a finger. He even petted the plant as though it were a puppy. But when we came to an intersection requiring a fast brake, the "puppy" spilled into a pool of crimson petals on the floor of the car.

Jordan looked up with horror and grief and guilt on his face. His hands raised before his face expressed the pain he was feeling: *Oh no, what have I done? I should have held it tighter. I should have prepared. I should have protected it more. I should have done better.* When his mother saw that gesture of hurt and shame, she instinctively reached out to him. She draped his hands with her own to cover his hurt with her love. Yes, he could have done better, but his expression of pain and shame provoked only greater love from his mother. With her hands, she brushed away the dirt that now covered him, righted the crimson petals, and put the gift into his hands again.

How much more our God cares for you! He shows it not by offering you a plant but by offering you an infant. Our tendency in this season is to hold the Savior in our imagination as a little puppy, cooing over him and patting his head. But our errors required him to come here, and our faults would spill his blood. The shame of that horror is ours. On our hands is the guilt of Christ's death. Because of our sin, crimson droplets from his hands, feet, and side would pool on the earth beneath a cross. When we see what we have done, our hands rise up to shield us from the horror of our actions and the shame of our sin. But when our heavenly Father sees such expressions of pain, his automatic gesture is to reach out to touch us with his love. The dirt on us does not distract or repel him. He brushes it away with the ministry of his Son. And with the cleansing blood of that same Son, he . . .

Drapes us with his purpose,

Covers us with his love, and

Makes us shine with heaven's glory.

As tinsel can decorate a twig with beauty, our heavenly Father covers our shame with Christ's glory. In the images of the season, he puts his Son again within your reach to receive and to cherish. If your faults and failures make it seem unlikely or improbable or impossible that he would deal so beautifully with you, then you must remember the message of Christmas that is blowing 'round again this year. He who sent his Son for sinners loves to decorate. He even puts tinsel on twigs like me—and like you.[13]

---

13. The final words are meant to include the preacher as one who needs the grace of God in order to encourage others to claim the same. Redemptive vulnerability can be a powerful means of communicating the wonders of the gospel.

Preparatory Christ-Centered Interpretation

(A Dead End Example)

Not every aspect of a prophet's message is predictive. As stated in the introductory comments to the preceding message, the prophets spoke about their time and about the future. When the prophets speak to their time, the message may have content that is ethical, corrective, rebuking, warning, or that contains a host of other kinds of instruction. But the instruction never implies that people's improvement will merit God's affection. God's Word is always preparing his people to understand the nature of his redemption. He may bless obedience, punish rebellion, or warn of consequences, but he doesn't wait to love his people until they stop sinning; he doesn't start loving them because they have achieved perfection. God is always turning his people from sin to himself and embracing the unlovely before their faces reflect his holiness. Though they are faithless, he abides faithful. His love precedes their sinlessness, and his mercy covers their sin.

The implicit message always glimmering within the explicit content of Scripture is that God cares for his people despite their sin and provides for them despite their imperfections. After all, if he didn't care for his people, he wouldn't speak, wouldn't discipline, wouldn't call them to repentance, wouldn't warn, and certainly wouldn't send a Redeemer. If we only look at God's ethical instructions or the sad consequences of ignoring them in the Old Testament, then we will struggle to see the Christ-centeredness of all Scripture. But if we learn to see how passages are preparing God's people to understand their great need and God's greater provision, then the grace of the gospel will begin to glimmer in some of the most unlikely places.[1]

The following sermon from a portion of Isaiah's prophecy demonstrates how God's people are being prepared throughout biblical history to understand how amazing the grace of God is in contrast to spiritually deadly alternatives. The prophet's words provide a "doctrinal statement" of the nature of grace that will make Christ's words and work more understandable in the future.[2] Again, it is important to remember that a sermon is not made "Christ-centered" by forcing a passage to mention Christ but rather by demonstrating how a passage prepares God's people to understand the grace that he ultimately provides. In this case, God's provision is highlighted by contrast to the people's pursuit of forms of idolatry that are a dead end for spiritual sustenance.[3]

1. For a further description of Christ-centered interpretation of how God's people are being "prepared" to see the grace of God that will culminate in the person and work of Christ, see the introduction to this book and the author's *Christ-Centered Preaching: Redeeming the Expository Sermon*, 2nd ed. (Grand Rapids: Baker Academic, 2005), 282–84; hereinafter *CCP*.

2. For a further description of how "doctrinal statement" in some passages enables Christ-centered interpretation, see the introduction to this book and *CCP*, 306–8.

3. For a further description of how some biblical passages identify "dead ends" for spiritual sustenance in order to turn the people of God to his gracious provision, see the introduction to this book and *CCP*, 305–6.

Grits and Grace

Isaiah 44:9-23

Scripture Introduction

You would not want Isaiah's job. He represents God as a prosecutor against Israel. Isaiah speaks of coming judgment—first upon the northern kingdom of Israel, and then upon Judah. He wants to turn them from their idolatry. Instead, his message seems to harden their hearts. But God's heart is not hard. When dealing with his people, God has a gracious purpose even in his judgments. Thus, through Isaiah, in the first few verses of Isaiah 44, God declares that he is the One who creates, sustains, rules, and redeems. He reminds his people that he is the origin and the end of all things, and that apart from him there is no other God. The culminating reason for these declarations comes in verse 8 (NIV), where the Lord asks, "Is there any God besides me?" and then answers, "No, there is no other Rock; I know not one." These statements about the power and uniqueness of God simultaneously set up the following passage about the impotence and futility of idolatry. Isaiah wants God's people to realize that the gods of the world are a sham, and there is no hope in them. But the lesson is more than a warning against trusting wood and stone; it is a warning against trusting in anything human to make us right with this one true God.[1]

---

1. This Scripture introduction has the dual challenge of giving the context of a text that will be obscure to most people and creating longing to hear about material idols that will seem irrelevant to many contemporary people. Thus, the Scripture introduction first deals with the historical context and then ties it to universal human concerns.

Scripture Reading

Read with me this lengthy passage from Isaiah 44:9–23:

All who fashion idols are nothing, and the things they delight in do not profit. Their witnesses neither see nor know, that they may be put to shame. Who fashions a god or casts an idol that is profitable for nothing? Behold, all his companions shall be put to shame, and the craftsmen are only human. Let them all assemble, let them stand forth. They shall be terrified; they shall be put to shame together.

The ironsmith takes a cutting tool and works it over the coals. He fashions it with hammers and works it with his strong arm. He becomes hungry, and his strength fails; he drinks no water and is faint. The carpenter stretches a line; he marks it out with a pencil. He shapes it with planes and marks it with a compass. He shapes it into the figure of a man, with the beauty of a man, to dwell in a house. He cuts down cedars, or he chooses a cypress tree or an oak and lets it grow strong among the trees of the forest. He plants a cedar and the rain nourishes it. Then it becomes fuel for a man. He takes a part of it and warms himself; he kindles a fire and bakes bread. Also he makes a god and worships it; he makes it an idol and falls down before it. Half of it he burns in the fire. Over the half he eats meat; he roasts it and is satisfied. Also he warms himself and says, "Aha, I am warm, I have seen the fire!" And the rest of it he makes into a god, his idol, and falls down to it and worships it. He prays to it and says, "Deliver me, for you are my god!"

They know not, nor do they discern, for he has shut their eyes, so that they cannot see, and their hearts, so that they cannot understand. No one considers, nor is there knowledge or discernment to say, "Half of it I burned in the fire; I also baked bread on its coals; I roasted meat and have eaten. And shall I make the rest of it an abomination? Shall I fall down before a block of wood?" He feeds on ashes; a deluded heart has led him astray, and he cannot deliver himself or say, "Is there not a lie in my right hand?"

> *Remember these things, O Jacob,*
>   *and Israel, for you are my servant;*
> *I formed you; you are my servant;*
>   *O Israel, you will not be forgotten by me.*
> *I have blotted out your transgressions like a cloud*
>   *and your sins like mist;*
> *return to me, for I have redeemed you.*

> *Sing, O heavens, for the* LORD *has done it;*
>   *shout, O depths of the earth;*
> *break forth into singing, O mountains,*
>   *O forest, and every tree in it!*
> *For the* LORD *has redeemed Jacob,*
>   *and will be glorified in Israel.*

Sermon Introduction

Here is one of the most practical hints that I have ever related in a sermon: you can get grits at Waffle House restaurants for thirty-five cents. And I do not mean just a dab to decorate your plate with a little Southern charm. You can get a heaping, big bowl of real grits, slathered in butter, and dripping with cheese for only thirty-five cents. When I saw that big bowl of grits, I didn't even want the waffle that came with it. I knew that those grits would be a meal in itself—and for thirty-five cents! That's almost as good as free. And getting a heaping bowl of cheese grits almost free—that's about as close to seeing grace in real life as you can get.

Since I discovered this amazing grace while my family was on vacation, I immediately began to calculate how inexpensively we could travel across the country if we frequented Waffle House restaurants on the rest of our trip. I even began to consider how the rest of our lives might change. We wouldn't have to wait for anniversaries and birthdays to eat out. We might even give my wife, Kathy, a break once or twice a year from dinner preparations on a regular weekday! My miserly contemplations almost had me in cheese grits heaven, until my eyes landed on the small print on the menu.

Printed at the bottom of the plasticized list of waffles, pancakes, and fried eggs were these disheartening words: "Cheese grits 35 cents *with* any full entrée." Yeah, the cheese grits were *almost* free, as long as you purchased something else. Suddenly I knew that I was looking at the kind of grace too many of us in the church actually believe in. It's good, it's sweet, it's wonderful, as long as you add something more. It's almost free. It's grace that is yours only if you add a little more of your own efforts and accomplishments to deserve it. Such grace seems sufficient until we discover that we really don't have more to give and that the grace we "deserve" isn't grace that can help us at all.[2] Faith in "almost free" grace is actually what Isaiah

---

2. The fallen condition focus (FCF) for this message is stated informally and colloquially. If it were stated in formal terms, the FCF might be something like, "We tend to believe that the grace we get is the

is warning Israel about. The way he does so will first surprise you, then make you question his theology, and finally lead you to praise his God for a grace that—unlike my cheese grits—really is totally and amazingly free![3]

I. The Nature and Futility of Idolatry

The Nature of Idolatry (vv. 9–11)

Idolatry occurs whenever we begin to believe that something produced by human effort has divine power. People practice idolatry when they claim something of the created world can create a new world for us. In essence, idolatry substitutes gods we create to serve our purposes for *the* God who created everything for his purposes.[4]

Isaiah gives three examples of such idolatry: he describes products made by a blacksmith, a carpenter, and a cook. Each description has a particular nuance that tells us a bit more about the nature of idolatry.

Blacksmith

The blacksmith (v. 12) forges an idol with fire, tools, and "the might of his arm" (NIV). But ultimately the process makes him hungry, tired, and thirsty. Instead of helping him out, his idol wears him out. This lesson is simple: looking to anything other than God to remake our world will ultimately wear us out. Seeking more recognition, more salary, more pleasure, or more security solely by our own efforts and designs may work for a while, but trying to remake our world by depending solely on the things we can produce will ultimately deplete and exhaust us.

---

grace we deserve." Instead, this FCF is developed over several short sentences and leaves some tension about what "almost free" grace is about. For more information on the FCF's role in redemptive approaches to preaching, see *CCP*, 269–72.

3. The proposition is also informally stated and implied. A formal proposition would be something like this: "Since the grace of God is totally free, we must not claim his grace by pointing to the reasons we deserve it." Instead, this implied proposition asks the listeners to hang with the preacher for a while to find out why Isaiah's definition of grace is so surprising that it will make us question the prophet's theology. This approach intends to present a proposition that creates interest by intrigue rather than by explicit statement. For further discussion on implied propositions, see *CCP*, 147–49.

4. The challenge of this message is to make ancient pagan idolatry seem relevant to modern listeners. Thus, "principle-izing" Isaiah's examples (i.e., identifying what universal truth principles may be elicited from his specific examples) occurs early to demonstrate relevance and keep listeners engaged before the examples are dissected.

Carpenter

The carpenter (v. 13) measures and marks wood before carving his idol and putting it in a shrine that is also the work of his hands. Isaiah's language choices are meant to be instructive: the carpenter roughs out the idol with chisels and refines it with compasses—it really is a work of art—but ultimately he fashions it "into the figure of man." Even though the form is of "the beauty of a man" (i.e., a man in all his glory), it is still just the reflection of a man, a work of the carpenter's hands. Our idols inevitably mirror our thoughts and abilities. They cannot be more or provide more than we can devise. Our idols will always reflect our image and possess our limitations.

I remember a college professor responding to a student who was challenging the truthfulness of Scripture. The professor handed the student a pair of scissors. "Alright," he said, "you cut out everything you think does not belong in God's Word, or is not worthy of being there. But you should recognize that, when you are done, the Bible you have will only reflect your wisdom. It will really be just your word. It will only be a reflection of your own thoughts and opinions." In my mind's eye I saw the pages of the Bible appearing as a collection of paper dolls, all looking like that student.[5] All products of our wisdom and efforts are ultimately just a reflection of us.

We can make cars go faster than we can, telescopes see farther than we can, and computers calculate faster than we can, but still we are inextricably bound to the natural—and all we create will reflect natural limitations that are far short of God's supernatural power and identity. Thus, though idols are created to escape our limitations, they reflect our humanity, and their worship can only pay homage to our own limitations. All idolatry is ultimately worship of our own reflected image.

Cook

But what if the idols we fashion from natural resources could be used to conjure or control the supernatural? This proposal Isaiah answers with his description of the carpenter turned cook. The prophet's gentle mockery makes it clear that if the maker of the idol cannot control the forces that provide his idol, then it is foolish to expect the idol of his making to have more power. The cook (who is really just the

---

5. Relevance of the ancient account is also maintained by showing how its truths are exhibited in a modern context such as a classroom.

carpenter preparing his meal in vv. 14–20) begins his work by cutting down trees whose growth requires the rain of heaven—which the cook can't control (v. 14). Then the cook uses the wood he could not cause to grow to make a fire to warm himself from the elements he cannot regulate and to bake bread for the hunger he cannot stop from recurring (v. 15). In essence, Isaiah teases, "The wood serves him, yields to his hand, and performs his bidding. Why would he think that he should worship it?" And to make the point further he adds, "Half of it [the wood] he burns in the fire. . . . And the rest of it he makes into a god, his idol" (vv. 16–17). Since the cook destroys half of his own idol, why would he think it can save him? In logic later made notorious by the Pharisees, Isaiah similarly asks, "If your god cannot save itself, why would you think it can save you?" (cf. Matt. 27:42).

The Futility of Idolatry (vv. 18–20)

The futility of idolatry exposed through the images of a blacksmith, carpenter, and cook now erupts from the prophet in exasperated tones: "They know not, nor do they discern . . . they cannot understand" (v. 18). Idolaters trust an idol they control to take control of a world beyond their control.

Isaiah concludes that the man who trusts an idol "feeds on ashes" (v. 20). The same materials his fires consume are those he tries to use to feed his lusts and longings. Such ashen consumables won't fill you up, won't nourish you, won't satisfy you—they will just make you want to rinse and spit. If you have tried to find happiness in the ashes of relationships or possessions or acclaim, then you know exactly what the prophet meant. You just want to rinse and spit out the disappointment—and find something else that does not turn ashen in the crucibles of life.[6]

Isaiah is intentionally leading God's people on such a search—a search they would not ordinarily initiate. After all, in a Jewish culture it was not much of a radical idea to teach that we should not trust created things to control the Creator. Though we can appreciate the cleverness of Isaiah's discussion of idols, we need to go a bit deeper into why this discussion is where it is. The reason has to be that Isaiah wants to expose what is really behind the idols of some people's hands in

---

6. A key discovery for most preachers is the principle of mutual condition (see a discussion of FCF in *CCP*, 48–52). When the preacher shows that the people in the biblical context are experiencing human pain, emotions, or struggles that are common in our own context, then we feel compelled to listen to what the Bible says about our mutual heart condition, even when our external circumstances differ.

order to make us all face the real idols of our hearts. To make the idolatries of our hearts evident, the prophet talks not just about the nature of idolatry (in terms that we expect) but also about the nature of redemption (in terms that surprise us).

II. The Nature of Redemption

Why does Isaiah spend so much effort exposing an idolatry his people are unlikely to approve? The prophet knows that until we understand the nature of all humanity reflected in every idol, we will not understand how inclined we all are to our own idolatries. Only when we understand how free God's grace is of any human contribution will our hearts discover the redemption that rightly motivates his worship and our lives. Describing the true nature of such redemption is the prophet's next task.

God Remembers His People (v. 21)

Most commentators say that by the time Isaiah writes this portion of his book, there remains only a remnant of Israel, the people who are either facing a Babylonian takeover or are already in Babylonian slavery. God's people are in dire straits. They must wonder if God will help them, if their sin has sent him away forever, and if he has *forgotten* them. Isaiah responds with these beautiful words: "Remember these things, O Jacob, and Israel, for you are my servant; I formed you; you are my servant; O Israel, you will not be forgotten by me" (v. 21).

The people forgot their God and abandoned loyalty to him, but God says, "I formed you . . . I will not forget you." He also addresses them by their covenant names: Jacob and Israel. The names remind the Jews that they are the people of promise, the nation God prepared for his purposes, and the precious treasure of his heart. God's statement that he will not forget his people is more than a promise of mental recall; it is a declaration that he will act according to his covenant promises in their behalf.[7] The centuries of care he has given them, as well as the promises that he will fulfill through them, are in accord with the pledges God made to the

---

7. These sweeping statements regarding God's covenantal faithfulness are important reminders of the faithfulness of God despite the frequent waywardness of his people. In this general way, Isaiah *prepares* the ancient readers and the contemporary ones to understand God's redemptive nature and plan. God's covenantal faithfulness is clearly an aspect of his relational interaction with his people that displays his gracious nature, but there are even more explicit doctrinal statements of this truth to come.

patriarchs that state God will never forget or forsake. Though Jacob's descendants have turned from trusting his provision (they made alliances with pagan kingdoms when the nation was threatened), God will not turn from them.

God Forgives His People (v. 22)

Not only are God's covenant people remembered despite their abandonment, they are also forgiven despite their sin. God says, "I have blotted out your transgressions like a cloud and your sins like mist; return to me, for I have redeemed you" (v. 22). The words are beautiful and precious, and I will try not to spoil them by technical discussion; but part of their beauty lies in the precise ways God expresses his mercy.

After Sin

First, God says that he forgives his people *after* they have sinned. The people turned from God to self-preserving devices of their own making. How does God use his sovereign power in response? He blots out their offenses, as a cloud can be swept out of a portion of the sky or from an entire mountain over which it settles. Additionally, as the sun melts away the morning mist, so God's mercy dissolves his people's guilt.

These beautiful images are not randomly chosen. The Lord knows how sin can cast a cloud over our lives and take the light from our hearts. When we really understand that our sin has been blotted from the sight of heaven, and the mist of our shame has been melted away by the warmth of God's mercy, then a new day dawns for us. Our hearts brighten and our steps quicken with the realization of God's provision for a forgiven past and a fresh start. God promises to remember us and not our sin. So, though it may sound sappy, the possibility of sunny days of sin swept away means everything. If you have only known gray days, you know how powerful such light can be.

In her book *Traveling Mercies*, novelist Anne Lamott describes the feeling of being remembered despite sin and, as a consequence, having the clouds of life clear:

> [The minister] was about the first Christian I ever met whom I could stand to be in the same room with. Most Christians seemed almost hostile in their belief that they were saved and you weren't. What did it mean to be saved? I asked. . . .

"You don't need to think about this," he said.

"Just tell me."

"I guess it's like discovering you're on the shelf of a pawnshop, dusty and forgotten and maybe not worth very much. But Jesus comes in and tells the pawnbroker, 'I'll take her place on the shelf. Let her go outside.'"[8]

That was the promise of new light and a new day just in being remembered, not forgotten on the shelf because of sin. But the mist still had to dissipate for Lamott. She writes:

> I wanted to fall on my knees, newly born, but I didn't. I walked back home . . . and got out the Scotch. I was feeling better in general, less out of control, even though it would be four more years before I got sober. I was not willing to give up a life of shame and failure without a fight. . . .
>
> Slowly I came back to life. I'd been like one of the people Ezekiel comes upon in the valley of dry bones—people who had given up, who were lifeless and without hope. But because of Ezekiel's presence, breath comes upon them; spirit and kindness revive them.

I love those words: "spirit and kindness revive them." They remind me of Romans 2:4 (NASB): "the kindness of God leads you to repentance." Yet, though the words are dear, something seems wrong here. Anne Lamott was reminded that she was not forgotten, *before* she repented. She experienced kindness *before* the end of the drinking that was destroying her. *Before* the turn from ruin, she began to experience God's remembrance and mercy. We can't tell people they are forgiven before they repent, or else they may take advantage of God's mercy—right!?

No, not right. The beauty of grace on display here is not simply the statement that God's people are forgiven *after* sin; they are actually forgiven *before* repentance. Does that sound impossible and dangerous? It might be. But consider how Isaiah presents a grace so amazing that even believers have trouble believing it.

Before Repentance

What does repentance mean? An Old Testament word for repentance is *shuwb*, and it means "to turn." Repentance means to turn from sin to God. Knowing this

---

8. Anne Lamott, *Traveling Mercies: Some Thoughts on Faith* (New York: Pantheon Books, 1999), 41–44 with some wording variations for sermon structure.

helps us more carefully examine the wording of Isaiah 44:22. God says, "I *have* blotted out your transgression like a cloud and your sins like mist." What tense is that assurance, and when is the mercy extended? Already. God's sweeping away of his people's offenses is a past, accomplished act. Then, what are the people to do in response? God says, "Return to me." When does that happen? It hasn't yet happened at the time that Isaiah is writing.

At the moment when God reminds his people of the mercy he has already granted them, they are facing discipline for their sin and haven't yet turned back to him. In fact, not only is their situation about to get worse, the people are about to get worse. Their sin and rebellion will deepen. God will not forget them, but they will forget God. How can this be true? How can the people's sins be swept away before they have turned back to God? The answer is in the next phrase: "for I have redeemed you." What tense is that? The Lord's redemption is a past, completed action. There could hardly be a clearer exhibition of a heart of unconditional love or clearer evidence of a covenant made and maintained by God rather than by human accomplishment. God has redeemed before his people have repented.[9]

One of the joys of serving on a seminary campus is seeing so many couples with young children. When you mix theology and family, babies seem to result. That means I get to watch a lot of babies take their first steps. You know the scene: a parent kneels *beyond the reach* of the child, but reaches toward the child, saying, "C'mon. I will catch you. Come to my love. Come to my arms." Very few parents turn their backs, cross their arms, and say, "When you can stand up on your two legs and walk over here, then I'll love you." Love comes first. Such love is not made conditional on the performance of the child. Rather, the love that precedes proper performance beckons and draws the child forward in the way he should go.

To move from this simple parental example to the poignant spiritual implication, consider the difference between what John Calvin called "evangelical repentance" and "legal repentance." Legal repentance presumes that God's mercy depends on

---

9. Many of the best sermons that we preach will have a pivot point, a crucial idea that, once stated, really is the fulcrum on which the power of the sermon is leveraged. This is such a point. Though this portion of the message does not contain the formal proposition, the immediate insight that is based on the grammar of the prophet enables the preacher to articulate an aspect of grace that will seem surprising (if not impossible) to believe for many steeped in traditional religious thought. Showing that grace is absolutely free and undeserved is the *raison d'être* for this sermon, and this exegetical observation proves that point. This distinguishing feature of grace *prepares* generations prior to Christ and all those in the ages after his earthly ministry to understand the defining nature of his grace—and how amazingly good it is.

the adequacy of one's repentance. We attempt to activate his mercy by our actions (investing sufficient words, tears, or time). We look for our salvation in the sufficiency of what we do. In contrast, evangelical repentance—what we would probably call "gospel (i.e., good news) repentance"—is a consequence of God's mercy. We repent (turn from our sin to God) because we have grasped that the mercy extended to us is already present, full, and free. The knowledge of a love greater than all our sin, of forgiveness despite our rebellion, of mercy despite the inadequacy of our repentance, breaks us, beckons us, and builds in us the joy that is our strength—apart from the adequacy of anything in us.

Anne Lamott again clarifies with the example of her own experience. She speaks first of the god she had unknowingly made in a form of idolatry, from which she had to turn in order to discover the God who already loved her:

> Mine was a patchwork God, sewn together from bits of rag and ribbon, Eastern and Western, pagan and Hebrew, everything but the kitchen sink and Jesus.
>
> Then one afternoon in my dark bedroom, the cracks webbed all the way through me. I believed that I would die soon, from a fall or an overdose. I knew there was an afterlife but felt . . . they couldn't possibly take you in the shape I was in. I could no longer imagine how God could love me.
>
> But in my dark bedroom . . . out of nowhere, it crossed my mind to call the new guy [the new minister] at St. Stephen's. . . .
>
> It took me forty-five minutes to walk there, but this skinny middle-aged guy was still in his office when I arrived. . . . He was really listening, . . . and so I let it all tumble out—the X-rated motels, my father's death, a hint that maybe every so often I drank too much.
>
> I don't remember much of his response, except that when I said, I didn't think God could love me, he said, "God *has* to love you. That's God's job."

I confess that the minister's response doesn't initially seem like a very good, theological answer. But years later the minister explained why he had put the responsibility of Anne's redemption entirely on God and not at all on what she had done or could do. Later he told her,

> Here you were in a rather desperate situation, suicidal, clearly alcoholic, going down the tubes. I thought the trick was to help you extricate yourself enough so you could breathe again. You said your prayers weren't working anymore, and I could see that in

your desperation you were trying to save *yourself*: so I said you should stop praying for a while, and let me pray for you. And right away, you seemed to settle down inside.

What settled Anne Lamott?[10] Not trusting in the god of her making or in the adequacy of her prayer, but letting another take the entire load of her salvation. She had to learn to trust that it was "God's job" to do everything that was needed to save her. In short, she needed to discover how free grace really is. God's mercy doesn't depend on the adequacy of our prayer, of our thought, of our obedience, or even of our repentance. God's love and forgiveness come first, even before repentance.

Despite Concerns

I know all of you listening to me are worried now. You are thinking, "If a preacher promises forgiveness before repentance, then people will do whatever they want and presume upon God's mercy. They will take advantage of grace." I must acknowledge, yes, that is certainly a possibility. But consider the alternatives:

1. *God's forgiveness depends on the quality or quantity of my repentance.* If God's forgiveness depends on my repentance, what will happen if I repent just a little? Will he forgive me if I murder a million people and then say, "Oh, sorry about that"? Most of you will say, "Definitely not. God will only forgive if our repentance is sincere, authentic, and from a heart that is really broken." In other words, what we all tend to think is that God's grace depends on the adequacy of our repentance.

But I have a question for those reaching the conclusion that God's mercy depends on the adequacy of our repentance: Exactly when do you think that our repentance will be sufficient to satisfy a holy God or merit his blood-bought forgiveness or activate his infinite mercy? Let's all agree that repentance *should* be sincere, authentic, and deep. But if God's grace depends on what we do, then we must realize that our theology actually states that divine activity is controlled by human accomplishment. Yet that conclusion is the very idolatry Isaiah has been warning God's people about in this passage. If our salvation depends on the quantity or quality of our remorse, then the object of our faith is not the sufficiency of God's mercy but the sufficiency of our repentance.

10. The appropriateness of using Anne Lamott will vary by congregation and pastoral context. Her own life story, even after her conversion, is not without murky issues. Whether her testimony is of benefit to the preacher may well depend on how deeply grace has touched the congregation—or needs to.

There are real consequences to making God's forgiveness conditional on the adequacy of our repentance:

1. We may base our spiritual status on the pride that our repentance is really enough to satisfy God;

2. we may require a purgatory in this life (in the form of depression or self-destructive behaviors) or in the next, out of fear of the inadequacy of repentance; or

3. we may simply presume, if our consciences are sensitive to the true inadequacy of our repentance to merit a holy God's approval, that hell is our future.

Hell begins in this life for all those who believe their repentance is the basis of God's love and yet face the truth that our repentance will never be enough, or fear that we have forgotten to confess something (which we all have), or dread that death may come too surprisingly or swiftly for us to adequately repent of the sins we can recall.

What is the alternative to such fear and dread? The alternative is to believe Isaiah's claim that forgiveness comes before repentance. Repentance does not earn forgiveness; rather, our repentance is the means by which we enter into the experience of mercy that is already above, around, and underneath us, surrounding us as a mighty ocean of divine love whose currents buoy us up and usher us to ever greater love for God. Such love binds our hearts to him, breaks them in true repentance for sin, and inclines them increasingly to yield to whatever pleases him.

2. God's unconditional forgiveness is only an Old Testament arrangement. Some may contend that God's unconditional willingness to melt away the mist of sin for his people is a unique arrangement of an Old Testament covenant with Israel. Such persons think this arrangement cannot apply to us because the New Testament says, "If we confess our sins, he is faithful and just to forgive us our sins and to cleanse us from all unrighteousness" (1 John 1:9).

To answer this concern, we must remember the difference between New Testament statements of fact and statements of cause. It is certainly true that if we confess our sin, God will forgive us. But the language is not of tit for tat, this for that. John is *not* describing a specific human act that gains or causes God's mercy.

Rather, the apostle uses the language of a continual confession (literally, "If we are confessing our sins . . ."). This is a description not of a specific act but of an attitude of life—a mind-set of contrition that is always pushing away from the adequacy of our work. Such an abiding attitude of confession is a steady dependence on grace, a state of humility before God, that allows us to experience the mercy that is always beyond our merit. This is not an indication of forgiveness earned by the merit of our repentance but of forgiveness savored in acknowledgment of our total dependence on God's mercy. I do not by my confession gain God's forgiveness; my confession is that his forgiveness is always beyond my contribution—it is really, totally free.

3. God's forgiveness requires adequate sorrow for and distance from sin. Some may believe that if we do not make God's forgiveness conditional on our contrition or correction, then we will encourage cheap grace—presuming on God's forgiveness regardless of any real change of heart or action. But Isaiah clearly does not say that unconditional mercy should encourage little remorse or less repentance. God says to his people through Isaiah, *"Return to me,* for I have redeemed you" (Isa. 44:22b). He expects a change of behavior because he has redeemed his people. He commands action that is consistent with their saved status. God clearly expects genuine contrition to accompany petitions for forgiveness. This is reinforced in the chapter immediately before this one we are studying; there God denounces his people for sacrifices that do not reflect true sorrow for sin (43:23).

The Lord expects correction and contrition for sin from the repentant. These are the marks of repentance. They are the evidence of devotion to him. They are the path to experiencing mercy and knowing his forgiveness. But they are not the *cause* of God's forgiveness and do not merit it. Knowledge of the prior and perpetual mercy that God promises without condition is the grace that draws us to him and keeps us walking with him. We have no assurance of grace if we have no evidence of God in our lives, but that reality is not a denial of the source of the grace: God alone.

We must confess that a possible consequence of believing that forgiveness can precede repentance is presumption upon and abuse of God's grace.[11] But there are

11. One of the marks of preaching that is both compassionate and courageous is the willingness of the preacher to ask questions listeners would ask, if they thought that they could. Acknowledging the dangers of an absolutely free grace just proclaimed and then answering why it must still be so is one way of dealing with listeners' inner reservations.

also dangers in assuming that divine grace depends on and awaits sufficient human attitudes or actions. If God's mercy depends on the adequacy of my repentance, then any apparent lack of mercy (such as the trials and difficulties we all face) can only be presumed evidence of insufficient remorse on our part or ineffective grace on God's part. Conditional grace inevitably becomes questioned grace.

Consider where loss of faith in pure grace could have left my beloved missionary friend Ricky Grey as a consequence of recent events in his life. He and his family have had to return to the United States from Uganda because his seventeen-month-old son, Chase, has a brain malformation. The family does not know what Chase's future will be, or the future of their other child who is also handicapped, or the future of the family if they cannot return to the mission field. Ricky writes:

> With every hint of progress—a hand clap, a better bite, a new sound—our hopes rise. But with every ongoing struggle—another decline in growth percentile, the drop of a toy, a stiffened leg—our hearts sink.... Consequently, depending on the moment, we vacillate back and forth between fear and faith.... When dark thoughts about the Lord's goodness and greatness threaten to undo us, we are learning the best heart medicine is a blood-stained cross and an empty garden tomb. (Mission letter July/August 2008)

No one writes that way whose status with God depends on the adequacy of human confession. You can't admit the vacillations of fear and faith, dark thoughts and comfort, questions about God and clinging to his Word, if God's favor depends on expressing sufficient faith. You can't risk the confession of continuing fear, doubt, and anger if God is only merciful to those whose confession is adequate, sufficient, and right. But if God's mercy is infinitely prior, full, and free (really free—not dependent on how perfect are our words and thoughts), then we can approach him as we really are, put our real heartache close to his heart, and really experience the love of God that surrounds us despite God's knowing the worst about us.

J. I. Packer explains the blessing of such pure, unearned, and honest grace:

> There is tremendous relief in knowing that His love to me is utterly realistic, based at every point on prior knowledge of the worst about me, so that no discovery can disillusion Him about me, in the way I am so often disillusioned about myself, and I quench His determination to bless me.[12]

12. J. I. Packer, *Knowing God* (Downers Grove, IL: InterVarsity, 1973), 42.

Do you hear that? You cannot quench God's determination to bless you because his mercy, his blessing, his forgiveness was never based on what you do or the adequacy of it. Knowledge of such a God breaks us, beckons us, and builds in us the desire to confess our sin and walk with him. This is why Isaiah speaks of such a gracious God in order to turn a rebellious people back to him.

We are forgiven after sin, before repentance, despite concerns, and also . . .

Through Consequences

Note that while the prophet says forgiveness is prior to repentance, he does *not* suggest there are no consequences for sin. In Isaiah's case, Babylon still will have its day. The people of Israel still will have their time of exile as a consequence of turning from the God who has redeemed them eternally and could rescue them at any time. But consequences come to correct the people and turn them from the sin that could damage God's greater purposes for them and us (after all, the Messiah will come through Israel). God's people, though they are being disciplined by Babylon's conquest, are loved no less. Listen to God's heart through Isaiah's words of both prosecution and hope:

> Sing, O heavens, for the LORD has done it {redeemed};
>   shout, O depths of the earth;
> break forth into singing, O mountains,
>   O forest, and every tree in it!
> For the LORD has redeemed Jacob,
>   and will be glorified in Israel. (Isa. 44:23)

Even when God's people are in the throes of the worst discipline heaven can bring, they are loved no less. The same is true of us. Even when we are in the midst of the chastisement we deserve, God loves us no less. The aim of his correction is to turn us back into his arms, to return us to the paths of blessing, and to bring us close again to experience his love. How do I know this is true for people in this age as well as for people in ancient times? I know because this is the same God who has redeemed his people through the blood of his Son. We are redeemed by the Messiah that Isaiah prophesied. His work for his people is finished; all that he intended is accomplished. I am forgiven because he was forsaken, not because my confession passes muster. I am loved because he cherished me before the foundations of the world were laid, not because I have performed well enough today. I am welcomed because the Father sacrificed his Son in my place, not because I wept long enough over my failures. He has been gracious to me before I even faced my sin and long after my repentance for it failed to merit his mercy. When I know so great a grace from my God, I want to confess my sin, walk with him, and tell the world about his gospel.[13]

Conclusion

This passage of Isaiah, which so beautifully portrays grace principles of the fullness and freeness of our redemption, reminds us how the Bible consistently prepares God's people to understand our standing before God solely based on the grace of Christ. Such an interpretation does not require us to extricate any passage from its original context and purpose but rather to see its relation to the ultimate good news provided by our Savior. His love is not conditioned on the adequacy of anything in us. As we lean entirely upon his mercy, his grace surrounds our lives, makes provision for our insufficiency, and supplies forgiveness for our sin even before we are able rightly to request it.

I sometimes think of our forays into the Old Testament as analogous to walking along a path that leads to a party to which we were long ago invited. The party is an old-fashioned hayride. For such a party, people pile into a hay wagon to sing and play as they make their way to a place of celebration. As they travel, they gather more friends along the way, and even more friends travel the route the hay wagon has passed, anticipating that they will join the party already under way. Most of us are walking along the path toward the celebration that has already begun, and we sometimes wonder if we are worthy of the gathering—if we have come too late or strayed too far now to be welcome. But as we see the little clumps of hay from those who have traveled this path before us, and as we hear strains of distant music, we begin to understand that the party didn't get canceled and hasn't ended because we weren't there when it began.[14]

13. This paragraph summarizes the amazing grace that Isaiah has prepared God's people to understand and depend on.

14. Sermons have strengths and weaknesses. I am unconvinced of the strength of this conclusion. It was presented in a context in which I was committed to demonstrating that all of the Old Testament *prepares* us to understand the grace of God. As a consequence, the closing illustration becomes more a reflection of that larger concept than the best fit for climaxing the specifics of this message. I have kept the conclusion here for the purposes of this chapter (showing how Old Testament passages prepare us to

Finally, we break into a clearing where the party is in full swing, the fire is bright, the food is great, and the band leader gathers us all into his dance. Whether we came early or late, or have the right shoes to dance, or don't have the skills to dance well, we still get invited to join the party. In fact, the leader of the dance invites us to join in even though we wonder if we should. He acts as though he knew all along that we would show up at different times, in different ways, sometimes stumbling, and sometimes still wearing the wrong shoes. He doesn't send us away or lessen his welcome because of our missteps. He keeps playing the music and calling the dance even though we've not yet got all the moves down or apologized for stepping on the toes of our partners. He seems to be all right with us before we have gotten everything all right before him.

The clumps of hay and music along the path are the principles of grace throughout Scripture that tell us about the gospel joy to which our Savior invites us. The party in full swing—that's the New Testament gospel of Christ's mercy and victory being enjoyed by his people. And the leader who invites us to dance is our Savior, who isn't looking at the time of our arrival or the adequacy of our dress but looks only at our names on the invitation that he wrote. It doesn't seem to matter that we missed the wagon when it passed our street, or turned the other way when he reminded us to follow him, or don't have enough money to pay for the music he provides. All that seems to matter to him is that we are now at the party that he always planned for us to attend.

But, of course, our joining the party is not the end of the story. This is a hayride, and that means the party will eventually move on down the road to gather more friends. So now that we are part of the party, we get to invite more and more people to join the celebration of Christ's grace. And the more we delight in this grace, the more we rejoice that there is so much of it and that it is really free. Grace so abundant and so free keeps us dancing in the light of the gospel to the glory of the Savior. We yield our lives to him because he has given such amazing grace to us. You who know this grace, keep dancing to the tune of the gospel, and invite someone else to the dance.

---

understand the grace that culminates in Christ), but I would substitute material more personal if preaching this sermon again.

Reflective Christ-Centered Interpretation

(Narrative Passage)

The following sermon multiplies our understanding of ways to provide a Christ-centered interpretation of an Old Testament passage (and some New Testament passages). In the two previous sermon examples, we have considered how Old Testament passages may be predictive of, or prepare for, the person and work of Christ. This sermon demonstrates how the truths of grace may be "reflected" in an Old Testament passage, even one which initially may seem to have few redemptive qualities on display.[1] Again, no attempt is made to make Jesus "appear" in the narrative; rather, the preacher points out aspects of grace that will have their full expression in the person and work of Christ. The passage points to Christ not by mystical mention but by reflecting aspects of our nature and God's that help to disclose the grace ultimately needed and provided in Christ.

---

1. For a further description of how grace "reflected" in some passages enables Christ-centered interpretation, see the introduction to this book and the author's *Christ-Centered Preaching: Redeeming the Expository Sermon*, 2nd ed. (Grand Rapids: Baker Academic, 2005), 284–86; hereinafter *CCP*.

This message also demonstrates the importance of not simply preaching a "be like" message.[2] "Be like" messages are one form of the "Deadly Be's" that sting listeners with unqualified moralism. A "be like" message identifies the exemplary features of a biblical character's life and then simply encourages listeners to be like that person. Such "biographical preaching" highlights the deeds of heroes of the Bible. The problem with such messages that only focus on the exemplary behavior of heroic figures is that there is only One entirely exemplary person in Scripture. The Bible takes care to tarnish almost everyone else so that we will know our hope is in our Savior and not in our behavior.

Of course, the Bible uses heroes to teach us about righteousness, courage, and sacrifice, but all truly godly people in Scripture put their hope in God. The heroes are meant to teach us about godly dependence as well as godly behavior. Thus, "be like" messages are not wrong *in* themselves; they are wrong *by* themselves. Without underscoring the grace that enables godliness and redeems its lack, messages on biblical heroes can only drive God's people to pride ("I can be like that") or despair ("I can never be like that"). The following message on the life of Moses demonstrates how the greatest of biblical heroes still needs the grace of God—as do we.

Finally, readers should note that the following message is an example of an expository sermon prepared for a narrative passage of Scripture.[3] The message does not follow a typical "three-points-and-a-poem" structure because it seeks to reflect the flow of the biblical narrative's plot.[4] As a consequence, this message has four points, with a "surprise" ending intended to reflect how Moses's story would have impacted original readers.[5]

2. For further discussion of "be like" messages and the other "Deadly Be's," see the introduction to this book and CCP, 289–95.
3. For a further description of preaching expository messages on narrative passages, see CCP, 122–23, 156–57, and 187–88.
4. For further discussion of sermons based on narrative forms, see CCP, 162–68; for further discussion of sermons with more than three points, see CCP, 155.
5. Astute preachers will also note that there is an implied fifth point, if one counts the short "misdirection" immediately before the first main point, where I address a road not taken (i.e., dealing with the wrongdoing of the people instead of the mistakes of Moses).

A First Repenter

Numbers 20:1–13

Scripture Introduction

For almost forty years Moses and the people of Israel have wandered in the desert, preparing to enter the Promised Land. Before their wanderings, the people were poised to enter the land. Then they sent men ahead to spy out the blessings and challenges of the new land. The spies brought back reports of a land flowing with milk and honey, but there was just one little problem: really big people. The people of Israel trembled and turned back. Now, after four decades of desert misery, they are almost ready to try the Promised Land again. But there is another big problem: no water. And no water means somebody must have led them badly. All fingers point to Moses. How he responds is not only a lesson in leadership but a lesson in how God's grace can show up in the most unexpected places—for the most unlikely people.

Scripture Reading

Read with me Numbers 20:1–13:

> And the people of Israel, the whole congregation, came into the wilderness of Zin in the first month, and the people stayed in Kadesh. And Miriam died there and was buried there.
>
> Now there was no water for the congregation. And they assembled themselves together against Moses and against Aaron. And the people quarreled with Moses

and said, "Would that we had perished when our brothers perished before the
LORD! Why have you brought the assembly of the LORD into this wilderness, that
we should die here, both we and our cattle? And why have you made us come up
out of Egypt to bring us to this evil place? It is no place for grain or figs or vines or
pomegranates, and there is no water to drink." Then Moses and Aaron went from
the presence of the assembly to the entrance of the tent of meeting and fell on their
faces. And the glory of the LORD appeared to them, and the LORD spoke to Moses,
saying, "Take the staff, and assemble the congregation, you and Aaron your brother,
and tell the rock before their eyes to yield its water. So you shall bring water out of
the rock for them and give drink to the congregation and their cattle." And Moses
took the staff from before the LORD, as he commanded him.

Then Moses and Aaron gathered the assembly together before the rock, and he
said to them, "Hear now, you rebels: shall we bring water for you out of this rock?"
And Moses lifted up his hand and struck the rock with his staff twice, and water came
out abundantly, and the congregation drank, and their livestock. And the LORD said
to Moses and Aaron, "Because you did not believe in me, to uphold me as holy in
the eyes of the people of Israel, therefore you shall not bring this assembly into the
land that I have given them." These are the waters of Meribah, where the people of
Israel quarreled with the LORD, and through them he showed himself holy.

Sermon Introduction

The sermon had gone very well, if he did say so himself. The pastor, whom I will
not mention by name, later wrote of how he was basking in the glow of encouraging words and enthusiastic handshakes that greeted him after the morning service.
In the sermon, his exegesis revealed the implications of a Greek word not even
noted by his seminary professors. The illustrations were as diverse as a reference
to the martyrdom of an obscure Puritan and an observation about the docking
mechanism on spacecraft. And the applications—ah, the applications—had been
so poignant that even the engineers in the congregation got misty eyed. The sun
was shining, the choir sparkled, attendance was up, the sermon was done (and
done well). It was a perfect Sunday!

Only one thing bothered the pastor as he drove home. He realized that his wife
had not added her voice to the chorus of compliments. Her oversight began to niggle
at him, and he couldn't let it go. He knew that he couldn't just come out and directly
ask for a compliment. That would be too obvious, and maybe even unspiritual. But

there she sat, looking out the window, saying nothing. It was obvious that she needed some help to do the right thing. So he decided to help her by simply asking a question that would lead her to a proper response. With a nonchalant voice, intended not to put his wife on guard or embarrass her in any way, he asked, "Honey, how many really great preachers do you suppose there are in the world today?"

She did not answer but continued to gaze out the window. Perhaps, the preacher thought, she had not heard him. She was probably still lost in the euphoria of the worship and depth of his message. So he asked again, "Sweetie pie, how many truly great preachers do you suppose there are in the world today?"

This time she answered: "One less than you are thinking right now, honey."[1]

The account may be a bit funny, but it's a lot more scary. What's frightening is how easy it is to shift our worship focus from God to ourselves. Right in the middle of serving God, and serving him well, we can get caught up in serving our own self-interests and not even notice the problem. We think we are directing glory to God only to discover that we are directing worship to ourselves.[2] Such self-idolatry sounds so awful that you would think it would be easily avoided by mature spiritual leaders. Yet Moses's experience reminds us that directing worship to ourselves can be a temptation at any stage of ministry. This familiar account of Moses reminds us of a fairly simple lesson: leaders of God's people cannot obey God and be God at the same time.[3] That's the simple lesson, the more difficult truth is as important to know but harder to accept: our susceptibility to mixing up who gets God's glory is greater than we may dare to imagine.

Of course, we all agree that humans cannot obey God and be God at the same time. Moses, the inscriber of the Ten Commandments, would have agreed too. But by the end of this account, the Lord says to Moses, "You did not believe in me, to uphold me as holy in the eyes of the people" (Num. 20:12). That announcement tells us that something subtle can invade good intentions to lead the best

1. Adapted from James L. Snyder, "How Many Really Great Preachers Are There?" *Ministry International Journal for Pastors*, September 2000, www.ministrymagazine.org/archive/2000/September/how-many -really-great-preachers-are-there. I cite the source that generated this illustration, not intending to indicate that my version is identical to what was published. A sermon is not a research paper. We give proper (and necessary) credit by indicating that the ideas did not originate with us, but in this oral context we are not bound by strict rules of citation unless we indicate we are giving a direct quote.

2. The fallen condition focus (FCF) is directly stated in this sentence with implications unfolded in the surrounding paragraph.

3. The proposition is directly stated in this sentence, though not in the most formal structure. Rather, it is stated directly but informally as is most common for my preaching.

of us terribly astray. Understanding what went wrong with Moses's ministry, and understanding how God treats him to teach us to turn from similar paths, is an important message for every stage of ministry.

What did Moses really do that was so wrong? That's not an easy question to answer. What the people do wrong is more obvious.[4] They complain—again. At the beginning of this account, the Bible records the death of Miriam, Moses's older sister and inconsistent supporter, to signal the passing of the generation of people who previously balked at entering the Promised Land (v. 1). Now forty years have passed. And what does this next generation do as it prepares to enter the Promised Land? They complain as their parents did (vv. 3–5). The people of God have received God's provision in the desert for forty years, they are about to enter the land promised to their forefathers, the Shekinah glory will lead them—and they are complaining. That's wrong, but it's not Moses's sin. So what is his misstep, and what do his actions teach us along the way?

I. The Ministry of Leadership

In the face of the people's sin, Moses seems to do many things right.[5] In fact, his pastoral practice is so exemplary that it probably keeps him from even considering whether he should take his spiritual temperature. His exemplary pastoral practice includes:

Intercession (v. 6)

Moses and Aaron go from the assembly of the people to the entrance of the tent of meeting (v. 6). There the leader of God's people (with the high priest of God's people) falls down on his face before the glory of the Lord. The message is clear: the calling of a godly leader is to humble himself before God on behalf of his people. They grumble; he humbles himself to pray for them. They complain about him; he appeals to God to forgive them. They sin; he intercedes for them.

4. Both questions, "What did Moses do wrong?" and "What did the people do wrong?," are asking essentially the same question: "What does this text reflect of human nature that requires redemption?" This question is one lens in our interpretive "spectacles" that allow us to see the reflection of grace in the Old Testament. (see CCP, 284).

5. The first half of this sermon could well function as a typical "biographical sermon," explaining the heroic attributes of Moses that we supposedly should emulate. For the dangers of such sermons that *only* extol the positive attributes of human figures with exhortations to "be like" them, see CCP, 289–91.

From Moses, we learn that a godly leader is a *first intercessor*. Instead of lashing back at the people's complaint, he leads them by praying for them.

Moses provides a wonderful example of pastoral intercession, for the pastor troubled by the gossip of his congregation or the weakness of his elders. The example can also apply to a counselor seeking to help a young mother in despair over the drudgery of child care, or a parent reaching out to God for the heart of a rebellious child. The sin may be the fault of others, but the duty of godly leaders is to intercede, not to complain.

Forgiveness (v. 6)

Moses's plea for these people is even more instructive when we recognize that the people's complaint is not about their circumstances alone. They are complaining against Moses. They blame their plight on the one who delivered them from Egypt, fought for them, prayed for them, risked his life for them, sacrificed his royal heritage for them, and lived in the desert for forty years because of their sin. Moses's willingness to intercede for those who abuse his love is evidence of a remarkably forgiving heart.

Moses's forgiveness is a difficult but necessary lesson for all who would lead God's people. Though we want to believe that because we have served others, they will serve us—or at least appreciate us—the fact is that people will fail us over and over. If we cannot forgive them, then we cannot lead them. We do not wait for others to make the first move, acknowledge their wrong, or even ask first for forgiveness. A godly leader is a *first forgiver*.

I have pastored long enough to know that being talked about, ridiculed, lied to, and betrayed by those closest to you is par for the course. It happens, and happens regularly, because people are people. Even God's people will *really* do such things. That is why they need godly leaders. But we cannot lead if we bear grudges, return evil for evil, or cannot look past a matter for the sake of the kingdom. God's leaders are *first forgivers*. Consider the church planter who discovers that the mature church no longer desires his entrepreneurial gifts, the sacrificing mom whose child says she never cares, the meal organizer whose needs are forgotten when her child is sick, the pastor who does his best to be fair but whose motives are misjudged as being self-serving or dishonest. All of these kinds of leaders must learn that personal abuse does not excuse leaders from forgiving

God's people—even the ones who don't deserve it. Christ's priorities do not flourish when his leaders do not forgive.

Risk (v. 10)

Moses exhibits additional spiritual maturity by rejecting the impulse to please people for personal gain. He is willing to address hundreds of thousands of Israelites with this challenge: "Hear now, you rebels: shall we bring water for you out of this rock?" (v. 10). Oh, that's not very politic. But Moses is not leading for the sake of approval. In this regard he demonstrates another mark of God's leaders: they are not people pleasers.

Godly leaders do not mince words when truth must be spoken. They do not change course simply because more people would approve. True leaders are willing to put themselves at risk by confronting others with their sin, even before the guilty have indicated a willingness to turn from their sin. Such willingness to take a risk first is displayed in the life of the apostle Paul, who said, "As we have been approved by God to be entrusted with the gospel, so we speak, not to please man, but to please God who tests our hearts" (1 Thess. 2:4). A godly leader makes petitions for God's people but is not a people pleaser. Leadership that prioritizes righteousness demands leaders willing to be *first riskers* for the sake of God's honor before people's approval.

No one can effectively pastor, or parent, or counsel, or teach who *needs* to be liked. *Wanting* to be liked is actually a good thing. Such desire indicates that we take pleasure in the human relationships that God uses to communicate his own heart. But *needing* to be liked inevitably forces one to be a servant of human opinion rather than a leader of God's people. Leading without the priority of pleasing others can be quite lonely, but God's people need leaders secure enough in their relationship with God, settled enough in matters of the spirit, and sufficiently confident in the purposes of the Word to dare to confront, correct, and challenge to further God's priorities. Moses here displays what it means to be the first to take a risk for righteousness' sake.

So if Moses was so well portraying the leadership characteristics of selfless intercession, forgiveness, and risk, what did he do that was so wrong? The answer lies in understanding how the independence that kept him from relying on people's approval ultimately led him to act without relying on God.

II. The Idolatry of Leadership[6]

Some of the ways that Moses substitutes personal initiative for divine guidance are easy to see. God tells Moses to take his staff and speak to the rock to bring forth water (Num. 20:8). Moses does take the staff, but instead of speaking to the rock, he speaks to the people and strikes the rock—twice (vv. 9–11). This wasn't exactly what the Lord said to do, but it's hard to see what was so wrong with it. God seems to overreact when he says Moses will not enter the land of promise as a consequence of such a slight misstep. The people are more obviously and seriously sinning with their ungrateful complaining (v. 12). So why does Moses pay so high a price for his slips? The answers become clear only as we consider precisely how Moses strayed from God's instructions. Ultimately we will see that he substituted other words, deliverance, and authority for God's and, in doing so, did just as God charged: Moses did not uphold God's holiness before the nation (v. 12).

Substitute Words

The word substitution that Moses performs is obvious. God said to speak to the rock; instead, Moses rebuked the people, calling them "rebels." God gave a word of relief, and Moses gave the opposite—a word of rebuke. Maybe we think that the people deserved it. Moses certainly did, but it was not his choice to make. As God's spokesman, Moses was supposed to say what God said. Instead, Moses made himself the originator of the message God's people heard. In this sense, Moses became his own prophet, substituting his words for God's Word.

Substitute Deliverer

Moses's actions were a bigger problem. God told Moses to speak to the rock while holding the staff that had been used repeatedly for divine deliverance. This was the same staff that Moses held when he brought Egypt's plagues and parted the Red Sea. The rod represented God's power and presence, showing that the Lord was delivering his people through means beyond human initiative or ingenuity. So when Moses condemns the people and strikes the rock with God's staff, but without God's permission, Moses indicates that he doesn't need God to deliver

---

6. This portion of the message exposes Moses's sin and makes clear why a "be like" message should not be preached.

these people. Moses now not only becomes a self-proclaiming prophet; he also becomes a self-declared priest of his own status as Israel's deliverer.

Moses's substitution of himself as Israel's deliverer becomes more obvious in the light of earlier parallel events. Something quite similar to this episode of water coming from a rock has already happened. In the previous generation represented by Miriam, God taught his people a lesson that they and Moses now seem to have forgotten. The earlier generation also complained about their deprivations in the desert, and God commanded Moses to take his staff and strike a rock in the desert to bring forth water. Moses did it, but God did something too.

God said that he, who had previously represented himself in a cloud of glory, would stand before the rock that Moses struck (Exod. 17:6). The language is shadowy, but the term for "stand before" is typically used for a servant in a subservient position. If God were humbly to stand before—inevitably surrounding—the rock in his glory before Moses struck the rock, then that would mean the blow would have to strike God before it hit the rock. The Creator God delivered his people by allowing himself to be humbled and struck to provide for their needs.[7] The punishing blow that the complaining people deserved God took on himself, as their mediator, in order to bring forth the water of their deliverance. New Testament believers do not miss the implications. The apostle Paul tells us that the people of Israel "drank from the spiritual Rock that followed them, and the Rock was Christ" (1 Cor. 10:4).

By bringing the people rescue through his own humiliation, God prefigured the nature of the provision that he would make in Christ Jesus. But when Moses struck the rock this time, without the instruction or presence of God before the rock, the human leader acted as though he were his people's deliverer.

The result was that Moses robbed the people of the divine grace God intended for them to experience. Moses's actions implied that God's provision was not enough. The satisfaction for their sin apparently came through striking them with the "rebel" accusation—the very thing that God did not allow to happen when he took the blow that they deserved earlier.

As their mediator, God interceded for his people by taking the blow that they deserved. Now Moses seems to indicate that their rescue will come from renewed

7. In the subpoints of this main point, the descriptions of God's work in behalf of his people are answering the question, "What does this text reveal about the nature of God who provides redemption?" This question provides the second lens in the "spectacles" that allow us to see grace reflected throughout Scripture (see CCP, 284–85).

guilt and his own mediation. In essence, Moses becomes the priest of another gospel—the gospel of his own power and provision.

Substitute Authority

As noted earlier, Moses addressed the people and struck the rock—twice—with the staff of God in his hand. That staff was also the mark of God's authority. It represented divine permission and power. Moses held the staff when he addressed Pharaoh, received the law, and defeated enemies. To hold that staff while saying and doing what God did not command was to assume God's authority. Moses does not speak for God but stands with Aaron when he says, "Hear now, you rebels: shall we bring water for you out of this rock?" (Num. 20:10). Moses indicates that the power of rule over the covenant people is his and his brother's. He thus positions himself and his family as the true royalty of God's people—with himself as the one with the most authority in that royal clan.

This is the final puzzle piece in determining why Moses's failures were so serious. His sin was not simply a small burst of temper and a spiteful lashing out. Moses disqualified himself from godly leadership by giving himself the status of prophet, priest, and king. Moses presumed to speak with a voice equal to God's, denied the sole efficacy of the mediating work of God, and did it all claiming the authority of God. Yet, the Bible makes it plain that no individual except the Lord Jesus can fulfill the offices of a prophet, priest, and king for God's people. By claiming all these offices for himself, Moses substitutes himself as the Redeemer of Israel. Thus, God says to Moses, "You did not . . . uphold me as holy in the eyes of the people of Israel" (v. 12). The word "holy" communicates God's unique, separate, and pure nature that is necessary to deliver his people. By substituting his own words, deeds, and rule for God's, Moses denied God's unique nature and authority needed to save his people. By his words and actions Moses communicated that the people were not dependent on God for their salvation—Moses could substitute.

Once we understand how serious was Moses's sin and how subtle was its entrance into his heart, we begin to see why there are lessons from Moses's life that Christian leaders still need to take to heart:[8]

---

8. Often aspects of application are attached to each main point, but in this message the previous applications are minor and the developed application unfolds in multiple dimensions in this one main point. However, the length and complexity of this discussion should not distract us from the realization that the heart-lever for motivating the application is yet to come. Since application must answer four

1. *We should take care not to depend on our pastoral practice apart from God.* It is always tempting to turn ministry into mere ritual and routine. We get so busy about the business of the church that our thought processes begin to run this way: "If I answer my correspondence, run these programs, organize well, practice the right church-growth methods, set the right vision, and preach good sermons, everything will turn out all right." No one would say such mechanical thoughts really reflect their spiritual/theological commitments, but the daily pressures of ministry can make us process daily ministry in just this way. Ministry becomes a matter of exercising skills rather than seeking God. For example, a minister friend in trouble for plagiarism told me that, over the course of years, making sermons was just a routine—nothing more spiritual than a carpenter taking up his hammer and nails to do a job.

Moses's experience teaches us to take great care to maintain our dependence on the Spirit of God as we minister to others. Our hearts should ring with the refrain: "No other word; no other deliverer; no other authority. May Christ be the only prophet, priest, and king known through my ministry."

2. *We can be tempted to make people prioritize our honor rather than be dependent on God.* The distinction between having people honor your message and having them honor you is often very subtle and very seductive. There is a level at which God's people should honor godly leaders as representatives of God's care. But when people begin to look to you rather than through you, there is great danger. Our goal is to make disciples of Christ, not disciples of ourselves. Divisions in churches frequently come when people are loyal to leaders more than to God, and many of the most wounded people in the church are those who entrusted themselves to leaders who were not capable of being God. Always our message must be: "Honor the Word, trust in God alone for salvation, and be led by no authority but his." Not only will God's people need this message, godly leaders will also.

III. The Erosion of Leadership

Moses probably would have agreed with all of the conclusions we have reached so far about the priorities of ministry. He would not have advocated making substitutions

---

questions (what to do, where to do it, why to do it, and how to do it—see *CCP*, 214–22) to be complete, the spiritual power of this message is lacking until something is added that creates loving and compelling motivation to do what God requires.

for God's Word, deliverance, or authority. So how did his ministry erode so badly? Practical scrutiny of Moses's life story provides some answers.

Moses has been fighting for survival and sustenance for more than forty years amidst some of the world's most difficult terrain, dangerous nations, and stiff-necked people. After meeting so many challenges for so long, there is yet another community crisis: no water and a flood of complaints. All crises have the ability to make you stronger. They also take their toll. Although Moses has made it so far, being responsible for the lives and souls of hundreds of thousands of people must have created tremendous stress and pressure—and occasionally some fear and doubt too.

Making matters worse, the people do not merely complain; they blame. They "quarreled *with* Moses" (v. 3) and hounded him with accusatory questions: "Why have you brought the assembly of the LORD into this wilderness, that we should die here, both we and our cattle? And why have you made us come up out of Egypt to bring us to this evil place?" (vv. 4–5). The people attack Moses, the one who gave up so much to save them. The people seem to have no appreciation for him and all he has gone through for them.

Perhaps another reason this crisis gets to him is that he has been here before. This is how the people grumbled forty years ago. And even though a new generation is on the scene, the same old sins appear and have to be dealt with again. Time seems not to have improved these people.

Community difficulty, personal attack, and unappreciated fatigue dig into Moses's heart. Commenting on the Israelite leader's response, the psalmist says that Moses spoke "rashly" (Ps. 106:33). In plain terms, Moses got mad. That's what happened. It got under his skin that he had given so much, sacrificed so much, and led so long, and now the people turned on him—again. They would not listen to him. They were not honoring him. So he turned on them.

Much has been written about pastoral burnout in recent years. Initially researchers believed that increasing demands on pastors' families, finances, and energies were responsible for many pastors leaving ministry. More recent research, however, indicates that the problem is anger, as much as fatigue. Feeling isolated, overworked, and unappreciated at the same time that we are fearing failure, embarrassment, and conflict leads many pastors to live in a constant state of low-level anger or resentment that ultimately erodes energy and desire for ministry. These realities make Moses's problems seem remarkably contemporary.

As we read of Moses's anger, we are faced with the reality that "bitterness is the acid that eats its own container." If we are experiencing resentment about ministry demands, we should ask God to help us learn to pace our lives, prioritize our tasks, and forgive those who have hurt us, so that we continue honoring him in the way we lead God's people.

Even as I say these things, I am very much aware that what I caution against can and, more frequently than I wish, does characterize me. I know the pain of personal attack, the pressure to succeed, and the disappointment of not meeting others' expectations. I know how bitterness can grow in me when complaints multiply in others. I know that in order to continue to minister, I need to be a *first repenter*. I have to confess to the Lord the sins of pride and self-concern that make me want to tell others how much they should honor me. I have to ask the Lord to keep me dependent on him, or I will try to minister out of my gifts rather than through his Spirit. All of this I am ready to confess, but I still struggle with something. I don't struggle to confess the sin of Moses; I struggle to understand why God's punishment of him was intense—and I wonder if something similar might await me. After so many years of service, God did not let Moses go into the Promised Land. I want to ask: Where is the second chance? Where is the mercy? Where is the grace? Can we really preach grace if we do not see and experience it in the life of Moses or in our own lives?

The answers lie in seeing that, although Moses substituted himself for God, God mercifully substituted himself for Moses. In a most surprising way, Moses's account teaches us that grace covers leaders like me who need it.

IV. The Redemption of Leadership

Moses failed miserably. What did God do in response? God redeemed the ministry and the man.[9] Here's what we learn as we examine the history surrounding this provision of water in the desert.

9. This last portion of the sermon is its gospel pivot point. The goal is not only to touch the heart with the evidence of God's grace toward Moses and his people but to stimulate love for God, which is the motivation and power to exhibit the aspects of leadership (discussed in the first part of the sermon) that are impossible apart from the grace of God (see CCP, 320–23 and 326). Frequently in redemptive preaching, the motivating aspects of the gospel come later in the message to provide grace-based power for the applications and to keep the sermon clearly redemptive. The temptation is simply to "tack on"

God Provides for His People Despite Leadership Flaws

Moses messed up. He spoke rash words to the people and struck the rock when he was supposed to do neither. What did God do then? He brought forth the water anyway. It wasn't a trickle; a torrent of blessing came despite Moses's flaws.

In Sunday school literature you often see artist depictions of this scene. Water streams from the rock in a sedate little trickle for the dozen or so people and animals that gather around. But we need to remember the numbers that we are really talking about. Six hundred thousand fighting men left Egypt with their families. That means, if you count those men and their extended families, about two million people left Egypt with Moses. Now they have been wandering for forty years. Are there fewer people due to the deprivations, or have they multiplied? No matter how you estimate, there are still hundreds of thousands of people needing to drink in the desert. Imagine that each person drank a gallon of water a day (and you need at least that much to survive in the desert). If there were only half as many people as left Egypt, then that would mean they would need a million gallons of water a day, forty-two thousand gallons an hour, seven hundred gallons a minute.

But don't forget the animals mentioned in verse 9. The livestock had to be watered too. If every family had a sheep, a goat, and a camel (and many would have had much more), then you would have to triple the flow of water to provide for them all. The reason the Bible says that the water "came out abundantly" is that the nation couldn't have survived on a trickle; there had to be a gushing flood of water—at least two thousand gallons a minute. Now, I don't know just what two thousand gallons a minute looks like, but it doesn't come out of your shower that way, and it doesn't come out of a fire hydrant that fast. This is a flood! God provided a flood of blessing to his people, even though Moses went about it all wrong.

I love this message that God continued to bless his people despite the flaws in their leader. I need to remember that when the sermon did not go well, when I have botched a relationship, failed in my duty, overreacted to a crisis, underprepared for an event, neglected my family, or doubted my God. Despite all my failures, God still rules and can still bring blessing out of my mistakes. He can work past my faults to show his grace. He is able to draw a straight line with a crooked stick. He can pour his grace out of a very earthen vessel.

---

the redemptive components, but with well-integrated thought, such gospel endings give proper gospel weightiness to all that has preceded in the sermon's most climactic and impacting moments.

I thought of God's use of earthen vessels last week when my daughter disobeyed me and went to a neighbor's house after I told her she could not. I am not used to being disobeyed. I got very angry and later felt awful about my reaction. I wish that it had never happened. At this stage of life and ministry I should be more mature. I hate to face the sin that is still in me, yet I tell you this now for two reasons. First, I tell you so that if you have acted improperly toward your children or toward others of God's children committed to your care, you will remember that God can deliver his people even through flawed leadership. He does not abandon his people because you have failed them. So all is not lost. Confess your sin, ask for his help, and lead as he says. But I also tell you of my errors for a second reason. I want you to know that there is continued provision not only for God's people but also for God's leaders when we fail. And that gracious truth was a wonderfully needed and pleasant surprise that came to me from the study of this account of Moses.

God Provides for His Leaders Despite Leadership Flaws

At first, this account troubled me, as it may be troubling you, because of what happened to Moses. Yes, the people were blessed, but look what happened to Moses. God said to him, "You shall not bring this assembly into the land that I have given them" (Num. 20:12). Wasn't there enough grace left for Moses? Yes, he got to look into the Promised Land (Deut. 34:1–4), and a few Bible scholars will point out that he eventually made it there through his appearance in the Transfiguration with Jesus (Matt. 17). But somehow that seems insufficient consolation for one who led so long and well during Israel's times of hardship.

I do not think that I understood the grace that was present until I thought of this account from its author's perspective. Moses misguides his people, disgraces himself, denies his God, and is denied entry into the land of promise. Who tells you all of these terrible things about Moses? Moses. This is one of the five books of Moses. The one who rats on Moses is Moses! He confesses, records, and publishes this account of his own sin.

What does this self-disclosure tell us? To answer this, I considered when such admission of fault is most likely to happen in my family. When my brothers and sister and I get together for the holidays, we play Monopoly so late into the night that we get exhausted and giddy. In those giddy moments, we occasionally tell tales of our misdeeds of the past. Some of those misdeeds were discovered years ago (such as when my father discovered my brothers smoking in the garage, or when my mother discovered my sibling's secret way out of the house). But some other misdeeds have just now come to light, as one or another of my brothers confesses taking a car without permission, or tossing garbage cans on a neighbor's roof for a Halloween prank, or putting chocolate syrup in our sister's mascara.

Often when we tell these revealing stories, my parents still gasp, "You did what?!" But what does it mean to you when you hear me say that my siblings and I are able to speak of these missteps now? It means we trust that, despite our past misdeeds, things are okay now between us and our parents. There may be disappointment or exasperation, but there is no condemnation. We openly confess sin when we know that love and acceptance are not jeopardized by it.

So when Moses tells us of his sin, there is not only evidence of confession but also evidence of reconciliation with his Lord. The evidence is not simply in Moses's openness about his errors but in the Lord's willingness to keep using Moses. The Lord has continued to use the books of Moses for millennia to tell us how the world came to be, how the covenant people were formed, how godly people should live, and how the Messiah would come. Yes, in essence, God said to Moses, "I can't let you lead my people into the land of promise if they think you can do it without me. Belief that you are their deliverer wouldn't be good for you or for them. There is only one Redeemer of Israel." But God wasn't done with Moses. He continued to use Moses to lead the people, to write their history, and to greet Jesus on the Mount of Transfiguration in the Promised Land.

What does Moses's confession and continued acceptance indicate? It indicates that things are okay between him and God, despite Moses's sin—and that's the grace that is so surprising and so good in this passage. God not only blesses his people despite their leader's flaws; he also blesses the leader despite his flaws. That's a grace I long to hear, need to hear, and delight to see in the life of someone as greatly flawed as Moses and me.

Conclusion

The implications are scary, I know. To acknowledge that confession of our flawed humanity gives others confidence in God's grace means that ministry is not just about looking good; it's also about acknowledging our personal need of grace.

Preacher Steve Brown tells the account of a little girl who came home from school, slammed the kitchen door, and declared, "Phew, boys!"

"Why do you say that?" asked her father.

The story unfolded that one of the boys had brought a *Sports Illustrated* swimsuit edition to school. Giggles and snorts erupted in that corner of the room, followed by crude remarks to the girls in the class.

The father was about to take the safe path. He started to tell his daughter about the difference between how boys are visually tempted and how girls imagine idealized relationships in similar ways. But then he did something quite unsafe. He said something that was hard for his daughter to hear but necessary for her to know if she would understand the grace of her God. "Honey," he said, "you know that I am a boy too."

"No, Daddy, you are not like them," she protested.

"Yes, Honey, a part of me for which Jesus died is just like them."

Maybe you think that fatherly confession was unwise, or that it is not good for a daughter to know such things about her father. I confess that's a tough call; it would depend on knowing a lot more about the father and daughter. But this cannot be denied: when that daughter knows that one flawed like her father is not only loved by her but by Jesus too, then she has learned something important about the grace of her God. And there will come a day when she will need to know that grace too. When a father tells of his sin, when Moses tells of his idolatry, when I tell you of my flaws, there is a part of us that is very uncomfortable with the realization that God's leaders could be so flawed. But with that discomfort, something else grows—the assurance that God's grace is greater than all our sin. When our flaws have been discovered, God isn't done. While there may be consequences to my sin, God is still my God. A godly leader who will dare to say so is a *first repenter* whose testimony will lead others to the grace of repentance that all the world needs.

Resultant Christ-Centered Interpretation

(A Macro-Approach)

Thus far we have examined Old Testament prophetic and narrative passages that exhibit aspects of the gospel by predictive, preparatory, or reflective means. We have considered different scriptural genres to demonstrate that God's grace can be preached from each. A question remains, however, as to whether these examples are exceptions. Is the message of God's provision of grace for his people really the consistent message of Scripture? Does the entire Bible really bear witness to the message of redemption, the apex of which is in the provision of Jesus Christ?[1]

These questions are addressed by the next two sermon examples. The first considers a New Testament passage in which the apostle Paul states his own biblical theology, identifying what he believes the entire Bible teaches. In this message, we will also consider the last means that I will suggest to help us preach the gospel from all the Scriptures. The gospel truths of some passages are possible only as a

---

1. For further discussion of how biblical theology informs our interpretation of all Scripture, see the author's *Christ-Centered Preaching: Redeeming the Expository Sermon*, 2nd ed. (Grand Rapids: Baker Academic, 2005), 275–80 and 300–306; hereinafter *CCP*.

result of what Christ has accomplished.[2] Thus, preaching aspects of grace resulting from Christ's work becomes another way of demonstrating the Christ-centeredness of all Scripture. By making this final suggestion, I do not mean to contend that the predictive, preparatory, reflective, and resultant approaches exhaust the means to demonstrate the Christ-centeredness of all Scripture. However, with these approaches in mind, preachers will have basic tools necessary to excavate grace from every portion of Scripture.

In order to see this pervasive grace, preachers still need to remember that "context is part of text." In contending that we can uncover grace in every portion of Scripture, I do not mean to imply that every word, phrase, or paragraph specifically refers to some aspect of redemption. Rather, in its context, every passage of Scripture is part of the unfolding story of God's provision for human inadequacy. That story finds its culmination in the life and ministry of Christ, but the story is not fully told in every passage of Scripture. The task of Christ-centered preaching is to indicate where we are in the unfolding story of God's grace and to show how each particular passage contributes to this story.

The gracious nature of God's provision may need to be gleaned from the wider context of a passage (a *macro*-perspective), or there may be evidence of the grace of God within the narrow contours of the text (a *micro*-perspective).[3] This first sermon that takes a resultant approach to biblical theology deals with grace from a macro-perspective, reflecting Paul's own desires to disclose the purpose of "whatever was written in former days" (Rom. 15:4). The sermon after this one (the ninth sermon) will show grace within more narrow contours. These approaches remind us that both approaches to expounding a text—distilling truth from a large portion of Scripture or exploding truth from a small portion of Scripture—are legitimate expository approaches.[4]

2. For a further description of Christ-centered interpretation that is a "result" of the grace of God expressed in the person and work of Christ, see the introduction to this book and *CCP*, 286–88.

3. For further discussion of macro- and micro-interpretations, see the introduction to this book and *CCP*, 306–8.

4. For discussion of the legitimacy of both expository approaches, see *CCP*, 60–61.

Hope's Journey

Romans 15:4

Scripture Introduction

At the intersection of two rural highways in eastern Maine lies one of our nation's most photographed churches. The church is small and remote, sitting between nondescript fields. But that very isolation seems to have given those in the church a sense of responsibility for helping passersby locate their place and time in the world. The little church has an enormous steeple with a large clock face on each side. I don't know what to compare it with—an ant carrying a banana, or a toddler with a tuba? It seems so out of proportion. Yet that out-of-proportion design is what forces people to pay attention to the church, orients them to their location, and keeps them from losing their way. In a rather curious way, that church helps us understand what's going on in this passage. Here we see the church in Rome made small by bickering. People from both Jewish and pagan backgrounds have become Christians, and they are getting lost in little squabbles over what they should eat or drink or celebrate. The petty debates seem only to need a little refereeing from the apostle Paul. But instead, he writes of an enormous truth, stating the purpose of the entire Bible. Though the concept is contained in one verse, the truth is so massive that the little church will be forced to abandon its small-minded ways and reorient itself to the great gospel purposes of every church in every age.[1] This

1. A common critique of redemptive preaching is that it creates egocentric Christians, only concerned about relief of their own guilt. While such an incomplete gospel result is possible (as all forms

is what Paul says to make a small church think and act in accord with the great purposes of the gospel.

Scripture Reading

Read with me Romans 15:4.

> Whatever was written in former days was written for our instruction, that through endurance and through the encouragement of the Scriptures we might have hope.

Sermon Introduction

In the 1929 Rose Bowl game, Georgia Tech and the University of California were locked in a defensive struggle. The score was zero–zero, when "Stumpy" Thomason, quarterback for Georgia Tech, fumbled the ball and University of California defensive center Roy Riegels got the chance of a lifetime. The ball bounced into his arms with open field ahead of him. As a defensive player, Riegels was not accustomed to handling the ball, but he was determined to do everything right. He tucked the ball, ducked his head, and ran for all he was worth. He crossed midfield, the forty-yard line, the thirty, the twenty, and then, on the one-yard line, his own teammate, Benny Lom, caught up with him and screamed, "You ran the wrong way!" Before he could run the other way, Riegels was smothered by Georgia Tech players, setting up a two-point safety that was the deciding play in the game. For the rest of his life, the poor defensive center was known as Roy "Wrong Way" Riegels.

The story of Wrong Way Riegels seems especially sad because he tried so hard to do everything right. He did just as he should: tucked the ball, ducked his head, and ran as fast as he could. His only problem was that he lost track of his goal. Something similar is happening to the church in Rome in the apostle Paul's time. Everyone is trying to do the right thing. They want to eat and drink the right

---

of Christian immaturity are possible), it is not the normal pattern for those in whom the Spirit dwells. When the grace of God fills us with love for Christ, we love what and whom he loves. As a consequence, Christ's love for the unlovely, oppressed, undeserving, and different becomes the believer's love and concern also. All Christian relationships and ethics are ultimately a consequence of living out our love for Christ, which is motivated and enabled by his grace.

things and to celebrate the right holy days. But as commendable as those desires may be, the church goes astray because it has lost sight of its goal. That is why Paul here writes so plainly of the purpose of all the Scriptures that the church is supposed to be representing. In essence, he is plastering a huge signpost on the church so that people neither then nor now lose sight of the goal that will keep them oriented to the gospel's highest priority. What is that highest priority? *The purpose of all Scripture is hope.*[2]

Paul says that whatever was previously written under the inspiration of the Holy Spirit was intended to give God's people hope. The implications are at once vast and specific for those of us who wish to honor God's Word. Discussions about duty and doctrine are necessary and inevitable, but if we do not provide hope to the people of God, we have missed the purpose of the Word of God. Our instruction may be valid, our facts may be accurate, our doctrine may be correct, our truth may be true, but without providing hope we have missed the message God means for us to share.[3] To keep the main thing the main thing—to keep the good news of the gospel really good—we must never lose sight of its goal: hope.

I. All Scripture Is for Our Endurance

The journey toward hope begins with a startlingly comprehensive claim. Paul looks back across the millennia of scriptural instruction that precedes him and says that everything that was written in the past was written "for our instruction." In the narrowest sense, he is simply justifying his use of Psalm 69, just quoted in the preceding verse, Romans 15:3. There Paul reminded his readers that all who seek to serve their neighbors—even neighbors with different backgrounds and preferences—will have to put up with some "reproach," even as Jesus did (Rom. 15:1–3). The quotation from the Psalms reminds everyone of the need to sacrifice for the sake of others, and Paul's immediate task is to defend his use of this instruction from the Old Testament. But this little justification of a quotation is just the beginning of how the apostle will urge the church to take its bearings from the earlier Scriptures.

2. A simple and straightforward proposition.
3. In this case, for rhetorical flow, the fallen condition focus (FCF) follows the proposition, the shorter form of which then is repeated prior to the first main point.

Aid in Enduring Others

Paul says that the Old Testament instruction first functions by providing us endurance (v. 4).[4] Why endurance is needed we understand from the context of the passage. The Jewish and gentile Christians are running out of patience with each other. Their backgrounds, traditions, and habits are so different, and the Jewish converts must be wondering why they have to put up with such grief from the ignorant "newcomers" to the covenant. Paul will spend some time reminding everyone that the endurance and encouragement needed in the church come from God (vv. 5–7). Then the apostle drives home this point: the presence of these newcomers was God's purpose from the beginning.

Addressing the Jewish believers, Paul writes, "For I tell you that Christ became a servant to the circumcised to show God's truthfulness, in order to confirm the promises given to the patriarchs, and in order that the Gentiles might glorify God for his mercy" (vv. 8–9). The apostle reminds the Jewish believers that God promised he would make Abraham a father of many nations. The presence of gentiles worshipping the one true God with Jews is the fulfillment of the ancient promises given to the Jewish patriarchs. Time and trial may seem to have denied that God would fulfill these promises, but God endured in his purposes, and now it is time for these Jews to endure with all his people.

Paul knows that it will be hard for some of his Jewish brothers and sisters to accept gentiles as fellow members of the covenant, so he reminds them of their heritage. He adds instruction from other portions of the Old Testament, portions that they will recognize.[5] The first is this: "Therefore I will praise you among the Gentiles, and sing to your name" (v. 9b). This is a quotation from David's Song (2 Sam. 22:50). David wrote this psalm at the end of his life, after he had sinned with Bathsheba, murdered her husband, raised rebellious children, and numbered his troops in pride. In essence, David says, "I have failed, but God will not fail.

4. In essence, Paul states the *result* of God's grace first, saying that all the Scriptures were intended to enable us to endure (our trials of circumstances and relationships) and to be encouraged for the challenges that gospel living will bring. Then he unfolds a summary of the redemptive truths in this chapter that provide that result (although these truths have been discussed at length in the preceding chapters of Romans; see also *CCP*, 286–88).

5. Paul's biblical theology (seeing all of Scripture as a unified message of God's redemptive purpose) is remarkable in this portion of Scripture, as he demonstrates from each portion of Scripture how consistent is God's intention to fulfill his covenantal promise to redeem a people for himself from the nations.

Our God is a God of promise. He will be honored among the Gentile nations and fulfill his purposes for all people."[6]

Next Paul quotes from Moses's Song (Deut. 32:43): "Rejoice, O Gentiles, with his people" (Rom. 15:10). At the end of his life, after the sin of bringing water from a rock without God's authorization, Moses still writes of God's faithfulness to his promise to include gentiles with his people. The message is the same: "I have failed, but our God is a God of promise. He will not fail to fulfill his purposes."

Then Paul quotes from Psalm 117: "Praise the Lord, all you Gentiles, and let all the peoples extol him" (Rom. 15:11). Long after the nation of Israel has been divided and dispersed, the Jews continued to sing this portion of their biblical hymnbook. The words reminded them that their failures were not the end of God's faithfulness. He would still be true to his promises and would be honored among all the peoples of the earth.

Finally Paul quotes from Isaiah 11: "The root of Jesse will come, even he who arises to rule the Gentiles; in him will the Gentiles hope" (Rom. 15:12). In this great prophecy of the Jewish Messiah, the prophet includes hope for the gentiles. The message is made more poignant by the realization that Isaiah is also prophesying judgment for Israel because of his nation's sin. Thus, the message is again of God's faithfulness to his promises despite the failures of his people. Always God has endured in his purposes.

In these verses just cited, Paul scans the genres of Scripture (Pentateuch, history, poetry, and prophecy) to demonstrate that the promises God made to his people across millennia have been fulfilled in this generation of believers.[7] The validity of biblical theology is demonstrated not only by the message of the grace for all nations extending throughout the Bible but also by the Jews and gentiles gathering together in the church in Rome.

Surely it had seemed for centuries that God's promise to bless the nations of the gentiles through the Jews would never occur. Yet God did not fail in his promises. Though time and trial often seemed to deny God's faithfulness, he remained

6. Each of the examples Paul cites indicates not only that God is faithful in expanding his grace to the nations but also that he is faithful through persons whose sin and failure are clear. The gospel is evident not only in the extension of grace to many but also in the application of grace to sinners.

7. This macro-approach to biblical theology considers not only different types of Scripture but also different eras in which God unfolds his redemptive truths. Paul's approach provides both method and permission for us to explain how God is unfolding redemptive revelation as we expound particular portions of Scripture or compare different portions of Scripture to make God's redemptive purposes plain.

true to his promises for the nations. God endured for his people; therefore Paul urges us to endure with each other in Christ's church despite our differences of background and culture. We should not give up the hope of getting along with each other because together we fulfill ancient promises.

Aid in Enduring Trials

Not only does Scripture's testimony of God's faithfulness to his promises enable us to endure each other; it enables us to endure our difficulties. The knowledge that time and trial do not annul God's purposes means that our circumstances need not be our barometer of God's care. We endure our own personal difficulties because all Scripture instructs us that God's promises to fulfill his eternal purposes through his people do not waver, despite earthly challenges and failures.

- When Abraham first responded to a divine call to be a father to many, walking from Iraq to Israel, *and* when he was almost a hundred years old and still did not have any children—God was still being faithful to his promise.[8]

- When Jacob's children were delivered from famine in Egypt, *and* when their descendents were delivered into slavery in Egypt—God was still being faithful to his promise.

- When David slew his tens of thousands in his progress to the throne, *and* when he murdered the husband of his mistress in a terrible abuse of the throne—God was still being faithful to his promise.

- When Solomon built the wonders of the kingdom of Israel, *and* when his children and grandchildren divided the kingdom—God was still being faithful to his promise.

- When the Son of God was born in a manger, *and* when he hung on a cross— God was still being faithful to his promise.

Time and trial do not annul God's promises. Ours is a God of promise. All the Scriptures attest to his faithfulness to work his eternal purposes through his people even when they must endure great difficulty. Consider how knowledge of this truth has powerfully affected Christian leaders in the past. William Carey

8. Though the repetition of these phrases reads poorly as prose, preachers can use such repetition with significant rhetorical power. Oral communication requires much more redundancy than written literature.

was challenged not only by the unbelief of masses in India but by the apathy and opposition of churchmen in England. Yet, inspired by the words of Psalm 22 ("All the ends of the world shall . . . turn to the LORD, and all the families of the nations shall worship before You," NKJV), Carey said,

> Though the superstitions of the heathen were a thousand times stronger than they are, and the example of the Europeans a thousand times worse; though I were deserted by all and persecuted by all, yet my faith, fixed on that sure Word, would rise above all obstructions and overcome every trial. God's cause will triumph! . . . The work, to which God has set his hands, will infallibly prosper. . . . We are neither working at uncertainty nor afraid for the result. . . . He must reign until Satan has not an inch of territory![9]

Two young Americans were deeply moved by Carey's message of God's promised victory. Their names were Adoniram and Ann Judson. They left the United States and sailed for India in 1812; she was twenty-three, he was twenty-four, and they had been married fourteen days. Neither could have predicted the hardship that awaited them nor the endurance that the promises of Scripture would give them.[10]

The economic and political intrigues of the British East India Company caused the Judsons to be denied entry into India. They traveled on to Burma. During the extended journey, their first baby was born dead. Their second child, Roger Williams Judson, lived seventeen months and died. The third, Maria Elizabeth Butterworth Judson, was born just before her father was thrown into prison under suspicion of being a British spy.

The conditions of the prison were so cruel and squalid, we struggle to describe them. Adoniram's cell was so crowded that some prisoners had to stand while others slept. They were deprived of sanitation and water. The heat was oppressive and the stench sickening. Torture was a daily routine, not only for punishment, but also for entertainment. Prisoners were hung from their ankles or thumbs until the pain broke their will to live.

Adoniram survived with heroic help from his wife. When fear made others abandon their spouses, Ann descended into the squalor of the prison and endured

---

9. William Carey, quoted in Iain H. Murray, *The Puritan Hope* (London: Banner of Truth, 1971), 140–41.

10. Material on the Judsons comes from various sources, including John Piper, "How Few There Are Who Die So Hard!: Suffering and Success in the Life of Adoniram Judson: The Cost of Bringing Christ to Burma," Bethlehem Conference for Pastors, February 4, 2003, www.desiringgod.org/resource-library/biographies/how-few-there-are-who-die-so-hard.

the jeers of the guards. With her eyes she poured love through the prison bars, and she refreshed her husband's soul by echoing the words of William Carey that had inspired their mission efforts: "Do not give up, Adoniram. God will give us the victory." When hope died in others, those oft-repeated words kept Adoniram alive.

Ann also used the visits to smuggle food to Adoniram. He did not realize that it was her only food and that she was slowly starving. Her milk for her baby dried up, and she would go through the streets at night begging other women to nurse her child. Then her visits to Adoniram stopped without explanation. As anticipation of her visits once kept him alive, now concern for her absence drove Adoniram to make it through each new day.

When political changes allowed his release, Adoniram began a desperate search for Ann. He learned that she was in a government refugee camp, and as he approached the tent assigned to her, Adoniram passed a child so filthy that he did not at first recognize her as his own daughter. Inside the tent, Ann lay without movement on tattered blankets. The illness had taken her hair and warped her features so that she was barely recognizable. Still, Adoniram knew the eyes and the heart that once again said the words of hope: "Do not give up, Adoniram. God will give us the victory." Ann died eleven months later, and their daughter died six months after that.

Despite the time of suffering and the trial he had endured, Adoniram ultimately claimed those words of victory based on the promises of God. Later he would write, "The religion of Buddha, of Brahma, of Mohammed, and of Rome, with all other false religions, will disappear and the religion of Christ will pervade the whole world." These words were not based on vain optimism or empty sentiment but on the testimony of God's faithfulness to his redeeming promises that pervade Scripture from beginning to end. God catalogs his grand march of redemption in every category of Scripture so that we will not lose hope during the battles we must endure. Time and again the Bible instructs us that although God's purposes seem annulled or delayed, they are ultimately fulfilled. God is always faithful to his promises. He will give us the victory. The victory may not come in the time we would like or even in our lifetime, but God records his promises and purposes in all the Scriptures so that we will not lose hope. "Whatever was written in former days" was written for our instruction so that we would have the encouragement to endure.

II. All Scripture Is for Our Encouragement

But what if we cannot endure? Yes, we want to endure, but life holds challenges deeper and times bleaker than anyone can anticipate. Even Adoniram, after the death of his wife and child, could not endure. He stopped his translation work, renounced his theological degree, and ordered that all previous correspondence related to his faith be destroyed. He built a hut in the jungle, moved into isolation, and wrote, "God is to me the Great Unknown. I believe in him, but I find him not." Such words remind me of Mother Teresa's journals, discovered after her death. There she wrote, "God forgive me, if there be a God. My prayers are as knives to heaven that return to pierce my soul." She referred to God as "the absent one."[11] And lest we be tempted to judge her harshly, we must consider what we would think if we had held starving infants in our arms for decades on the streets of Calcutta.

The Encouragement We Need

What does Scripture offer when trials overwhelm us and we believe we can endure no more? Paul answers by writing, "Whatever was written in former days was written for our instruction, that through endurance *and through the encouragement of the Scriptures* we might have hope" (Rom. 15:4). The Scriptures were written not only to help us endure but also to give us encouragement.

The word used for "encouragement" in this verse is similar to *Paraclete*, the "Comforter," a title used elsewhere for the Holy Spirit. Its root meaning is "to call alongside," as a comforter comes alongside someone grieving or fearful in order to give them encouragement. Paul's point is that the instruction of Scripture is not simply that we should "buck up" and "endure" but that we should take encouragement from the message the Holy Spirit inspires in God's Word.

We learn the content of Scripture's encouragement in the same place that we learn about the promise that fuels endurance—in verses 7–9:

> Therefore welcome one another as Christ has welcomed you, for the glory of God. For I tell you that Christ became a servant to the circumcised [i.e., the Jews] to show God's truthfulness, in order to confirm the promises given to the patriarchs, and in order that the Gentiles might glorify God for his mercy.

11. Helen Kennedy, "Mother Teresa's Letters Reveal Her Crisis of Faith," *St. Louis Post-Dispatch*, August 25, 2007.

The first message of encouragement is "Christ has welcomed you" (v. 7). For the believer there is no news that could be more encouraging. The Lord who knows faults and flaws has welcomed us. And that message is about to be expanded and its implications deepened. Paul says that though the Jews rejected Jesus, he served them; and though the gentiles crucified God's Son, he is merciful to them. Paul's simple but powerful message of encouragement is that God is not only faithful to his promises; he is also merciful to his people. This mercy includes gracious provision not only for his weak and rebellious covenant people but also for the people of the world who were once enemies of his covenant. Such mercy displayed throughout the pages of Scripture is meant to encourage us so that we would have hope when our challenges overwhelm us.

The message of God's mercy ultimately gave Adoniram Judson the encouragement he needed. In his isolation Adoniram received news of the death of his brother. The brother had been a desperate and unbelieving alcoholic. But with the news of his brother's death also came word of a caring body of believers that had witnessed to him of the mercy of Jesus. As a consequence, Adoniram learned that his needy brother had died as a believer in Jesus Christ. By the mercy of God, he would be made new in heaven without the guilt, shame, or torment of his addiction. Adoniram realized afresh that if God could be merciful to so desperate a sinner as his brother, then God could also be merciful to him despite his failures of faith.

This was the encouragement Adoniram needed. The message of mercy gave him hope again. There was hope that beyond the torment of his grief for Ann, beyond the sinful misery of thousands upon thousands who needed his New Testament translation, and beyond his own lapse of faithfulness there was still mercy that provided eternal healing, forgiveness, and glory. God's mercy encouraged Adoniram enough to return to his ministry, and thousands would come to know eternal hope through his work.[12]

The Hope We Need

The apostle Paul looks back over the whole of the Word of God and says all was written to instruct us that God is faithful to his promises and merciful to his

---

12. The example indicates how the hope of the gospel gives motivation and enablement to do what God calls his people to do. Grace is not license to do as we please but rather incentive and power to do what pleases God because pleasing him most pleases the ones who love him. And those who love him most deeply do so as a result of perceiving his grace most fully. Thus, obedience is a *result* of grace (see *CCP*, 228 and 326–27).

people. He also tells us why these truths are recorded: so that "we might have hope" (v. 4d). When we know that God is faithful to his promise (even when time and trials seem to deny it) and that he is merciful to his people (even when they deny him), then we have hope. Such hope is not merely optimistic wishing; it is confidence in the future, based on God's faithfulness in the past. Such hope is not produced by or characterized by fanciful good wishes for a carefree life. Biblical hope may have to be experienced through extended time and excruciating pain. We endure and are encouraged through such trials, not by empty and vacuous assurances that everything will turn out all right in life. Rather, in the face of awful circumstances or personal sin, biblical hope holds with a fierce tenacity to the confidence that God will accomplish his good and eternal purposes because the entire Bible demonstrates his unwavering faithfulness and mercy.

As *trust* is faith that is held in the present, *hope* is faith that is maintained for the future. Each is the confidence that because God is faithful to his promises and merciful to his people, he can be trusted to accomplish his good purposes for us despite adverse circumstances, inexplicable trials, or personal failures. Because yesterday, today, and tomorrow are in our faithful and merciful God's hands, whatever happens—whether it seems very good or very bad—we endure and are encouraged. Our God reigns for his glory and our good. With this hope, the promises of the future invade our present lives, giving us endurance and encouragement for whatever God calls us to face today.

Conclusion

I could not help but consider this hope when a choir from the Republic of Belarus sang in our church soon after the breakup of the Soviet Union. These people had lived under repressive Communism, been driven from their churches, been denied the opportunity to raise their children in their faith, and were now enduring runaway inflation, a failing economy, and few jobs. Yet when they sang their closing selection, the "Hallelujah Chorus" from Handel's *Messiah*, their voices resonated with power and hope.

The Belarusian choir did not realize when they began their final selection that our church choir had also been preparing the "Hallelujah Chorus" for our Christmas program. So when the first notes of Handel's music were played, singers from our congregation spontaneously went forward to join their Christian brothers and sisters. Together they sang the words of the chorus: "The kingdom of this world is become the Kingdom of our Lord and of his Christ."

The significance of these words being sung by this combined choir brought tears to my eyes. Not only were the suffering Belarusians proclaiming that this world *is become* (i.e., is already characterized by) the kingdom of our Lord and of his Christ, but suffering choir members from our own church were singing this same hope. Handel's words powerfully echo the apostolic contention that faith in God's future kingdom gives us the hope we need to face present trials. The faces of those singing said the same.

I watched as fierce tenacity mixed with tears for a couple raising a Down's syndrome child, their voices declaring the kingdom to come in which that child will be made whole. I treasured an older man singing with zeal for his Lord's kingdom, although his wife has just had a leg amputated from complications of diabetes and might never return home. I was inspired as two parents held each other and declared the mercies of God in hope for a child who has abandoned them and is facing a prison sentence. They all sang "Hallelujah," praise the Lord, because they have hope in a God who is faithful to his promises and merciful to his people. Hope in the realities of his eternal kingdom gives them the endurance and encouragement they need for the realities of today.

Proclaiming this hope not only helped our church members; it united them with members of Christ's church from Belarus. Christians of different backgrounds and experiences united in the goal of declaring the hope of the gospel. In those moments, we all knew there was nothing more powerful or precious. The most important goal of our worship, preaching, service, and counsel is to give hope. Affirming that the God of promise and mercy is at work in our world and that his kingdom shall prevail will unite and empower the church. All the Scriptures give us reason for this hope. We must not lose sight of this goal because "whatever was written in former days was written for our instruction, that through endurance and through the encouragement of the Scriptures we might have hope."

Example SERMON NINE

Resultant Christ-Centered Interpretation

(A Micro-Approach)

This is an example of an expository sermon prepared for a complementary command, parable, and narrative that appear together in Scripture.[1] This sermon suggests ways of preaching commands, parables, and narratives, helping us consider how to preach multiple genres (i.e., types of biblical literature) together.

A frequent task of the preacher is to communicate why the biblical author arranged his material as he did. The Bible tells us that Jesus said and did much more than is recorded (John 21:25). So the biblical authors had to be purposeful in their choice of material. Not only do individual passages communicate truths of the gospel, but the way passages follow and coordinate with each other may also intentionally communicate the author's concerns. In this portion of Scripture, Jesus gives a command to his disciples, then follows it up with a parable; next, the author of the text narrates a story about Jesus's actions, which further illustrate and emphasize an aspect of his command and his parable.

---

1. For a further description of expository sermons, see the author's *Christ-Centered Preaching: Redeeming the Expository Sermon*, 2nd ed. (Grand Rapids: Baker Academic, 2005), 131–33; hereinafter *CCP*.

The following sermon leverages this command/parable/narrative interplay to emphasize the message of grace that the author communicates by putting all three side by side. In this case, the message of grace is gleaned not from the wide historical context (the *macro*-perspective demonstrated in the previous sermon) but from the immediate context and content. This *micro*-perspective helps us see how grace may be evident in the words or actions within a specific text.[2] Micro-perspectives demonstrate that the preacher does not always need to refer to the wider context to demonstrate the gracious character of God that culminates in Christ and is a result of Christ's ministry.[3]

2. For further discussion of macro- and micro-interpretations, see the introduction to this book and *CCP*, 306–8.

3. For a further description of Christ-centered interpretation that is a "result" of the grace of God expressed in the person and work of Christ, see the introduction to this book and *CCP*, 286–88.

To Make God Come Down

Luke 17:1–19

Scripture Introduction

In our church, a couple who had been dating and who seemed so right for each other, recently broke up—dashing the hopes of all the matchmakers in the congregation. Then one Sunday, after weeks of coming to different services and sitting in separate pews, the couple came to the same service and sat in the same pew *together*! There was a message in their being together that everyone understood. Here in the Gospel of Luke, there are accounts of a servant not getting thanks and a leper giving thanks. The accounts are quite different, but they sit side by side; and, like our couple, there is a message of grace in their togetherness.[1]

Scripture Reading

Read with me Luke 17:1–19:

> And he said to his disciples, "Temptations to sin are sure to come, but woe to the one through whom they come! It would be better for him if a millstone were hung around his neck and he were cast into the sea than that he should cause one of these little ones to sin. Pay attention to yourselves! If your brother sins, rebuke him, and if

---

1. This Scripture introduction informs listeners that the arrangement of the biblical material, as well as its content, can communicate redemptive truths.

143

he repents, forgive him, and if he sins against you seven times in the day, and turns to you seven times, saying, 'I repent,' you must forgive him."

The apostles said to the Lord, "Increase our faith!" And the Lord said, "If you had faith like a grain of mustard seed, you could say to this mulberry tree, 'Be uprooted and planted in the sea,' and it would obey you.

"Will any one of you who has a servant plowing or keeping sheep say to him when he has come in from the field, 'Come at once and sit down at table'? Will he not rather say to him, 'Prepare supper for me, and dress properly, and serve me while I eat and drink, and afterward you will eat and drink'? Does he thank the servant because he did what was commanded? So you also, when you have done all that you were commanded, say, 'We are unworthy servants; we have only done what was our duty.'"

On the way to Jerusalem he was passing along between Samaria and Galilee. And as he entered a village, he was met by ten lepers, who stood at a distance and lifted up their voices, saying, "Jesus, Master, have mercy on us." When he saw them he said to them, "Go and show yourselves to the priests." And as they went they were cleansed. Then one of them, when he saw that he was healed, turned back, praising God with a loud voice; and he fell on his face at Jesus' feet, giving him thanks. Now he was a Samaritan. Then Jesus answered, "Were not ten cleansed? Where are the nine? Was no one found to return and give praise to God except this foreigner?" And he said to him, "Rise and go your way; your faith has made you well."

Sermon Introduction

"Mom on strike." That was the sign thirty-six-year-old Debbie Tribble of Collinsville, Missouri, put in her yard.[2] Tired of the whining, back talk, and lack of cooperation from her family, this young mother went on strike. She put the sign in the front yard and moved out of the house . . . into a tree house in the backyard. From there she vowed not to come down until things changed in her home.

Some local television reporters picked up the story and interviewed the family. Debbie's comments were interesting, but I found her husband's responses just as fascinating. He said, "I have the kids doing their chores again. And I've told them to cool it with the sarcasm. We are trying to make amends and do whatever we can to get her to come down."

2. The account is true; specific names and details have been changed.

On a human level, the husband's remarks make perfect sense. When we have had a problem with people, have failed to meet their expectations, or have caused their upset, we typically resolve to make amends. This perfectly reasonable human response runs us into trouble, however, when we try to approach God in the same way. When we know we have failed or frustrated him, we long to make amends because we do not want God to be on strike. We long to do what will make him come down from whatever "tree house" of heaven he occupies and reenter our lives with his care, power, and blessing. But what will cause this? How can we make God come down when his standards are so high?

To get a view of how high his standards are, you have only to glance at the opening verses of this chapter. First, Jesus tells his disciples that they must *cause no sin* (Luke 17:1–3a). Next, he says they must *confront others' sin* (v. 3b). Finally, he says that they must be willing to *forgive any sin* (vv. 3c–4). These really are high standards!

The disciples know what we also know: the standards Jesus has outlined are high—so high as to be unreachable.[3] In response to Jesus's standards regarding sin and forgiveness, they say, "Increase our faith" (v. 5), which is just a sanctified way of saying, "You are going to have to help us out here, Lord. If these really are your expectations, then you will have to give us the faith to believe and do what you require."

Jesus says the disciples are correct in assuming the power required to serve him is a matter of faith. He says, "If you had faith like a grain of mustard seed, you could say to this mulberry tree, 'Be uprooted and planted in the sea,' and it would obey you." (v. 6). Yes, the power of God does come down as a result of faith. But faith in what? The parable and the narrative account that follows are designed to answer that question by revealing the nature of our God and helping us know what will move him to act in behalf of those who discover his standards are beyond them.[4] The message already displayed in the disciples' plea for more faith is this: God is not moved by our deeds but by our desperation.[5]

---

3. This statement of the fallen condition focus (FCF) connects the experience of the apostles to "us," transforming the passage from an abstract, third-person observation to a direct, first-person experience (see *CCP*, 51–52 and 299).

4. Note that this sentence establishes a redemptive perspective by addressing the nature of God who provides redemption and the nature of humanity who requires it (see *CCP*, 284).

5. The proposition is both a negative and a positive, setting up the conceptual structure of the following sermon that will first deal with answers that don't work before turning to the provisions of the gospel.

I. The Motive of God's Goodness

What will move God to favor his people with his power and his presence? Jesus begins to explain by annulling some all-too-common misconceptions. His parable tells us that . . .

God Is Not Moved by the Deeds We Do

The parable Jesus tells troubles us. The master that Jesus uses to represent his own attitude seems so unsympathetic. Not only does the master not invite the servant who has worked all day to his table; Jesus says the master owes the servant no thanks. In fact, Jesus says of the servant, as well as of those who would honor Christ, that even when we have done all that we should do, we should still say, "We are unworthy servants; we have only done what was our duty" (v. 10).

Perhaps these harsh-sounding words will make more sense if we transfer the parable to a more modern setting.[6] Imagine that you were to go into a restaurant and be served by a waitress who had been working hard all day. Even if you were to acknowledge that she was doing a good job and had a right to be weary, you would still be surprised if along with your meal she were to bring an extra plate and chair to your table. You would be further amazed if she then sat down to dine with you. Her serving you well would not be reason enough for her to think that she had earned a place at your table. She was simply doing her job, her duty, and that would not make her suddenly worthy of joining your family.

This far-fetched example is actually not quite as bizarre as the point that Jesus is making in the context of his culture. At that time, being invited to a nobleman's table was a high honor, tantamount to having all the privileges of the man's own household. A more accurate modern analogy (than the restaurant example) would be a realtor who, after arranging the purchase of your home, thinks she has a right to move in. Consider this scene: Your moving van has just unloaded your furniture into your new home, and suddenly another moving van pulls into the driveway. In the passenger seat is your realtor. You ask the realtor what's up, and she says, "Since I helped you buy this home, now I am going to enjoy the fruits of my labor

---

6. Putting the details of the ancient narrative in a contemporary situation often helps listeners see how the biblical material connects to their lives. The effort of the preacher to make this connection also evidences compassion and credible understanding, which contributes to the persuasive power of the preacher's *ethos* (see CCP, 34–41).

by moving in." You would reply, "Now, wait a minute. You were just doing your duty, and that does not earn you the right to my house." Jesus is saying something very similar to his disciples and to us: Simply because you have done your duty does not give you a right to the household of heaven.

While these modern analogies may help us make more sense of his words—we agree that it would be inappropriate for a realtor to expect to move in—we still need to understand that Jesus *intends* to offend his listeners. Remember Jesus is speaking to his own disciples, not the Pharisees. His words are meant to turn them from ever considering their obedience (however great its measure or duration) as qualifying them for heaven's household or making them worthy of divine acceptance. The same message applies to us. Our efforts before God will never earn us entry into his kingdom or require the favor of his heart. However much we may want—or feel the need—to advertise our good works in order to merit God's acceptance, our accomplishments remain incapable of obligating God's approval of us.

A few weeks ago, I visited a pastor who had various large game trophies from Africa displayed around his home: a zebra skin, an antelope hide, the foot of a great elephant turned into a sitting stool. All these trophies were very impressive, and I asked the pastor to tell their origin. He began to explain where each animal was taken, but then, as the minister was speaking, it became obvious that he also was sensing the hidden questions on my and other guests' minds. We were thinking, *Aren't these endangered species? Though these are impressive, large game trophies, isn't there something inherently wrong in displaying them?* Sensing our questions (which he had probably answered for many previous guests), the pastor offered qualifications for each of the trophies he presented. He said, "These animals were shot before they were rare, before there were restrictions on such hunting, and I personally did not shoot them. My father-in-law did." In effect, the pastor was forced to apologize for the very trophies that he displayed.

Jesus's parable forces us to do the same. Though we may want to display the trophies of our righteousness, obedience, and stewardship, we are forced to recognize that there is not sufficient goodness in anything we do to require God to move in our behalf. Initially, this is not a pleasant discovery. We want to be able to compel God to honor us by comparing our goodness to the actions of others. We who innately think that we have achieved more consider ourselves more deserving of divine favors. We instinctively put our faith in our performance to garner God's blessing. Thus, when we find that we cannot promote our good works without qualification, we become frustrated for two reasons: we discover we have lost our basis of comparison with others, and we have lost our basis of leverage with God.

For these reasons we can identify well with Luther who said that "rising up from works righteousness" to belief in grace "is an exceedingly bitter thing" because it robs us of all cause for pride in self and all resources for brokering control of God's gifts.[7] We discover that because of the "great disproportion" (as the *Westminster Confession of Faith* says) between our best works and God's true holiness,[8] we are unable to trade our righteousness for God's favors; our bargaining chips of good works have no currency with God. I cannot bank on a great career because I vow to study hard; I cannot guarantee an absence of family difficulties because my devotions are consistent; I cannot secure success with my faithfulness. God will be no person's debtor. Our attempts to barter for his kindness with our goodness, great efforts, and long-standing resolutions will not move him.

In my humanity I do not always want to believe this. I want to believe that God will be good to the seminary I serve, to the family I love, and to the career in which I strive because I am good. My reasoning abandons me, however, when I truly compare my righteousness to Christ's standards and ask, "Have I really caused no sin, confronted others' sin, and forgiven any sin?" When I face the reality of the inability of my works to merit God's favor, then I recognize I must depend on his goodness and not mine.[9] At times this dependence is scary because it lifts control from me, but there is no other choice when I recognize the true character of even my best works: according to Scripture they are only "a polluted garment" (Isa. 64:6).

John Calvin said, "To man we may assign only this: that he pollutes and contaminates by his impurity those very things which are good. For nothing proceeds from a man, however perfect he be, that is not defiled by some spot. Let the Lord then call to judgment the best of human works: he will indeed recognize in them his own righteousness by man's dishonor and shame."[10] In repeating this quotation I do not want you to think that God never desires or blesses our goodness. Walking in ways that reveal God's character to us is itself a blessing. My concern is that we all recognize that God's blessing flows from his mercy rather than from our merit, and we cannot guarantee that the mercy will flow according to our plans

7. Martin Luther, from the sermon "The Sum of the Christian Life" (Wörlitz, November 24, 1532).
8. *WCF*, XVI.5.
9. The radical nature of the gospel requires us to face the inability of our best efforts to merit God's acceptance or control his actions.
10. John Calvin, *Institutes of the Christian Religion*, III.xv.4.

simply because we conform in some degree to God's standards. Our works do not obligate God to care for us in the way that we think is best. God is not leashed by our goodness nor at our command through our merit. We should not put our faith in our works as the basis for seeing his power in our lives.

But if our works in themselves will not move God to care for us, what will? The Bible makes it clear in the narrative account that immediately follows this parable. In Jesus's dealing with the ten lepers, we learn that while God is not moved by the deeds that we do . . .[11]

God Is Moved by the Desperation We Confess

As Jesus travels along the border between Samaria and Galilee, a group of lepers begin to call out to him "in a loud voice" (Luke 17:13 NIV). Do you remember why their voices had to be "lifted up" in this way? According to the customs of that day, when persons had leprosy, they had to leave home. They could no longer know the warmth of their own family's touch. Further, they could no longer seek comfort for their soul in a temple or synagogue. Such people had to isolate themselves from all others, go outside the walls of the city and, lest anyone get close enough to contract the contagion, call out, "Unclean, unclean!" Lepers were not only deprived of health but were also denied any touch that would bring comfort to their body, heart, or soul. In this desperate condition, ten lepers cry out, "Jesus, Master, have mercy on us" (v. 13).

And what does he do? What does Jesus do when these desperate people plead with him to show them mercy? He does. Jesus shows pity to those who have nothing to claim but desperation. He is moved by a desperate cry for help.

What is the message to you and to me? God is not moved by the deeds that we do but by the desperation that we confess.[12]

11. I frequently introduce new main points in this way: restating the preceding main point in summary, then continuing the sentence with the new main point in parallel wording. Often the first main point mentioned is preceded with a "not only," and the second with a "but also." However, in this instance the first main point is introduced as a negative, setting up the positive implications of the second main point (see CCP, 262–63). This structure is aided by the arrangement of the biblical material that also demonstrates the negative in parable form before demonstrating the positive in narrative form.

12. Here is the gospel pivot point of this message, turning listeners from dependence on human performance to dependence on grace as indicated by Christ's willingness to bless a cry of desperation. Note that the redemptive truths are evident within the bounds of the passage. In this case, it is not necessary to move to the wide contours of Scripture's historical developments to see the grace so clearly on display in the immediate passage (see discussion of macro- vs. micro-interpretations of redemptive truths in CCP, 306–8).

Our own human relationships may reveal how powerful is the claim of desperation in moving a heart toward the mercy that we need. My wife and I have friends whose son in his middle teens lived in rebellion against them and against God. During those years, their son made countless protests of innocence regarding his unacceptable conduct and innumerable promises of "straightening up," "doing better," and "living right." But each rationalization or justification, though it initially may have made sense, turned out to be a veil for actual wrongdoing. Each promise, though it may have been briefly honored, was broken. So much pain, embarrassment, and discouragement were inflicted on these parents that the wife confided to us that she did not know if she loved her son anymore. Her heart had grown hard against her own child.

One day the son sat in the family's living room looking at a photo album of better and happier days past. He came across one picture that he asked his mother to look at. The picture showed the teen as a young child under the approving smile of his mother. The teen pointed to the photograph and said, "Mom, when I look at this picture, I understand why you don't love me anymore. When I look at this picture of you, there is such hope in your eyes for me, but I have dashed all your hopes. I don't know how to fix who I am and what I have done. Still, Mom, please forgive me that I have dashed all your hopes." And what did she do? Her hardness broke, and she embraced him, with her heart renewed in love for him. She did not delude herself that there would be no more troubles. What moved her were neither protests of not having really done anything wrong nor fresh promises to do better. What moved her was the statement of absolute desperation from her child. This is what moves God also.

God's heart is moved not when we protest our innocence with good works that fail to recognize how far short of his holiness they actually fall, nor when we promise that we will do better in the future. The nature of the gospel that we confess is that though there is no reason for God to love us, yet he does. Until we recognize that there is no reason that God should be moved to love us other than the need we bring, we have no gospel to preach or claim. Our faith is most evident not when we boast about our goodness but when we cry out, "Jesus, Master, have pity on us!"

The one who cries out in desperation is in more hope of divine favor than the ones who would claim their own righteousness before God. What this means is that the gay activist, dying of AIDS, who in honest desperation says, "Sexual attraction was not the primary reason for my lifestyle; I would have loved anything that loved me back," may be closer to heaven than I am on the days that I am so pleased with my preaching, my position, and my righteousness. The attorney who confesses absolute powerlessness to resist the gambling addiction that has destroyed his family may have more access to the Spirit of God than I do when I am so confident of my abilities that I do not even remember to pray before proclaiming others' need of God's help.

I must confess readily and repeatedly my own hopeless condition. What makes me willing to do this is the knowledge that it is my desperation that inclines God's heart toward my own. The awareness that he does not turn away from my desperation is what actually draws me to honest confession and deep repentance. When I know that God will not turn away from me when I cry out for his pity, then I am more willing to identify the monsters of sin in my heart—my avarice, my anger, my ambition, my lust, my lack of forgiveness, my doubt—and say, "You are mine. I own you. You are why I am so desperate for my Savior's mercy." Such honesty is what moves God's pity.

I recognize that this is dangerous preaching. To claim that what we do has no inherent power to move God will immediately cause some to question whether we are obligated to do anything for God. If what we do has no power to move God to favor us as members of his house, then why should we move to honor him? Along with understanding the motive of God's goodness, we need to learn . . .

II. The Motive of Our Goodness

What should motivate our goodness?[13] The actions of the leper who returns to give thanks to Jesus instruct us. These actions that Jesus commends teach us that a proper willingness to honor God springs not from a desire for gain but rather from a delight in gratitude.

Turning from a Desire for Gain . . .

. . . is evident in the leper's return to Jesus. There is sacrificial risk in the leper's willingness to return that we may not recognize in our overfamiliarity with the story. He risks both a change in his health and a change in his physician's demeanor.

13. In this message the motivation of application becomes a separate main point because gratitude is so critical to the progress and point of the narrative (see *CCP*, 219–20 and 320–27).

The risk of a health change is a consequence of the rapidness of the lepers' changed condition. Recognizing that an aspect of the miraculous healing is its swiftness, Jesus commands the lepers to go to the priests, who will declare the ten cleansed of their disease (v. 14a). In the very process of going to show themselves to the priests, the lepers are healed. As they are on their way, the leprosy departs (v. 14b). Then, one leper seeing his cure, turns back to say thank you, notably *before* the priests make their declaration (v. 15). The risk in doing this, of course, is that what has changed so quickly could change back just as quickly.

Consider if you had been the one healed. If you had been denied family and affection for months or even years—without the warmth of home, neighbor, and worship—would you not have wanted above all other things to get the clean bill of health that would permit you to return to your home as soon as possible? Would you not have rushed to the priest who would declare you clean before something else happened? The leper has only to go a few more steps to stand before a man who has the authority to restore all that is precious in his life, yet the leper returns to fall at the feet of the One who helped him (v. 16a). Something more powerful than his own *self-promotion* motivates this leper that he would risk another change in his health to return to Jesus. But this is not the only risk.

The leper also risks a change in Christ's demeanor. To this point, the lepers have been treated as a group by the Jewish holy man who has healed them. But the one who returns to offer thanks is not Jewish; he is a Samaritan (v. 16b), a member of a race hated by most Jews. In returning to Jesus, the Samaritan can now be singled out. What if this Jew named Jesus were now to say, "Oh, I didn't recognize there was an infidel among the Jews I healed," and then he were to undo the miracle? *Self-protection* seems also to have vanished from this leper's motivations. There is no apparent personal gain in his return to Jesus, and there is great risk, which indicates that he is not motivated by self-promotion or self-protection.

This message coordinates with the one already made clear in the preceding parable. What we do for God cannot make God our debtor and should never be done primarily for our gain. Any other message actually precludes the possibility of our obedience honoring God. For if the primary reason that we are serving God is for our personal gain, then the one we are really serving is ourself. Too many Christians fail to realize this. They either serve God with the priority of getting a favor from him (in which case their primary motive is self-promotion), or they serve to keep "the Ogre in the Sky" off their backs (in which case their primary motive is self-protection).[14] In each of these cases, the motive behind the actions is nothing more than sanctified selfishness and, thus, the efforts do not actually honor God. What such people think is gaining them "points" with God is actually to their demerit in heaven's accounting, which considers the motives of the heart as well as the actions of the hand.

But now a dilemma seems to fall upon us. If our actions neither move God to love us nor should be pursued for our own gain, then why should we do them? The *Heidelberg Catechism* honestly asks, "[Since] we have been delivered from our misery by God's grace alone . . . , why then must we still do good?" The answer: "So that in all our living we may show that we are thankful to God for what he has done for us, and so that he may be praised through us." This is precisely the motivation evident in the leper. He turns away from the course of the others because of his compelling desire to express his gratitude to Jesus. By his actions and Christ's commendation, the leper teaches us what should move us to serve God: turning from a desire for gain and . . .

Turning to a Delight in Gratitude

The Scriptures record that the leper returned praising God in a loud voice (v. 15). The wording is important because it reflects the way in which the leper had previously called out his desperation, also in a loud voice (v. 13). The scriptural truth being echoed is that to the degree that we recognize our need, our praise of God will find appropriate expression. If we do not perceive our need to be great, then we will not rightly give ourselves to the praise of our Savior. Only when deep gratitude for the deliverance our Savior offers captures our hearts do we so fully fall before him and so gladly dedicate the strength of our lives to his glory.[15]

A long-time pastoral friend tells a similar story about the time a daughter brought home a chocolate teddy bear from a gift exchange at her school. The next day the girl's mother opened the door of her daughter's bedroom and found the girl's three-year-old brother where he wasn't supposed to be. He had been caught red-handed chomping his sister's chocolate teddy bear. Immediately the boy backed against the wall like a cornered criminal, knowing that there was no hiding his guilt (or his

---

14. See discussion of self-protection and self-promotion as inadequate motivations for holiness in CCP, 317–18.

15. The leper's actions in this regard are a delightful revelation of how the loving gratitude that motivates obedience is also the power of our obedience (see CCP, 220–22 and 326–27).

chocolate-smeared hands and cheeks). He began to sob uncontrollably at having been caught. Undaunted, the mother told the little boy that he would have to tell his sister what he had done when she came home from school.

The afternoon was torture for the little boy as each passing minute seemed like an hour of wondering how his sister would react to his crime. When his sister finally came through the door, the anxiety that had built in the little boy burst from him in a torrent of tears and confession. He cried, "Sally, I'm so sorry, I ate your teddy bear." He was a sorry sight standing there sobbing in his guilt. Blessedly, the one to whom he confessed was the kind of big sister who was always looking for a chance to love on her little brother. So she took him in her arms, kissed him, and said, "It's okay, Johnny, I will love you anyway and always."

Though he was still crying, the little boy began to giggle. Tears were still running down his cheeks for his shame, yet at the same time he was laughing for joy. With a vigor made stronger by his deep joy, he hugged his sister with all the strength that was in him.

This is a wonderful picture of every Christian who rightly perceives the nature of God's grace. When we face the reality and seriousness of our sin, we too are rightly broken to the point of tears due to our guilt. This degree of desperation only makes our joy deeper, however, when we recognize that our God is yet willing to say, "Do not despair, child; I will still love you anyway and always." The love and gratitude that such a gracious pardon generates then becomes the motive for embracing our Lord and his purposes with all the strength of our being. The joy that shines through the tears of repentance moves us to new obedience. In such renewed service we discover the truth of the biblical principle that "the joy of the LORD is your strength" (Neh. 8:10).

Conclusion

I mention the power of the joy of pardon because of its necessity in the gospel message all of us will share with others in the church, counseling room, class, kitchen, or workplace. If our teaching of grace causes us to make light of sin, to slight the requirements of the Savior, then we have not really understood the monstrosity of our sin, the vulnerability of our hearts, and the necessity of holiness in lives that would experience the blessings of righteousness. But if we have become mired in a guilty depression, have begun to equate orthodoxy with endless despondency over our shame, or have identified piety with unrelenting sadness, then we have not grasped the grace that marks the gospel and is distinguished by joy. We are obligated to proclaim the whole gospel, neither slighting the seriousness of sin nor shading the wonders of grace. This fullness of the gospel must also characterize our own lives and attitudes because those with whom we share Christ's living water will be affected by the springs from which we drink. I have discovered in my ministry these realities:

- Guilt-driven pastors produce guilt-ridden people.
- Guiltless pastors produce shameless people.
- Grateful pastors produce grateful people, zealous for God's purposes.

These same truths apply to counselors, teachers, parents, and all who spiritually nurture others. In order to share the gospel well, we must recognize that the tears of repentance *and* the joy of pardon are required to produce the gratitude that empowers the Christian life. This balance comes when we understand that God is not moved by the deeds we do but rather he pours his mercy on those who confess their desperation and delight in his praise.

The pouring out of mercy and power is evident in this leper's miraculous healing, but we need carefully to consider their source. Jesus said to the Samaritan, "Your faith has made you well" (Luke 17:19). What faith? The Samaritan has not repeated any creed or proclaimed the deity of Christ. All he has done is fallen at Jesus's feet and, in essence, said, "Everything that is now right about me, you did."

"Ah," you may say, "that's not very much faith. Why, that's practically a mustard seed of faith compared to the kind of mountainous faith that we expect to see in the Bible." But Jesus said that if you have faith "like a grain of mustard seed" (v. 6), then you will see the power of God come down. May the power of the gospel be evident among us because such mustard-seed faith characterizes our lives and our words. May the confession of our hearts be, "Everything that is right about me, Jesus did." When the wonder of his work alone is what we believe and proclaim, the power of the gospel will come down.[16]

---

16. The concluding wording forms a "wraparound" conclusion, echoing the language and image of the introduction and giving the entire message a sense of unity and purpose (see *CCP*, 259).

Gospel Application

Part Three will focus on the relationship between the indicatives of our relationship with Christ (*who we are* as redeemed persons) and the imperatives for the Christian life (*what we are to do* as those called from darkness into his marvelous light). The indicatives of the gospel assure us of God's love and strengthen us for his purposes despite our present weaknesses. The imperatives identify God's purposes and the standards we must follow in order to honor Christ and love as he loves.

An additional emphasis of Part Three is exploration of the relationship between the motivations and the enabling power of application. Even those who desire to serve God may struggle to find the ability to do as he commands. The struggle is aided by the realization that the power for Christian living comes not merely through greater resolve and discipline but through a reorientation of our affections. Sin has no power over us if we have no desire for it, and what displaces love for sin is a surpassing love for Christ. Thus, Christ-centered preaching should seek to discern those themes and practices presented in Scripture that grow love for Christ in us. The following sermons (especially Example Sermon Twelve) explore the relationship between the motivating and enabling truths of the gospel.

Because our preaching should be designed to fuel a preeminent love for God that provides the believer's greatest joy and strength (2 Cor. 5:9; Neh. 8:10)–and knowing this joy cannot be embraced without confidence in the truths of God's Word– the final sermon example in this section expounds the apostle Paul's own exhortation to "preach the Word."

Indicative/Imperative Dynamics

(Indicative Emphasis)

Our reasons for excavating grace from all of Scripture include more than laying claim to fresh interpretive insight or even showing that all Scripture prepares us to understand Christ's person and work. We reveal grace in order to generate love for God, which is the most powerful motivation for biblical obedience.[1] The indicatives (who we are) established by the grace of God generate the will and ability to follow biblical imperatives (what he requires).[2]

We love God most deeply—most compulsively—when the realities of his grace overwhelm us. And when we love him deeply, we desire to walk closely with him and daily honor him. This is why the gracious beats of the divine heart are sounded over and over in Scripture with an unwavering ardor. Commands are not absent, but we are called to obey God's imperatives as a consequence, and never as a condition, of divine love. The greatest commandment, under which all others are subsumed, is that we should love God supremely (Matt. 22:37). But why would we so love him? Scripture answers, "We love because he first loved us" (1 John 4:19).

---

1. For further discussion of how grace motivates the Christian life, see the author's *Christ-Centered Preaching: Redeeming the Expository Sermon*, 2nd ed. (Grand Rapids: Baker Academic, 2005), 313–16 and 320–23; hereinafter CCP.

2. For further discussion of how imperatives are based on the indicatives of our relationship with God, see CCP, 325–27.

The relationship that God establishes with us on the basis of his grace alone is the foundation of this compelling love. To quote Herman Ridderbos, "The imperatives are based on the indicatives and the order is not reversible."[3] God does not say, "You be good and then you will be mine." Through the work of his Son being revealed in all Scripture, God says, "You are mine, so follow me."

So many Christians confuse their "who" and their "do." They think *who* they are is determined by what they *do*, but the gospel says what you do is determined by who you are. God did not say to Israel, "You will be my people, if you obey my commands." He said, "I am the God who has redeemed you, and you are mine; therefore obey my commands" (paraphrase of the truths of Deut. 5:6). Always and everywhere in Scripture, the imperatives are based on indicatives. If the indicatives are not directly stated, they yet appear in context for those with eyes to see.

There may be no better place to test this proposition of the pervasive power and presence of Scripture's indicatives than Colossians 3. In this striking passage, the apostle Paul commands putting to death—mortifying—whatever belongs to the flesh. The imperatives could hardly be clearer or more powerfully stated. Paul demands holiness without compromise. Yet the force that drives these imperatives is not threat of rejection but assurance of our blessed status provided by various dimensions of God's grace. In the sermon that follows, we will see how the indicatives of grace—rather than being an excuse for sin—are the foundation for holiness.

3. Herman Ridderbos, *Paul: An Outline of His Theology*, trans. John Richard de Witt (Grand Rapids: Eerdmans, 1975), 253.

Dying to Live

Colossians 3:1–5

Scripture Introduction

A friend of mine is a pastor who has also spent many years as an Army Reserve chaplain. As a consequence, he is often consulted by young people considering whether they should serve in the military. He says, "I always ask, 'Are you willing to die for your country?,' because once you answer that question, everything else should be easy." But he adds that almost everyone says yes without even thinking. So he asks another question: "Would you be willing to kill for your country?" My friend says that question makes people pause. But imagine what the responses would be if he asked these young people whether they would be willing to kill *themselves* for their country. There might be flight rather than a pause. Yet the call of the apostle Paul is not so different in this passage of Colossians. He calls us to kill whatever is earthly *in* us. Let's read his words to discern why he calls us to such a mission and how we may have power to fulfill it.

Scripture Reading

Read with me Colossians 3:1–5:

> If then you have been raised with Christ, seek the things that are above, where Christ is, seated at the right hand of God. Set your minds on things that are above, not on

things that are on earth. For you have died, and your life is hidden with Christ in God.
When Christ who is your life appears, then you also will appear with him in glory.
     Put to death therefore what is earthly in you: sexual immorality, impurity, pas-
sion, evil desire, and covetousness, which is idolatry.

Sermon Introduction

When he was seven, his middle-class parents sent him away for a year of religious
tutoring. With nine other boys he lived in the home of a minister. Rising at
dawn, the boys spent each morning in religious instruction, prayer, and Scripture
memorization. Each afternoon they went to a crowded street to pass out religious
tracts and collect money for their ministry. In the course of the year, some of the
boys vowed to become ministers; all promised to serve God with fervor forever.
At the end of his year of religious instruction, this boy returned to parents who
enrolled him in a parochial school. He was fervent for a while, but then the teen
years came and the attractions of music, fun, and girls distanced him from his
parents' faith.

     Not until he was at a university did his faith reignite. The parties that at first
seemed so exciting became habitual and only left him feeling empty. He became
increasingly disinterested in studies that seemed only designed to give him the
social status of his parents. The only classes that captured his attention were those
that spoke of the inequities of world power and wealth. The decadent lifestyles of
his friends and family, and his growing sense of injustice at the plight of the poor
and powerless, led him to connect again with those who really believed that their
faith had answers to suffering and could make a difference in the world.

     He connected again with the faith of his youth, embraced the eternal promises
of Scripture, and began to pray with fresh fervor. For the first time in years, he
saw the worth of living for a purpose larger than himself. The knapsack on his
back ceased being a burden because his studies fueled the concerns that gave
him a new sense of purpose for life, new hope for the future—a deeper sense of
significance than he had ever imagined possible. That is why he again went to a
crowded street, pulled a string on his knapsack, and blew himself up—killing and
wounding scores for his faith.

     When committed Christians read government profiles like this of Middle East-
ern terrorists, we feel chills. The shiver is caused by more than the sense of horror

that a life so ordinary could be turned to a purpose so deadly. We may also feel a strange sense of personal shame. The thoughts of these terrorists are demented, their god is false, their methods are horrid—and yet they are willing to kill *and* to die for their cause. Their commitment to their religion can make our commitment to ours seem pale and limp in comparison.

We are supposed to be in a war against the rule of anything but the Savior over our lives. And yet in a culture that encourages self-satisfaction without restraint, we find ourselves willing to die to very little, and even less willing to consider killing in us whatever opposes Christ.[1] If false religion can make vibrant, young men kill and die for the rewards of Allah, how much more should we who know the glory of Christ's rewards be willing to give our lives for his honor.

What will ignite so much zeal for Christ that we are willing die to self and to kill whatever is earthly in us? The answer lies in this passage where the apostle Paul motivates believers to mortify (i.e., put to death) whatever opposes Christ by embracing the truths of his grace: our new position in him, our life's imperative from him, and our great power in him.[2] By these means, Paul bids us come and die, killing whatever is in us that would steal glory from Christ.

I. Our Position (What We Are—Already)[3]

Raised and Seated (v. 1)

Paul first sparks our zeal by reminding us of the position Christ already provides for us. The apostle says, "You have been raised with Christ" (Col. 3:1). This is resurrection language. Yet, because we are still living and because being raised requires a death, the statement seems inaccurate or, at least, premature. The premature nature of the statement seems even more pronounced because it is put in the past/completed sense.

---

1. This statement of the fallen condition focus (FCF) establishes the human dilemma that the gospel truths of the text must address.

2. This elongated proposition is a combination of a Scripture bond (*CCP*, 244–45), a statement of the sermon's purpose (*CCP*, 143–44 and 243–44), and a "billboard" (*CCP*, 264–65) of the sermon's structure. A more concise version of the proposition comes in the following sentence and is emphasized by vocal dynamics.

3. This portion of the sermon expounds the indicatives (i.e., the status and identity we have by virtue of our union with Christ) of the gospel that provide the foundation, motivation, and power for the imperatives that are also in the text—and are expounded in the second portion of the sermon.

How can we already have been completely resurrected when we have not yet even died? The apostle's reasoning is based on truths already made plain in the previous chapter. There he said that those who have identified themselves with the body of Christ by submitting to baptism have ceased being identified with their former associations and way of life.

Baptism did not physically kill the new believers, but it was the rite by which they identified themselves with a totally new life orientation and publicly acknowledged that they no longer held their old faith commitments and priorities. By their baptism, these new Christians declared that their former way of life was dead to them. Thus, Paul tells the Colossians, whose new faith puts to death their previous existence, that they "were also raised with him [Christ] through faith in the powerful working of God" (2:12). An old life is dead, but a new life has started. These new believers have entered a new life because they have put their faith in Christ. They are basing their present existence and future hopes on his provision. Their lives on earth depend on his life in heaven, as he rules and intercedes in their behalf. So identified are they with him that his life and his destiny determine theirs. They are united with him. So, as he is risen from the dead, they are also by virtue of their union with him.

Like those plucked by helicopters from the mud and flood of a community devastated by a hurricane, believers have been plucked from the mire of sin by our Savior. You may question, "How can it be true that we are plucked from the mire of this world if we still exist here?" Paul's point is that our rescue is so sure, and we are so secure, that we are already above the mire. Struggle is not done, but a new life has begun. Like the rescued hurricane victims that still must struggle with their new lives, we still have struggles, but we have the undeniable, inestimable privilege of being saved from death by the rescue that has already been secured by Christ's resurrection.[4]

Where is this risen Lord? The end of the first verse tells us: "seated at the right hand of God" (Col. 3:1c). Much gospel truth has been compressed into these few words. Jesus, who took our sin on himself, is now at God's right hand. The right

4. The purpose of this illustration is not so much to clarify what has already been said as to provide a "lived-body" experience of the meaning (see CCP, 183–85). Preachers who believe that the primary purpose of illustrations is to clarify will choose not to illustrate if the idea has already been clearly explained. Such reasoning mistakes the *primary* purpose of illustrations, which is to motivate rather than to clarify. This is why the Bible illustrates, in parable, narrative, or image, the commands that are already clear. See further discussion of the purposes of illustration in CCP, 185–86.

hand of God is a position of privilege. Being in that position indicates that Jesus has been received into the presence of the holy heavenly Father and that our sin, which he bore, has been put away. By his death he took the penalty for our sin; by his resurrection he vanquished our sin. The completeness of that penalty being paid and that victory being won are proven by Christ's being seated at his Father's right hand. But the implications extend beyond Christ. If Jesus has been so honored and fully accepted by God, and we are united with him, then that means that we are also acceptable to God despite all our sin.

To make the effect clear, Paul precisely indicates the posture of the Savior with whom we are united at God's right hand. He is "seated." He is at rest. The work of salvation is finished; there is no more to be done. The price for sin past, present, and future has been paid. Jesus died once for all, rose the victor over all, and now is seated with God. The writer of Hebrews reminds us of the importance of our Savior being "seated" when he describes Jesus as our great High Priest. We read in Hebrews, "Day after day every priest stands and performs his religious duties; again and again he offers the same sacrifices, which can never take away sins. But when this priest had offered for all time one sacrifice for sins, he sat down at the right hand of God" (Heb. 10:11–12 NIV).

Through various passages of Scripture we learn the articles of furniture of the Old Testament temple: the laver and seven-branch candlestick, the altar and show-bread, the Ark of the Covenant and its contents. We know the dimensions of the temple, the material of the walls, and the decorations of the robes of the priest down to minute detail. Still, one detail of temple furnishing is never mentioned. There is no mention of a chair. Why? Because "day after day every priest *stands* and performs his religious duties; again and again he offers the same sacrifices." The task of offering sacrifices for a people who kept on sinning was never done, so there was no sitting down on the job.

For over a thousand years the sacrifices were unending. There were annual Passover sacrifices, when lambs were slain by the hundreds of thousands. Other annual sacrifices required that bulls and goats be slaughtered, with their blood sprinkled on the altar. There were seasonal sacrifices of firstlings (firstborn animals) and firstfruits (first foods harvested). New moon sacrifices were offered monthly. Sabbath sacrifices were made every week. The priests offered daily morning and evening sacrifices. In addition, the priests made sacrifices for the personal sins of individuals who brought their sacrifices to the temple. Day after day for a thousand years and more, the sacrifices never ended, until one Lamb went to a hill called Golgotha and was slain for the sins of the world. Then the veil of the temple—representing the separation of God from his people—was rent from top to bottom, the fire on the altar of sacrifice was snuffed out, and our great High Priest sat down at the right hand of God.

Jesus's being seated at God's right hand demonstrates that the ceaseless striving and sacrificing to be acceptable to God is over for those whose faith is in Christ.[5] So complete is our acceptance with God that the apostle can speak of believers' resurrection as past tense, even though we are still walking on this earth. We are already partakers of the heavenly reality of being with God by virtue of our faith in Christ. Our past failures need not haunt us, our present sin will not destroy us, and our future sin will not deny our access to our Savior. We have been made right with God. Though we yet exist here, we are already raised and seated with Christ at God's right hand.

Dead and Hidden (v. 3)

Our present position reflects not only the resurrection privileges of our future life but also the separation from our past life. Paul continues his description of the position of the Colossians by saying, "For you have died, and your life is hidden with Christ in God" (Col. 3:3). While it may be confounding for living believers to hear, "You have been raised" (v. 1), it is even more disconcerting to hear, "You have died" (v. 3). How can this be?[6]

Our present death (though we are alive) can be explained in two ways. First, if we are united spiritually by faith to the One who died, then we died with him. By establishing our identity "with Christ" (vv. 1 and 3) "who is [our] life" (v. 4), Paul makes Christ's past experience inseparable from our own. Since Christ died, then we who are united with him died too. The second way that we have died has a much more positive and present implication. Christ is now alive at God's right hand. If you have a new life in union with him, then the life you had is gone. The apostle says this in various ways. In his letter to the Corinthians, he says that we are new creations and that the old has passed away (2 Cor. 5:17). To believers in Galatia, Paul says that we have been "crucified with Christ" (Gal. 2:20).

5. Notice how this small comment in the biblical text is explained by a macro-perspective on biblical history and the unfolding of redemptive truths over many centuries (see CCP, 306–7).

6. In contrast to the macro-exposition of the preceding subpoint, the exposition of this subpoint requires close inspection of the language and theology of the immediate text and context (see CCP, 307–8).

But what good is it to have died with Christ? The answer is that whatever once characterized a life apart from God—resulting in guilt, shame, and loss—is all passed away, dead. Our life is now "hidden with Christ" (Col. 3:3b). His identity has become our own, and our past identity—characterized by sin that would separate us from God—is dead. So the apostle says not only that "you have died" but also that "your life is hidden with Christ in God" (v. 3).

My daughter and I sometimes play a game at the dinner table before the dishes have been taken away. We call it "Napkin War." I wait until she is distracted. Then I wad up my napkin into a ball and bean her. She always retaliates, but I am a better shot than she is. So after a few volleys, she takes up a position behind her mother. My daughter knows that I will not throw a napkin at Mom. So, hidden behind her mother, I cannot see my daughter, and she is totally protected by my regard for the one who's identity I can see. You know the point I am making: when we are hidden with Christ, his identify covers us. The volleys of heaven's righteous wrath that could rightly be turned on us for our sin will never be thrown.

There is no sin so staining, no lifestyle so bleak, no shame so strong, no rebellion so abhorrent, no fault so dark, no failure so unforgivable, no weakness so overwhelming that it can deny the love of God to those whose identity is hidden in the One whom he loves. We are hidden with Christ in God, enfolded into the Father's care as he embraces the Son with whom we are in union. There is nothing in our past or present or future that will deny us God's love because our past is dead and we are now hidden with Christ in God.

Due to Appear (v. 4)

Paul makes a final statement of our position based upon our present identity and future events. He writes, "When Christ who is your life appears, then you will also appear with him in glory" (v. 4).[7]

"Christ . . . is your life." Don't you love those words? You will not stand before God having to justify your record or make up for your past because you already have your Savior's identity. You are dead, and Christ is your life. This is an amazing claim. It means that all the wonder that is him—his righteousness, his compassion,

7. The exposition of this subpoint requires both macro- and micro-perspectives, as well as the understanding made plain by the use of illustration from a noteworthy source. Each device has a proper place in biblical exposition (see *CCP*, 186–90 and 306–9).

his courage, his glory—is yours through faith that unites you with him. If you have hidden your life in him by faith, then you are dead and your old identity is gone. Now Jesus stands in your place to make the privileges and blessings of his identity yours. Christ is your life—what wonder, how amazing!

My identity in Christ becomes even more amazing when I remember the destiny of the One who is my life. He is coming again. He will appear in power and great glory at the conclusion of the ages. And because we are united with him, when he appears, we "will appear with him in glory." This "glory" the apostle mentions does not simply refer to the heavenly place we will have; it also refers to the heavenly status we will possess. By being united with Christ, we will be with him *and* we will be like him. Remember how the apostle John says this:

> Beloved, we are God's children now, and what we will be has not yet appeared; but we know that when he appears we shall be like him. (1 John 3:2)

We will be like Jesus in glory, not because we are deserving of such status but because we have it by virtue of our union with Christ.

C. S. Lewis attempted to capture this "Weight of Glory" in a famous message so named. He said that were we able now to see the most ordinary of persons in the heavenly status they will have, we would be tempted to bow down and worship them. It sounds improbable—maybe even heretical—but consider all the apostle Paul has just told us about our position. Through our union with Christ, we are already raised with him, seated at the right hand of God, dead to our sinful identity, hid with Christ in God, and now Christ is our life, so that when he appears, we will be with him in glory. There is an intentional crescendo here. The apostle wants us to understand the increasing magnitude of the grace of God that gives us such a glorious, present position, so that we will be moved to act on these heavenly assurances.

II. Our Imperatives (What God Calls Us to Do—Now)[8]

The apostle's goal of motivating us by the position God's grace provides is apparent in the progression of imperatives the apostle uses in these opening verses.

8. A frequent concern about grace-oriented preaching is that it ignores (or deemphasizes) Scripture's imperatives. Expository preaching that commits the preacher to say what God says in the text will not fall

Seek

Paul first says, "If then you have been raised with Christ, seek the things that are above" (Col. 3:1). Some Bible versions translate this phrase as "set your hearts on things above." We should recognize that the meaning is about dedicated pursuit or focus. Other translations use words such as "focus" or "search after." Being raised with Christ should cause us to seek after heavenly things with serious consideration of our standing before God.

Desire

In the second verse Paul says, "Set your minds on things that are above" (v. 2). This is an intensification of the "seeking" already mentioned. Various translations identify this intensified phrasing as meaning to "savor," "be intent," "have your mind controlled by," or even "have affection for." The various translations indicate that as Paul moves through the implications of our union with Christ, the apostle does not merely want rational reflection; he wants the reality of our union with Christ to grip our heart.

This movement from mere consideration of "things above" to intense passion for "things above" can be likened to the progression of emotions displayed by an actual Hurricane Katrina survivor in a television interview. The interviewer asked, "What happened?" The survivor responded in matter-of-fact tones: "I thought I could ride it out. But then the water began to come in. In less than five minutes it filled up the house to the ceiling. It drove me up to the attic and still kept rising. But then I kicked a hole out of the side of the roof . . . to keep from drowning." Everything this man said until that last phrase was said flatly, almost dispassion- ately—as though he were reading a story in a book. But when he said the words "to keep from drowning," the weightiness of the words that had just come from his mouth hit him. His voice cracked, and he wept as the reality of being rescued from death gripped his heart.

That engagement of the heart with the realities of heaven's rescue from hell's destruction is what the apostle strives to create with his words. In essence, he says,

---

into this error. Faithfully preaching the text will lead to faithful preaching of imperatives but never apart from the indicatives that are in the immediate content or surrounding context of every biblical text (see CCP, 312, 320–23) and thus must also be addressed according to the principles of expository preaching (see CCP, 113–14, 270, 275, 282).

"Concentrate hard on things above since you are raised with Christ, who is seated at the right hand of God." And then, lest we go, "Yeah, yeah," he grabs us by the collar and says, "Get captured by this reality: you died and your life is hid with Christ in God, and when he appears, you will be with him in glory."

Kill

Only when our hearts are gripped by the heavenly realities that are greater, more enduring, and more wonderful than the realities of this sad world are we ready for the final and most intense imperative that the apostle will give. In contrast to the focus on our heavenly position, he says next, "Put to death therefore what is earthly in you: sexual immorality, impurity, passion, evil desire, and covetousness, which is idolatry" (v. 5). It is difficult for our English words to capture the intensity of this expression. The King James Version translates, "Mortify . . . your members which are upon the earth." But "put to death" or "mortify," as noble a heritage as those terms may have in our theological traditions, may actually obscure the intensity of the apostle's imperative. What he says so powerfully might be better understood in the simple phrase, "Kill it!"

The consequences of sin lead to death and destruction. Treat such sin in your life no differently than it treats you. Do not think that Satan intends any less harm to you with the deadly temptations he brings. Do not consider sin lightly. Kill it, lest it deprive you of the life that your Lord intends for you.

On the afternoon of April 26, 2003, as he navigated up Blue John Canyon in Utah, rock climber Aron Ralston came to what he thought was an easy three-meter drop. It wasn't. His movement shifted the balance of an eight-hundred-pound boulder, crushing his right hand against the canyon wall. Six days later, the rock still had him pinned to the canyon wall, and he was dying of exposure and dehydration. Then he realized what he had to do to live.

Ralston wrote, "I poked my thumb with the knife blade twice. On the second prodding, the blade punctures the epidermis as if it is dipping into a stick of room-temperature butter, and releases a telltale hissing. Escaping gases are not good; the rot had advanced more quickly than I had guessed. . . . I lash out in fury, trying to yank my forearm straight out from the sandstone handcuff, never wanting more than I do now to simply rid myself of any connection to this decomposing appendage."

He declared of his now dead member, "I don't want it. It's not part of me. It's garbage." And he cut his hand off, removing from him what would otherwise have been responsible for his death.

As awful as that experience sounds, Ralston later wrote, "To me the amputation is the most beautiful experience I'll ever have in my life because it comes from the contrast of being dead in my grave for six days and [then] having my life back."

What Paul is saying to you and me through this letter to the Colossians is that God has given us a new life in Christ; so do not let Satan and sin spoil it. Love your life in Christ enough to put to death whatever binds you to your earthly nature. Because of such sin, Paul says that the wrath of God is coming upon the unregenerate (v. 6). Do not think that similar sin—though it cannot quench the Savior's love—will have no effect on you. Kill whatever would keep you from the blessed life God intends for you. The account of Aron Ralston is graphic but not stronger than the language Paul is using to compel us to rid ourselves of the sin that will damage our walk with Christ.

III. Our Power

The apostle knows how hard it is to rid ourselves of the habits, patterns, and sin that have become so much of our life. So his next words are intended to provide the power to kill the sin that attacks and attracts us at the same time.

The Power Is in Your Fight[9]

Paul's previous statements regarding our position are in the past tense: you have been raised (v. 1) and you have died (v. 3). But the imperatives are in the present tense: seek the things that are above (v. 1), set you minds on things that are above (v. 2), put to death what is earthly in you (v. 5). These words remind us that there are battles to fight in the present tense. The war with sin is not over even for these people whom the apostle has assured of their position in Christ. The simple message is that the fight is never over, and if we think it is, we will let down our guard to Satan's attacks.

9. Note that grace does not erase the need for human effort but rather provides the motivation and power for its expression (see CCP, 323–27).

In the famous devotional book *The Mortification of Sin in Believers*, Puritan writer John Owen writes that there are typically two times when believers are tempted to think that they will no longer have to fight temptation. The first is when they have just yielded to a temptation, and the aftermath of shame and guilt makes the sin repugnant even to the sinners. The second is when believers are in the midst of some crisis or tragedy that makes them resolve to abandon a persistent sin. In both cases, the temporary lessening of sin's power is due to the influence of present distractions that cause believers to think the sin will not tempt them so powerfully in the future. But all thoughts of a future life without the need to battle sin are deceptive. Owen writes that when the shame lessens and the crisis wanes, the temptation will renew in power.

While sin no longer has dominion over us and we have actual power to defeat it (Rom. 6:14), yet sin continues to act like an insurgent force in a vanquished country. The insurgency has already been defeated yet is still able to inflict terrible damage if those in power do not continue to fight. The vain hope that there will be no more struggle, no more need for resolve, no more need for caution, or no more need for the disciplines that fill us with Christ's strength—will weaken us. Therefore, Owen warns to give sin no foothold in heart or thought but continually fight it with the means the Spirit provides.

The need for vigilance in this war against the corruptions that could take back ground in our hearts is the reason for the apostle's list of sin warnings (Col. 3:5). Paul first tells us to put to death "sexual immorality," and then lists in progressive order the sins by which such evil enters our lives: first "impurity"—the crude conversations, jokes, and entertainments that we excuse as innocuous. Such impurity germinates earthly "passion" in our heart, and from this passion comes the actual desire for sin. "Evil desires" lead to "covetousness" (greed), a more general term for craving what God does not intend for us to have, which is "idolatry"—that is, putting other things above God's priorities. Paul warns, "On account of these [sins] the wrath of God is coming" against the unregenerate (v. 6). This warning does not deny that the grace of God will protect believers from God's ultimate wrath (as we are already "raised with Christ" and "Christ is our life"), but we should not think that what is so destructive in others' lives will have no negative effect on ours.

Paul is not only concerned about how our sin affects us individually. He wants our position in Christ to motivate us to reflect his love in our relationships with others. Thus, the apostle warns against the progression of sin in our community, urging believers to rid themselves of "anger, wrath, malice, slander, and obscene talk" (v. 8). These ultimately lead to deceptions (v. 9) and should be replaced by "compassionate hearts, kindness, humility, meekness, and patience" (v. 12). These latter traits reflect Christ's character in us, and through them we learn to forgive and to love one another in order to achieve unity with all believers who also reflect Christ—regardless of ethnicity or background (vv. 9–14).

In summary, Paul warns us to short-circuit at its earliest stages any process that would deprive us of the goodness of our lives in Christ. Immorality begins with simple allowance of impurity in our minds and mouths. Idolatry is the terminus of putting any priorities above God's. We should also give no foothold to the devil in our lives that would give him leverage in our relationships. In essence, Paul teaches that if you think sin is no threat, or that you can swim in its shallows or play along its fringes, then you will fall into Satan's clutches. If you believe that no fight is needed, you will not have the power that you need.

The Power Is in Your Faith[10]

If we must fight, how are we armed for the battle? Real power comes not simply in knowing that we have to fight but in the faith that we can have victory in the battle.

You must believe that you can be what you are called to be. You are raised with Christ who sits at God's right hand (v. 1). This means the resurrected Lord is petitioning his Father to provide for your needs. Further, because you are united with Christ and indwelled by his Spirit, his resurrection power fills you. Satan wants you to believe that you have no power over sin and that you cannot help what you do. These are lies meant to dispirit and weaken you. The Bible teaches that the One in you is greater than Satan's powers (1 John 4:4). The creature you once were, who was not able to resist sin, is dead (Col. 3:3). You are a new creation in Christ Jesus, and the sin that the Holy Spirit reveals to you, he also gives you power to resist. What this means is that you can have victory. Sin no longer has dominion over you. The battles you must fight, you can win. Tomorrow does not have to be like yesterday. Where there is such confidence, God's power resides.

The Puritans sometimes spoke about the obedient Christian life as "a walk of faith." To our ears this may sound like some work of super-spirituality whereby

10. For further discussion of the nature of power that is provided by faith and love, see CCP, 313–15 and 325–26.

faith was cranked into the human soul by extraordinary feats of saintly devotion. But the walk of faith actually is something quite different. This walk involves approaching life with the faith of a child—simply taking God at his Word. He says that you are a new creature, that resurrection power is in you, that you can resist, that he will hear your prayer, that he will instruct you in his Word, that his Spirit has already given you the will and the power to do what pleases him, and that his people are here to help you. God does not call us to exert any extraordinary energy, activity, or zeal to believe this. Yet his power accompanies such faith. If you believe that change is possible—or, more specifically, that change is within your power as one united with Christ—then you have spiritual power.

The Power Is in His Love

We have the power of our position and the power of faith, but why would we exercise them? The apostle answers by pointing us to the power of love. The dependence order of the believer's position and God's commands is pivotal for understanding the love implicit in this passage. The call to holiness—to set mind and heart on things above and to mortify the flesh—is based on the believer's prior status. Never is our status based on our performance of God's commands. We are to seek things above because we are already raised. We are to set our minds on things above because we are dead and hidden with Christ in God. We are to mortify the flesh because we are already alive to God and will appear with him in glory.

This passage demonstrates that the imperative (what we do) is based on the indicative (who we are). We obey because we are the Lord's. We do not become the Lord's because we obey. By making sure that we do not confuse our "who" and our "do," Paul ensures that God's gracious provision for us stimulates love for God, which makes obedience to him our delight. Never does our obedience *earn* his love. Instead, our obedience *expresses* our love.

We act upon the power and faith that are ours because our love for God motivates us to do so. Jesus taught us the power of such motivation when he said, "If you love me, you will keep my commandments" (John 14:15). Since nothing creates greater love for God than profound understanding of his provision for undeserving sinners, the grace that establishes our new identity in Christ is the power of the Christian life. Thus, as counterintuitive as it may be, grace does not release from obedience but is the compelling power of it. We long to please the One who has given us the status of his own child though we did nothing, and could do nothing, to earn this identity. Knowing who we are ultimately gives us the power to live as God desires.

Conclusion

The power of knowing who you are is portrayed well in the movie *Cinderella Man*. In the award-winning drama, a washed-up fighter named James J. Braddock struggles to find work during the Great Depression. Then, through a series of improbabilities, he gets a chance to enter the ring again despite being too old, injured, and arthritic. With his family's security at stake, Braddock wins an amazing string of bouts. An unlikely hero, he captures the imagination of the nation and actually gets an opportunity to fight for a championship title.

There's just one small problem: he will face a huge fighter named Max Baer, the reigning champion. Baer is a vicious fighter who has already killed two men in the ring. Braddock has to fight Baer for the title, and everyone knows the danger.

The night of the fight, tension fills the air. In the locker room, Braddock's handlers try to prepare him for the battle of—and *for*—his life. Wanting him to focus, one of them tries to stop Braddock's wife from entering the locker room minutes before the fight. She withers him with a look that clearly says, "Get out of my way," and marches to her husband.

Locking her eyes on his, she says these words: "So you just remember who you are . . . you're the Bulldog of Bergen, and the Pride of New Jersey, you're everybody's hope, and the kids' hero, and you are the champion of my heart, James J. Braddock." The message: Remember who you are, and fight like it.

The apostle Paul's words echo such encouragement. Paul does not hide from us the fact that the battle for holiness may be challenging and intense. But he calls us to the battle with a reminder of who we are. Listen to what he says: By your union with the crucified, risen, and reigning Lord who is seated at the right hand of God, you have been called to a battle requiring that you die to self in order to live for him. This battle will call for all of your strength, faith, and devotion. Your victory will require fixing your mind on the reality of who you are by the grace of

God alone. You are risen with Christ and united with the One who shares with you the affection and glory of God; you have a calling to live for him against all earthly challenges, and he has given you power to do so. He has put the heart of his champion within you despite his knowledge of your weakness and sin. Now that you know who you are, get out there and fight because through Christ you are the champion of God's heart.[11]

11. This final sentence attempts to meet the goals of a sermon conclusion, summarizing the content of the sermon while also exhorting its application: to die to self for the purposes of Christ because he has so privileged and loved us (see CCP, 254–56). The sermon also ends with the indicative emphasis of the passage—reminding us who we really are in Christ.

Indicative/Imperative Dynamics

(Imperative Emphasis)

Emphasizing the unconditional nature of the love of God in our preaching is quite concerning to many who rightly insist that Scripture demands holy living. They worry that if we do not make God's affection conditional on our obedience, we have, in essence, granted people liberty to disobey. When such concern is voiced, we who hold to the truths of the gospel have no choice but to concede the validity of the concern. There is a math of the mind that is unavoidable: If you tell me that I can sin and be loved no less by a holy God, then it may seem you have given me freedom to sin. But the math of the mind is not the chemistry of the heart.

The heart works beyond and above mere logic. Jesus said, "If you love me, you will keep my commandments" (John 14:15). Affection for Jesus makes us want to live for him and to turn from sin. The love of Christ compels us to do his will (2 Cor. 5:14). This is true because sin has power over us only because we are attracted to it. When the love of Christ supersedes love for sin, the power of sin is broken.

The biblical truth that generates the greatest love for Christ is his grace toward us. Grace is the constant theme of Scripture because its grasp has the greatest potential to produce love for God that is power for true obedience.[1] The consistency

---

1. For further discussion of how grace compels holiness, see the author's *Christ-Centered Preaching: Redeeming the Expository Sermon*, 2nd ed. (Grand Rapids: Baker Academic, 2005), 312–13; hereinafter *CCP*.

of the theme of grace does not diminish the demands of the gospel. Instead, those who love God are required to serve him. Their service does not merit or generate his affection; rather, obedience is the compulsion and delight of those who, in response to his grace, love him and consequently love those he loves (the best foundation for Christian ethics and mercy ministries).

Grace confuses us because most human relationships are consequential and reciprocal: we are paid because we work; we are rewarded because we perform; we are loved because we love. But the gospel of grace is something very different. While we were yet his enemies, Christ died for us (Rom. 5:10). When we are faithless, he abides faithful (2 Tim. 2:13). His love and his lasting affection are not offered on the basis of our past, present, or future actions. But this unmerited provision does *not* mean that God has no claim upon our behavior.

Those who are saved and maintained by God's grace are called to ever more dedicated expressions of his holiness in response to his unconditional love. In the preceding sermon, we focused on a passage of Scripture that emphasizes the indicatives that are the foundation of Scripture's imperatives.[2] In the following message, we will examine a passage that emphasizes the imperatives that flow from the indicatives. In both passages, the imperatives are founded upon the indicatives, but in this one the apostle Paul stridently reminds all who would abuse God's grace that the indicatives never annul the imperatives for those who truly love God.

2. For further discussion of how imperatives are based on the indicatives of our relationship with God, see CCP, 325–27.

Intolerant Grace

Titus 2:11–15

Scripture Introduction

Whatever happened to revival? A decade ago, Christian bookstores overflowed with books on the coming revival. Christian radio and television buzzed with talk of when and how revival would come. Articles and authors explored revivals of the past and plotted parallel paths necessary for a revival to come today. And now—virtual silence. Except for a few preachers still trying to whip up enthusiasm in congregations tired of praying for what has not come, the battle drum beats ever more softly and distantly. Why? Perhaps because in all the talk about revival we got a glimpse of what it would actually require, not of all those reprobate folk out there in a sinful society, but of us, the called people of God in the church.

My intention in this sermon is to beat the revival drum again, but not without counting the costs, lest renewed enthusiasm only lead to repeated discouragement. Living for others and denying the idols of sensuality are at least some of the means and evidences of revival among God's people. They are also the challenges Paul urges Titus to impress upon the church at Crete in order for that society to change. They remain the radical challenges facing us if our culture is to experience true revival through us. In the early verses of Titus 2 the apostle lists specific imperatives for God's people, and then—in the words on which I will focus—he explains why these mandates are necessary for us to experience a deluge of grace.

Scripture Reading

Read with me Titus 2:11–15:

> For the grace of God has appeared, bringing salvation for all people, training us to
> renounce ungodliness and worldly passions, and to live self-controlled, upright, and
> godly lives in the present age, waiting for our blessed hope, the appearing of the
> glory of our great God and Savior Jesus Christ, who gave himself for us to redeem
> us from all lawlessness and to purify for himself a people for his own possession
> who are zealous for good works.
>
> Declare these things; exhort and rebuke with all authority. Let no one disregard
> you.

Sermon Introduction

When El Niño's rain deluged Southern California during a recent winter, the
dangers of mudslides became a living nightmare for one family. While the family
was sleeping, a wave of mud tore through their house, ripping it apart and sweeping a sleeping baby out into the night. The parents began to search through the
darkness for the child. Tromping through the muck that had descended on their
whole neighborhood, they searched, dug, and called for their child throughout the
long night—without results. When the morning came, a rescue worker covered
in mud brought the parents a mud-caked bundle. In his arms he held the baby,
filthy but alive. You know what the mother then did. She clung to her child despite its filth, washed the mud away, and determined never to let her baby out of
her grasp.

This account helps me with concepts in this passage that are so opposed to our
common thought about the nature of God's grace. Grace, we know, annuls our
works as the means of securing or maintaining God's affection. The natural human
inclination, as a result, is to suppose that if our good works do not determine God's
affection, then there is no reason to do them.[1] Why be concerned about godliness
since we are saved by grace? Because, say the Scriptures, when the filth of my sin
was sweeping me in my helplessness to eternal death, my God came as a rescue
worker and as a mother. He covered himself in the muck of this world to claim me,

---

1. This sentence is the fallen condition focus (FCF) of this message (see *CCP*, 48–54).

embraced me despite my filth, and now wants me never again to be in the mire. Such cleansing grace should make us so love God that we cannot stand anything in our lives that would re-soil us or offend him. Biblical grace makes us intolerant of evil in our lives. The apostle Paul underscores this truth, saying that the grace of God teaches us "to renounce ungodliness and worldly passions" (Titus 2:11–12).

Grace—rightly perceived—compels holiness.[2] We must acknowledge that this is not natural logic. In the popular mind, those who are full of grace are supposed to say, "Okay, that's all right, fine, never mind, go ahead." But for this apostle, grace means we say, "No," to ungodliness and worldly passions. What kind of grace is this? The apostle answers by disclosing the power of Christ's rescue, the nature of his requirements, and the character of his redeemed.[3]

I. The Rescue of Grace (v. 11)

The apostle begins to explain the nature of transforming grace by reminding his readers of what God has accomplished and for whom. In the preceding section of this letter (vv. 1–10), Paul says that Titus should ensure that what "accords with sound doctrine" (v. 1) is taught to all kinds of people—older men, older women, young women, young men, slaves—who will pass along "the doctrine of God our Savior" (v. 10) to others. Now the reason for these imperatives follows. "For the grace of God has appeared, bringing salvation for all people" (v. 11). The context makes it clear that Paul is not contending that worldwide evangelism has already occurred but rather that the message of God's grace has been made available to all kinds of people. By reminding his readers that the message of the Savior has not been withheld from any on the basis of age, class, or gender, Paul defuses the discriminatory objections of those who would deny their testimony to others because of societal barriers.

Basis for discrimination is further removed when Paul reminds his readers of their own undeserved deliverance. The "salvation" (a predicate adjective describing God's "delivering" or "saving") made available to all kinds of people has been brought by "the grace of God" (a phrase used fifteen times in Paul's letters to

2. This sentence is a concisely worded informal proposition (see *CCP*, 148).

3. For the sake of smooth expression, the wording of this billboard is slightly different from the wording of the main points, but the identification of the main ideas is sufficient to alert listeners to the structure and content of the message that will follow (see *CCP*, 264–65).

describe unmerited divine favor). No one has been saved by what they themselves
have accomplished or vanquished. We are saved not on the basis of our goodness,
station, or class, but solely on the basis of God's sovereign action in our behalf.

Paul underscores this truth of our unearned deliverance, and expands its implications, by saying that this grace has "appeared." In Greek literature this word can
function as a technical term to describe a hero (or god) breaking into a helpless
situation to rescue people from danger (v. 11). Paul typically uses this terminology
to refer to the past or future coming of Christ to rescue his people (v. 13). When
the apostle uses the same word to describe the coming of grace, he so intertwines
who Christ is with what Christ provides that the two become inseparable in our
consideration. Grace is not some abstract doctrine or theological construct. Grace
comes as Christ does. Grace is as personal as he is. In fact, Christ is the grace to
which Paul refers. The unmerited favor of God is what Jesus is about, but it is also
who he is. We should thus see grace as a personal action by a personal God who
saves us from our helpless condition out of pure love.

Intimate affection from a majestic God is Paul's message, but intimacy is not the
entire message. The ancients would have understood a god who came to rescue
a person, group, city, or even nation from a crisis. The ancient Greek and Roman
plays employed the *deus ex machina* ("god from the machine"), where a god inter-
vened to rescue people from a specific crisis. But as has already been made clear,
this appearance is not limited in scope to a man or a clan. The unique Christian
message is that this God's rescue is offered and is sufficient for "all people," regardless of their human designation or demerit. Thus, the rescue that God our Savior
engineers is both intimate and immense.

II. The Requirements of Grace (vv. 12–13)[4]

Paul intends for the combined message of such an intimate and immense salvation to have an effect on us. Our hearts should flood with wonder, thanksgiving,
gratitude—and one more thing: determination. When we realize that we have

---

4. The wording of this main point—that there are requirements of grace—as well as the content of this
message, goes against the grain of common expectations about grace-based preaching. Many presume that
emphasizing grace necessarily deemphasizes the commands of God. The apostle's words (and this exposition of them) make it clear that the "rules" do not change in Christ-centered preaching, but the reasons
do. When grace captures our hearts, we obey God because we love him and desire to please him—not
to cause him to love and please us. For further discussion of the indicative/imperative relationships that

been rescued from the clutches of evil against which we were helpless, then our resolution is strengthened never to go back there. We never want to allow the evil to take hold again. That is why the rescue of grace results in requirements. This is not because the requirements rescue but because the rescued, who truly recognize the danger they were in, want to be forever free of such peril. Thus Paul describes both negatively and positively what is required of us to remain free of the dangers of sin from which grace has rescued us (v. 12).

To Say "No" (v. 12a)

First, Paul says that grace is "training us to renounce [the nuance of this word means to "reject on an ongoing basis"] ungodliness and worldly passions" (v. 12a). "Ungodliness" is a reference to a Christian's conduct—or, in this negative phrasing, one's misconduct. One commentator refers to Paul's use of "godliness" as "reverence manifested in actions," meaning our external behaviors. But the ungodly externals are not all that Paul says deserves our rejection. We are also to say "No" to "worldly passions." This means that we are to deny ourselves not only external conduct that betrays God but also similar internal impulses, what the older King James Version of the Bible simply described as "lusts." Other Bible versions variously translate these terms as worldly "appetites," "desires," or "cravings." There is no question that sexual compulsions are included in the term, but it also includes anger, hatred, ambition, and other urges that result in uncontrolled speech or behavior.

Now consider precisely from where these prohibitions come. They are not the means to get to God; rather, they are a consequence of the "appearing" of grace that is Christ, our God. When Isaiah saw the majesty and holiness of God, the prophet fell down and cried out, "Woe is me." He was devastated by his awareness of his own sin in light of the holiness of God. When God revealed himself to Moses in the burning bush, that deliverer of the covenant people similarly hid his face. Paul expects the "appearing" of God, made radiant by the grace of Christ Jesus, to affect us no differently.

When we have seen God clearly in the appearance of his grace, we have an intense awareness of our unholiness. Grace in this context "trains," as Paul says

---

inform, motivate, and enable Christian holiness, see *CCP*, 316–27, and the author's book-length treatment of this subject, *Holiness by Grace: Delighting in the Joy That Is Our Strength* (Wheaton: Crossway, 2001), esp. 91–158.

in the opening phrase of this verse. True apprehension of grace instructs us of the magnitude and repugnance of our sin. That is why Paul says that the grace of God that has appeared teaches us to renounce ungodliness. We want to be rid of whatever stains us before the splendor of God's glorious grace. But saying "No" is not our only obligation. Isaiah rose, asking God to use him; Moses walked from the burning bush to do as God required. There are positive compulsions that also arise from grace.

To Live "Yes" (v. 12b)

Grace teaches us to say "No" to ungodliness and worldly passions, but it also instructs us to live "Yes"—to live in assent to God's requirements. Such assent constrains Christians "to live self-controlled, upright, and godly lives" (v. 12b). The first two terms in this list could fairly be called the antithesis of ungodliness and worldly passions. The earlier, negative terms were about unrighteousness and lack of restraint; these first two positive terms are about control of passions (i.e., righteous constraint on one's impulses) and uprightness (i.e., righteous conduct in dealing with others). Because the emphasis in the verse thus far is on controlled behavior, the third term in the list of positive characteristics taught by grace— "godly"—has particular significance.

If being a Christian only involved self-control over our passions and upright behavior before others, then we might get the idea that the Christian life was only a matter of constraint, living within certain rules or standards. By adding the word "godly" to the ways that grace teaches us to live, the apostle reminds us that the Christian life is about the display of Spirit-provided power. Godliness is not a consequence of human resolution or willpower; it is the expression of relationship with God that results in an extraordinary life that honors God. Thus, taking the three positive characteristics taught by grace in order, we learn that the life of grace is comprehensive—involving oneself, one's relationship to others, and one's relationship with God.

To Act Now (vv. 12c–13)

How long are we expected to live according to these standards? Is holy living a matter only of the past, when people were under the law? No. Paul says that grace teaches us to live so as to honor God "in the present age, waiting for our blessed hope, the appearing of the glory of our great God and Savior Jesus Christ" (vv. 12c–13). We are not allowed to say that in this age of grace there are no standards for us to follow. Godliness remains our obligation until Jesus returns.

The future grace of Christ's return, when his glorious appearing will mark our deliverance (see the earlier discussion of "appear" in v. 11) from the evil and suffering of this world, is also identified here as our "blessed hope." The "appearing" and "hope" are introduced by the same definite article, indicating that they are the same event. What Paul adds by introducing the phrase "blessed hope" is explanation of what the glory of the appearing will include. When the elements of this phrase appear elsewhere in Paul's writings, they refer both to the multiple aspects of the deliverance that believers will know at Christ's return (for example, Rom. 8:24; Gal. 5:5; Col. 1:5) and to the renewed presence of the Deliverer who will bring those blessings—he who is "the hope of glory" (Col. 1:27). Thus, the elements of this blessed hope include Christ's return, the resurrection of those who have died in Christ, the union of living believers with Christ, the reunion of the faithful living and dead, and eternal life with Christ (1 Thess. 4:13–18).

The certainty of this hope is underscored by Paul's identification of the deliverer as "our great God and Savior Jesus Christ." Though the natural reading of this phrase has often been challenged for its direct affirmation of Christ's deity, it remains one of the most powerful New Testament proofs of Christ's divine nature that grants believers assurance of blessing (Titus 2:10–11; 3:4, 6). Not only is Jesus the Christ (i.e., the Anointed One, or Messiah, who came to fulfill past promises and provide present grace as the Lamb of God), but as our "great God" he is also able to deliver the blessings of the future grace for which the faithful hope. The knowledge that our God is coming creates expectancy in believers that stimulates faithfulness in daily endeavors and grants perseverance in times of trial. Because Christ is coming, we desire to live in fidelity to him, and knowing that he will deliver us from trial and vanquish all his and our enemies, we can. The glorious appearing of our great God and Savior, Jesus Christ, is our cause for godly living "in the present age."

In summary, the grace God provides in our past, present, and future requires that we say "No" to the world and "Yes" to God—now. Grace does not change the requirement of godliness in the Christian life. Still, because the categories of conduct the apostle has addressed are so comprehensive, Christians may be tempted to affirm their general obedience without really having examined the particulars of their lives. To force us to answer whether we are in fact willing to say "No" to the world and "Yes" to God now, we need to consider specific areas of our lives in which the world commonly challenges Christian faithfulness. Determining what God requires in a specific area, such as the entertainments we enjoy, will provide guidance for godliness in other areas of life.

A few weeks ago, my teenage son went to see a popular movie. Unbeknownst to him and to us—we had let him go to the movie based on the posted rating—the movie included a scene with a sexual encounter. My son walked out and took his friends with him. I was very proud of him for his principled leadership. Yet what happened to my son afterward has left me flabbergasted, discouraged, and, occasionally, angry. Over the next several weeks, the Christian friends and adult leaders in his life, almost without exception, told him that what he did was wrong. They said that such sexual material was not a valid reason for any really mature Christian with a well-developed world and life view not to watch a movie. The result, of course, was that my son felt confused and alone in his commitment.

How should Christians respond to such entertainments in the light of Paul's exhortation to respond to God's grace with godliness? Hopefully we will all recognize the folly of trying to establish a yardstick for flesh exposed (or lists of words used and themes addressed) in order to determine the appropriateness of works of literature and art for all Christians in all times. At the same time, the Bible requires that Christians now—in this place, culture, and time—answer to God regarding whether their entertainments, habits, and appetites exhibit a true commitment to say "No" to ungodliness and worldly passions and "Yes" to self-controlled, upright, and godly living. Our inability to draw hard and fast lines regarding artistic expression for all historical and cultural conditions does not remove our responsibility to determine if what we are consuming—and encouraging others to consume by our example—is damaging the cause of Christ.

Many knowledgeable evangelicals will question a challenge to examine the appropriateness of our entertainments. They remember the warnings of Christian philosopher Francis Schaeffer against living in a "corner culture." Schaeffer rightly contended that we should not shut ourselves into a Christian ghetto, listening only to ourselves and losing our ability to understand our culture, dialogue with it, and ultimately penetrate it with the message of the gospel. Such principles are profoundly true to the ethics and imperatives of Scripture. Still, Schaeffer was neither unconscious of the dangers inherent in our culture's values nor without warning about the indiscrete indulgence of what it offered. Schaeffer did not want freedom from legalism to lead to bondage to the intoxicants of the world. He wrote:

> Often, after a person is born again and asks, "What shall I do next?" he is given a list of things, usually of a limited nature, and primarily negative. . . . The true Christian life . . . is not merely a negative not-doing of any small list of things. Even if the list began as a very excellent list of things to beware of in that particular historical setting, we still must emphasize that the Christian life, or true spirituality, is more than a refraining from a certain external list of taboos in a mechanical way.
>
> Because this is true, almost always there is a reaction: another group of Christians begins to work against such a list of taboos; thus there is a tendency toward a struggle in Christian circles between those who set up a certain list of taboos and those who, feeling there is something wrong with this, say, "Away with all taboos, away with all lists." Both of these groups can be right and both can be wrong, depending on how they approach the matter.
>
> I was impressed by this one Saturday night at L'Abri, when we were having one of our discussion times. On that particular night everybody present was a Christian, many of them from groups in countries where "lists" had been very much accentuated. They began to talk against the use of taboos, and at first, as I listened to them, I rather agreed with the direction they were going. But as I listened further to this conversation, and as they spoke against the taboos in their own countries, it became quite clear to me that what they really wanted was merely to be able to do the things which the taboos were against. What they really wanted was a more lax Christian life. But we must see that in giving up such lists, in feeling the limitation of the "list" mentality, we must not do this merely in order to be able to live a looser life: it must be for something deeper.[5]

With Schaeffer there was certainly a push to make Christians aware of the values, concerns, and trends of our culture, but we must not forget why. Beneath the evaluation was outrage and grief. Schaeffer was outraged that the sophisticates of culture could take the noble things of creation and use them in rebellion against the Creator. Schaeffer's grief that young people were being led astray was intense and compelling. A life committed to their redemption (on their terms, if necessary) was the zeal of Schaeffer. It must remain ours. We must ask each other, "Is

5. Francis A. Schaeffer, *The Complete Works of Francis A. Schaeffer: A Christian Worldview*, vol. 3, *A Christian View of Spirituality* (Westchester, IL: Crossway, 1982), 201–2.

the reason that you are partaking of the entertainments that are poisoning the minds and morals of many in our society truly so that we can redeem them?" The Bible says that we must cling to the good but hate what is evil (Rom. 12:9). While we cannot read one another's hearts, we should be willing to examine our own hearts as to whether we truly hate what is illicit, immoral, or indecent on the screen. Are we outraged, out for redemption, or just out with the rest of culture for the Saturday show?

The ethics of grace require us to ask honest questions even about our own entertainments: Are we redeeming or simply imbibing? Are we being informed or simply being tranquilized to evil? Are we evaluating or simply enjoying? Are we living as though there is no difference between things sacred and things profane? Specifically, are we watching, reading, and listening to entertainments with the awareness that whether we are in a bright church, darkened theater, or secluded room, we are before the face of God? Do we act as though wherever we are, we are on holy ground? Does what we are doing really reflect the conviction that a holy God who rescued us from the death grip of sin is with us in every place and will appear in power and great glory? Are we doing everything in word and deed to the glory of God (Col. 3:17), or does our God go away when the lights go out?

These are hard questions even for the one who now asks them. I struggle to know all the answers in my own life, and I look for the means to evaluate my habits in these words. How do we examine and, if necessary, resensitize our consciences? How do we know if we have moved beyond the boundaries of God's requirements in our lives and are again in danger of being swept away by the mud—the filth of this world? Honest questions based on the apostle's instructions will help answer, if we will dare to ask them:[6]

1. Have we lost the ability to say "No"?
We must honestly assess our internal compulsions—our worldly passions. Do they control us? Do we see certain movies, watch certain shows, read certain books, listen to certain music not because of its aesthetic but because we need

6. Recognizing that these implications will be difficult for all and controversial for some, this application is more lengthy and structured than is ordinary—with analytical questions setting up each division of the application's discussion and each analytical question worded in the terms of the preceding exposition, so that the "expositional rain" (i.e., key terms of preceding exposition) gives both structure and authority to the imperatives (see CCP, 222–25).

a sexual fix or a violent adventure? Do we accept a job promotion only because we love the added power and prestige? No one can answer for us, but each of us must examine our own hearts with candor and rigor about these matters if we are to honor our Lord. Christ takes every idol of culture (sex, power, money) and requires it to bow before him.[7] If those idols are beginning to control our thoughts, actions, and anticipations, then we are bowing before them.

Something is wrong if our practices as Christians are practically indistinguishable from a culture that denies itself nothing. Francis Schaeffer cautioned us about our involvement in such a culture more than a generation ago:

> We are surrounded by a world that says "no" to nothing. When we are surrounded by this sort of mentality . . . , then suddenly to be told that in the Christian life there is to be this strong negative aspect of saying "no" to things and "no" to self, it must seem hard. And if it does not feel hard to us, we are not really letting it speak to us.[8]

If our understanding of the grace of God fails to teach us to say "No" to ungodliness, then we are living with the same perspective as the rest of the world—in contrast to Christ's calling.

2. Have we lost the concern to live "Yes"?

I expect that the reaction of many Christians to a renewed plea for purity and discretion regarding our entertainments will be, "You cannot take my liberty away. I am under grace. I am not under the law." I agree that I cannot judge the thoughts and motives of others and that this limits my ability and right to draw hard lines for others where matters are not directly addressed in Scripture. This limitation, however, does not allow me or any other Christian to stop being concerned for the effects of our actions on others. The Christian life cannot be lived autonomously. Our assent to live godly lives requires us to consider others as we make our choices.

---

7. This portion of the application briefly "unrolls" the principles of the imperatives to situations not previously identified by the preacher, so as not to limit the application to a particular concern or context. The goal of situational specificity in application is to make sure the message is not simply an abstraction; the goal of "unrolling" additional situations is to make sure the message is not "fenced in" by the specifics the preacher thinks to mention. By employing both situational specificity and unrolled situations that are nonspecific, we seek to make it clear that these imperatives have concrete, real-world application, but we do not limit the convicting power of the Holy Spirit to that single application (see CCP, 224–27).

8. Schaeffer, *A Christian View of Spirituality*, 216–17.

When Paul outlines the behavior God expects of those in the household of
faith, he reminds each member that they are not alone—the actions of each touch
others. Older men are to set an example for others (Titus 2:2). The older women
are to be reverent so that they can teach younger women (vv. 3–4). Titus himself
is to be an example to others (v. 7). The Christian life does not function indepen-
dently; we are part of a community, and our actions must be considered in light
of their effects upon others. Said Schaeffer,

> We are to be willing to say "no" to ourselves, we are to be willing to say "no" to things
> in order that the command to love God and [others] may have real meaning. Even in
> things which are lawful to me, things which do not break the Ten Commandments,
> I am not to seek my own, but I am to seek another['s] good.[9]

It is not enough to argue in the face of ungodly entertainment, "It doesn't bother
me." Maybe you are unaffected by the sexual content, violent fascinations, material
preoccupations, or societal disrespect that lace our culture's common distractions;
but our churches and our young people are not unaffected. Promiscuity and abortion among young people in evangelical churches is nearly equivalent to that of
those in the rest of society. Violence for fun and fame from those who seem no
longer capable of identifying with the pain of those they victimize is a growing
epidemic. And no church is distant from young people who, in growing numbers,
are estranged from societal norms and spend their days trying to stimulate listless
lives through pornography, gaming technology, self-mutilation, music immersion, drugs, alcohol binging, and dreams of stardom that will free them from any
responsibilities to take care of themselves or others.

As a result of these dehumanizing forces, sexual abuse, human trafficking, and
violent crime are staggeringly pervasive. Awareness of what the morals and mores
of our culture have produced forces us to ask the hardest question of all: In addition to being concerned about our communities as we see their devastation, are
we concerned about our complicity? The grace of God will not allow us to live
unconcerned for those God loves. Our practices and pleasures are examples to
others of our values and God's expectations. Our lives must evidence our assent to
his concern for others. If anyone says that it does not matter to God or his people
what we do, then that is selfish, ungodly, and damaging to the gospel of our Lord.

9. Ibid., 216.

3. Are we willing to act now?

Those uncomfortable with the notion that an ancient apostle might have some-thing to say about our modern society are likely to respond, "No one can take away my Christian liberty. My church will only run headlong back into legalism if I urge concern about these matters. Further, why should I limit my activities when no specific Bible verse addresses this specific activity, habit, or practice?" The biblical response to such statements is that, of course, no one has a right to bind another's conscience or judge another's actions where the Scriptures are not specific. But the principles that bind Christians in their love for God, his people, and his purposes are more about relationships than proof texts.

If we pursue our liberties with only ourselves in view, then we may profess a maturity that gives us rights, but it will not support the proclamation of God's grace toward those lost in the miseries of sin. The goal of the godly is to adorn the gospel with credibility and evidence of its power in their lives. The indulgence of ungodliness and worldly passions ultimately is a denial of the Word of God and the message of the Savior. If the grace of God truly creates in us a zeal to love him, then we will also love those whom he loves and will be willing to give of ourselves for their sake.

Where consciences made sensitive by the Spirit convince us that our conduct damages our heart's resonance with the Savior, or contributes to such damage in others' hearts, the grace we embrace will help us change our course. This is why godliness is so dependent on God. Without the convicting and renewing work of the Spirit in our hearts, we will always rationalize our sin and continue in its path. Yet, as we grow in our affection for God because of his grace, we increasingly grow intolerant of anything that distracts us from him and seek to guard our hearts from all that would distance us, or any other, from him.

III. The Redeemed of Grace (vv. 14–15)[10]

Having been explicit about the requirements God has for those claimed by his grace, the apostle now makes it just as clear that these standards are not the reason that God loves us.

10. In this message, the indicatives of the gospel (who we are by virtue of the grace of God) follow the imperatives (what we are to do as a consequence of our relationship with God). This is an inversion of the *sequential* order of these concepts as they appear in the preceding sermon in this book. However,

Our Status (v. 14)

We are awaiting the appearing of Jesus Christ "who gave himself for us to redeem us from all lawlessness and to purify for himself a people for his own possession" (v. 14). The work of salvation is his, and we are his. The apostle designs every phrase of this beautiful verse to exude the wonder of Christ's work and the consequent status of his people. Paul first reminds us that Christ "gave himself for us" (v. 14a). The words initially remind us that Christ's sacrifice was a gift neither earned nor deserved. Next we are reminded that the gift indicates that our God acted "for us." He became our advocate, acting in our behalf though we were yet sinners. This is some of Paul's favorite language used repeatedly to indicate the nature of God's unconditional favor for his people (e.g., Rom. 8:31–32; Gal. 1:4; 2:20), and it prepares us to understand what Christ's sacrifice accomplishes for his people.

Ransomed (v. 14b)

Christ gave himself for us "to redeem us from all lawlessness" (Titus 2:14b). The word "redeem" literally means to release upon the receipt of a ransom. Jesus speaks of himself as our ransom (see Mark 10:45, probably reflecting Ps. 130:8 and Ezek. 37:23), and Paul uses the concept explicitly (1 Tim. 2:6) to refer to our Savior giving himself to pay the price for our wickedness (literally, "every lawless deed"). The preposition translated "for" can even be translated "in the place of" to drive home the concept of Christ's rescuing us by becoming a ransom for sin in our place in order to satisfy divine justice and free us from our guilt.

Cleansed (v. 14c)

Not only did Christ give himself to redeem us; his offering was made "to purify for himself a people" (Titus 2:14c). The phrase reminds us of the various sacrifices and disciplines God established for his covenant people to demonstrate to them the need for cleansing from the taint of their sin. As the fulfillment of all these

---

the *theological* order remains the same: the imperatives are based on the indicatives, and this (theological) order is not reversible (see CCP, 325–27). The inversion of the sequential order allows an imperative emphasis that is sometimes thought to be denied by grace-based preaching but is very possible and, at times, necessary due to the nature of the text, circumstances, or sin being addressed (see CCP, 315–22). It is just as legitimate to say, "Do this because God loves you," as to say, "God loves you, so do this." Both patterns are found in Scripture, and neither denies the priority of God's grace as the motivation and enablement for Christian obedience (see CCP, 294–95 and 312).

practices, Christ's sacrifice and blood cleanses all to whom it is now applied by faith. The words remind us that God has cleansed us from the defilement of our sin by the sacrifice of his Son (2 Cor. 7:1; Eph. 5:26; Heb. 9:14).

Treasured (v. 14d, e)

Having redeemed and cleansed us at such a terrible price, our God's attitude toward us could be one of resentment or disdain. Instead, we are told that those whom he has purchased and purified he now claims as "his own possession" (Titus 2:14d). The Greek phrase reflects the wording of Exodus 19:5, where God identifies the covenant people as "my treasured possession" (see the earlier cited Ezek. 37:23; Eph. 1:11–14). The attitude of the Redeemer toward the redeemed is that we are precious to him despite the sin that required such sacrifice from him. These words breathe the grace that characterizes our God and should inspire us to do the good works that please our Savior. The people who are God's own by virtue of his unconditional favor and sacrifice are to be "zealous for good works" (Titus 2:14e). Here again is the theme that grace leads to godliness.

These statements that characterize our status as a result of Christ's work are our great protection against legalism and our great propulsion toward godliness. Because Christ's work alone purchases our salvation through the redeeming price of his blood, and Christ's work alone purifies us through the cleansing that blood supplies, we do not look to our works as the basis of acceptance. Doing what God requires does not make us his own, but having been made his own by no work of ours, we now love to love him who first loved us (1 John 4:19). Such love has a profound effect on our attitudes and actions.

My youngest daughter once said to her mother, "Mommy, I love you with all *your* heart." I realize why a three year old says such things. She tries to show her love by mistakenly echoing her mother's frequent endearment, "Katie, I love you with all my heart." But it is no mistake that here in Titus, God teaches us to love him with all his heart. He pours before us the signs of divine love so that we will love and respond to him (and others) with the kind of love he displays.

What does being a loved people do to us? It makes us more sensitive to sin. We should note well the order of the apostle's descriptions of God's work and response. God's people are first ransomed by his work, then purified to be his own, *then* they are "zealous" to do good. In some ways this message turns upside down a common perception of how the Christian life operates. We tend to think that we cannot see the love of God until we perceive the degree of our sin, but Paul here makes the point that perceiving the love of God enables us to see our sin.

Apprehension of the mercy of God in Christ makes us so long to love him and reject what hurts him that we become intolerant of sin in our lives. I understand this more as I look at my progress in marriage. The longer I am married, the more I marvel at my wife's love for me despite my early coldness and continuing selfishness. The more I see how much she loves me, the more conscious I become of my insensitivities and the more eager I am to please her. And the more I perceive her love, the more I cannot stand my sin against her. In the same way, the more we see how wondrous is Christ's love for us, the more sensitive we become to the sin in our lives, and the more we long to do what pleases him.

This dynamic of the love of God for us creating an intolerance for sin in us is what the Christians in previous generations called the "power of new affections." What will ultimately make us holy is not willpower, nor guilt, nor an inspiring message, but deep apprehension of the mercy of God in Christ. The resultant love for God drives out and replaces our natural love for sin. Believers in the early decades of our nation's founding taught this truth with the illustrator of the live oak, a variety of trees not found in Europe. The live oak's leaves—though dead—stick to its branches through the winter. What eventually forces the leaves from the tree is not the abuse of the cold or the beating of the wind but the new life springing up within and replacing what is dead. In a similar way, affections for evil remain in God's people even after our conversions. The way these evil affections are replaced is by an eagerness for good as apprehension of Christ's grace wells within us and ultimately drives out the old affections with the new life that is fueled by profound love for him.

Our Standard (v. 15)

So wondrous are these truths that Paul insists they must be the standard message of Titus. Paul tells him, "Declare these things" (Titus 2:15a). What are "these things"? The context indicates that they are the message of grace that enables Titus to "exhort" (*parakalei*, also meaning "comfort" or "encourage"; see 1 Tim. 6:2; Titus 1:9; 2:6) where the encouragement of the gospel mercy is needed, and to "rebuke" (or "refute," see Titus 1:9, 13) where others have to be reminded of the gospel's intolerance of sin. Both instructions remind us that grace is no gift if it fails to rescue us from and warn us of a destructive way of life.

Paul's final exhortation reminds us that if we teach "these things" (i.e., grace despite sin and obedience through grace), there will be those who accuse us of promoting license on the one hand and those who accuse us of being legalists on the other hand. Still, we must not cease from making the message of grace and godliness our standard. Whether he is accused of being a prude or a profligate, Paul says the leader of God's people should not let anyone "disregard" him (2:15b). We are required to say with authority *all* that Scripture says, whether or not the words seem pleasant to others.

Conclusion

Some months ago, a pastor friend took his family to the beach. After a few hours of enjoyment, the family beach was invaded by a rougher crowd that began to engage in immoral activities in plain view of all, including the pastor's children. He gathered his family to leave and, as they were leaving, told the apparent leader of the group that the families on the beach did not appreciate the immorality. This was not a smart thing to do. The group was a gang, and the leader responded to the pastor's complaint by knocking him to the ground and threatening to kill him. While other gang members restrained their leader, the pastor's wife ran to call the beach patrol, and the pastor was able to get away with his children.

As the family members were getting into their car a few minutes later, one of the gang members menacingly approached them with a broken bottle in his hand. He said, "I kept my friend from hurting you, so why did you call the beach patrol on us?"

The pastor replied, "I did not call the beach patrol, but my wife did because she was scared. And I do appreciate you holding back your friend. I did not mean to set him off, but I am a father and I was concerned for my children because of what you were doing on the beach."

The simple honesty made the gang member hesitate. "I am a father too," he said, "but I messed up and my wife kicked me out. I haven't seen my kids in years."

The pastor responded, "I am sorry. I am a Christian and a pastor. Can I pray for you?"

The man said yes, and after the prayer he threw himself on the pastor, sobbing, asking forgiveness, and asking to hear more of the gospel of Jesus Christ that would release him from the misery of the life he was leading.

This is the way the gospel is supposed to work. It does not ignore sin but expects the expression of the unconditional love of God to break people of their addictions to the filth of this world and to lead them into lives characterized by the joy of eagerness to serve God.

If you proclaim this message of grace that seeks to break people from their love of sin, I cannot promise your life will be blessed in human terms. In fact, I can virtually guarantee that you will be attacked from all sides—from those saying that you are a legalistic prude who does not understand grace, and from those saying that you are a grace fanatic who has no standards. Still, I say to you, "Let no one disregard you." Make grace clear and tolerate no evil, for your sake, for the sake of the people of God, and for the sake of the gospel of Christ. Revival will not come without the price of our discomfort and the cost of personal attack. No revivals of the past have come without dramatic change in the lifestyles of those in the church, as well as the reformation of society.

Extricating ourselves and our people from the mire of cultural sins that now characterize our habits, appetites, and homes will not come without struggle within and without the church. Still, we must proclaim the unconditional grace of God as the motive and power for standing with an uncompromising commitment to godliness. The reason should be clear: others will need the encouragement of being able to look through a misty dawn of revival with the assurance that God's leaders are still willing to carry more of God's children from the muck that threatens their eternal lives. We must not tolerate a gospel not founded on grace, nor a grace that does not inspire holiness. May you so powerfully believe and proclaim the love of Christ that affection for him drives out the affections of this world.

Union with Christ

Motivation and Enablement

In the last two sermons, we explored the ways in which the indicatives of grace motivate and empower the imperatives of Christian obedience. Thus far, however, we have chiefly explored the *human* responses operative in the obedience process. The preceding messages emphasize how grace stimulates love that motivates believers to obey God in order to express their gratitude and thanksgiving. We have also discovered that when this love surpasses all other affections, the power of sin's attraction is broken in the human heart. Thus grace not only motivates obedience but also empowers it.

Still, the love that motivates holiness and the surpassing affection that empowers it are forces that emanate from the human heart. As important as these forces are, they are limited by our humanity. Human affections waver. The human will can wither and wilt. Unless God provides power that is beyond human limitations, our spiritual adversary will yet overcome our determinations to honor God.

The following sermon details more fully the needed power for obedience that is ours by divine provision: union with Christ. By this union, believers have not only a new identity separate from their past but also a new power that enables them to resist the challenges of sin. Further, this union makes us colaborers with Christ in his purposes for the entire world. We would have no capacity to repel sin, or hope to participate in our world's redemption, apart from this union with the One who creates and maintains the universe. The power made available through our union with Christ not only enables Christian obedience; it also provides additional motivation for us to act on the power we have been granted by this great grace.[1]

---

1. For further discussion of the enabling and motivating power of our union with Christ, see the author's *Christ-Centered Preaching: Redeeming the Expository Sermon*, 2nd ed. (Grand Rapids: Baker Academic, 2005), 287–88, 294–95, and 312 (hereinafter *CCP*); and "United for Life," in *Holiness by Grace* (Wheaton: Crossway, 2001), 39–65.

Union with Christ

Romans 6:1–14

Scripture Introduction

The apostle Paul has just made a wonderful declaration . . . that is about to get him in serious trouble with his critics. He has just said, "Where sin increased, grace abounded all the more" (Rom. 5:20). The natural question his critics then raise is, "Well, if grace abounds where sin increases, then should we sin more that grace may abound more?" The author W. H. Auden reflects such an attitude in writing, "I like committing crimes. God likes forgiving them. Really the world is admirably arranged."[1] Is the apostle Paul really advocating something similar? His answer is clear in Romans 6:1–14.

Scripture Reading

Read with me Romans 6:1–14:

> What shall we say then? Are we to continue in sin that grace may abound? By no means! How can we who died to sin still live in it? Do you not know that all of us who have been baptized into Christ Jesus were baptized into his death? We were

1. From Herod's speech in W. H. Auden's long poem, *For the Time Being* in *Collected Poems*, ed. Edward Mendelson (New York: Random House, 2007), 394.

buried therefore with him by baptism into death, in order that, just as Christ was
raised from the dead by the glory of the Father, we too might walk in newness of life.

For if we have been united with him in a death like his, we shall certainly be
united with him in a resurrection like his. We know that our old self was crucified
with him in order that the body of sin might be brought to nothing, so that we
would no longer be enslaved to sin. For one who has died has been set free from
sin. Now if we have died with Christ, we believe that we will also live with him. We
know that Christ being raised from the dead will never die again; death no longer
has dominion over him. For the death he died he died to sin, once for all, but the
life he lives he lives to God. So you also must consider yourselves dead to sin and
alive to God in Christ Jesus.

Let not sin therefore reign in your mortal bodies, to make you obey their passions. Do not present your members to sin as instruments for unrighteousness,
but present yourselves to God as those who have been brought from death to life,
and your members to God as instruments for righteousness. For sin will have no
dominion over you, since you are not under law but under grace.

Sermon Introduction

Does grace lead to license? This question gets debated incessantly in pastoral seminars,
but I have witnessed how ordinary people may answer in sad ways in real life. For
example, I saw grace work powerfully in the lives of a young couple that had begun
attending our church. She came from a family of nominal faith. He was totally un-
churched. They became part of our church family, as counseling we provided helped
them work through some marriage problems. But when some health problems led
to her hospitalization, she was visited by another man—an old flame. Her husband
did not approve. She called her husband ridiculous for being upset. In anger, he
stomped away, picked up an old girlfriend, and moved into her trailer. Doing my job
as a pastor, I went to knock on the trailer door and urge him to go home so that he
and his wife might have a chance to work out their problems. I will not soon forget
his response: "God will forgive me later. I'm gonna stay right here for now."

"God will forgive me later" is the same theology we whisper to our hearts
whenever we as believers determine to run away from the Lord.[2] We rationalize

---

2. Note how this statement of the fallen condition focus (FCF) is made relevant to listeners and is
applied to those described in the introductory illustration. The best FCFs not only identify a dilemma

our separation from God for a season, a relationship, a pleasure, a recognition, or an advantage with the assurance that God will excuse us when we get around to asking his forgiveness. As we type in the dangerous URL, or drive down the forbidden street, or write down the false figure, or ignore the pain of another, we are counting on abounding grace to cover out-of-bounds hearts.

But what is really wrong with this thinking? The logic cannot be denied, and the grace should not be denied. God really does forgive later. But that reality should not drive us to sin; it should drive us from it. Here in Romans 6 the apostle Paul is making that precise point. He has just explained the wonder and power of the reign of grace that God provides for sinners like us. But the apostle's purpose is far different from providing a cover for licentiousness. Paul wants us to understand that grace frees us from the power of sin. Anger, lust, greed, bitterness, fear, ambition—they all become compulsions, driving us, preoccupying our thoughts, constraining the pursuits of our lives. But such bondage does not have to be our plight. If we will perceive sin as the slave master it is, then we will understand that the grace of Christ is the power of freedom from bondage, not the incentive to return to it. Under the reign of grace, we are united with him who frees us from bondage to sin. He is the antidote to sin's guilt *and* power. So Paul's conclusion is clear: because you are united with Christ, you can and must turn from the sin that would enslave you.

In order to experience this freedom, we have to understand how "abounding grace" unites us to Christ and how this union gives us power to break the bondage of sin. To give us such understanding, Paul describes this union as the means by which Christ gives us a new *identity* and a new *calling*.

I. Our Union with Christ Gives Us a New Identity

What does this union specifically provide? Some initial qualifications are needed to start us down the right path of answering that question.

---

created by humanity's fallen condition but also indicate how that dilemma affects those hearing the sermon; i.e., it is a problem of the first person (*us*) not just the third person (*them*). See discussion of similar matter in CCP, 106 and 151–53.

Not a License to Sin (vv. 1–2a and 15)[3]

The apostle makes it clear that whatever this union provides, it does not provide a license to sin.[4] He could hardly speak more strongly. He first dares to ask the question that those who are twisting his earlier words (namely, "where sin increased, grace abounded all the more") would ask: "What shall we say then? Are we to continue in sin that grace may abound?" (v. 1). Then, he answers that question as forcefully as can be expressed in the Greek language: "By no means! How can we who died to sin still live in it?" (v. 2). And to make sure we have not missed the point, Paul repeats his emphatic denial at the end of his discussion of this matter: "What then? Are we to sin because we are not under law but under grace? By no means!" (v. 15).

With these strident words the apostle Paul directly addresses the controversy that confronts preachers of grace in any church era. When we teach that salvation is by grace and through no merit of our own, there is a ready assumption (or accusation) that we are teaching that godly behavior is optional. Paul denies this leap of logic by reminding us of the realities of our existence as believers. We who have died to sin cannot continue to live in it without dire consequences. Understanding the reality of these consequences and the opportunity believers have for an existence free of sin's bondage are the subjects the apostle now undertakes.

But a Death Certificate

The new existence we have through our union with Christ begins with the issuance of a death certificate. The apostle says that those who have received grace have "died to sin" (v. 2), and the certificate of that death is the believer's baptism!

We don't tend to think of baptism as a death certificate because we don't think of the ceremony as marking a death. But Paul says that "all of us who have been baptized into Christ Jesus were baptized into his death" (v. 3). To say that we have been "baptized into Christ" means that we identify ourselves with his cause and purpose. And since he died, to be identified with him means that our existence is in some sense marked by death also.

3. Often a helpful way to organize main points and subpoints is to identify the negative and positive aspects of an idea—even identifying what the text does *not* mean (e.g., common misperceptions) before turning to what the text does mean.

4. The apostle begins as many grace-oriented preachers still must: denying that grace leads to license. If we are tempted to despair by having to defend ourselves from similar accusations, it helps to know that even the apostle Paul was required to travel this road.

Union with Christ's Death

The apostle Paul's explanation makes more sense if we put ourselves in the context of the first-century believers he is addressing.

Separated from the Past

Paul uses similar baptism language to refer to the identity of the Israelites after they left Egypt. He says that they "were all under the cloud, and all passed through the sea, and all were *baptized into Moses* in the cloud and in the sea" (1 Cor. 10:1–2). What happened when the Israelites followed God's directions under the cloud and through the sea? They were separated from Egypt and separated unto Moses—from slavery and into freedom. They now identified their cause, purpose, and new life with Moses rather than with their former life in Egyptian shackles. Some commentators think references connecting baptism and death necessarily support the practice of immersion baptism (with the action of immersion reflecting the burial and resurrection of Jesus), but in 1 Corinthians it was not the Israelites who were immersed, but the Egyptians. The Israelites' baptism was not one of immersion but one of separation from a painful past and identification with a better future (a closer analogy to the full significance of baptism). The past of slavery was dead, and a new life of freedom was the present reality.

We tend not to see baptism as a certificate of the death of a sinful past because we live in a culture where baptism is an accepted tradition whose significance has been lost. But if we were a first-century pagan or Jew, we would well understand the connection. By submitting ourselves to the rite of baptism in that era, we would be separating ourselves from all past family and faith. By identifying ourselves with those who put their faith in Jesus, we would likely suffer rage and rejection from all who once held us dear. The situation may still occur today when followers of Islamic, Hindu, or other faiths become Christians. When such people identify themselves as Christians by baptism, their families may actually say to them, "You are now dead to us." In the autumn of 2011, a Muslim convert in Morocco was stabbed outside his new church and left for dead. A Christian family ministered to him and eventually arranged asylum in the United States, only to discover that his biological family had arranged the attempt on his life. His baptism not only made him dead to them but made them willing to seek his death. Baptism for many in our present world, and for everyone in Paul's time, and for we who rightly understand the ordinance, becomes a certificate of death for an old way of life.

Identified with Christ

But baptism not only signifies the end of a past life; it also identifies believers with the one who died.[5] Paul says in Romans 6:

- We were "buried . . . with him [Christ] by baptism" (v. 4);
- "we have been united with him in a death like his" (v. 5);
- "our old self was crucified with him" (v. 6).

There is spiritual mystery here beyond our ability to explain in simple terms, but the death of our former selves is more than a separation from past *circumstances*. The *person* that we once were, "our old self," is also dead because we identify with the one who died. Who is the "old self" that Paul says has been crucified with Christ? We are aided in answering by understanding that the word translated "self" is also the word for "a person" (i.e., a *man* in generic reference, *anthropos*). Paul has used this word earlier to speak of our humanity, identifying us by our relationship to our natural predecessor, Adam:

- "Sin came into the world through one *man*, and death through sin, and so death spread to all *men* because all sinned" (5:12);
- "because of one *man's* trespass, death reigned through that one man" (5:17a);
- "one trespass led to condemnation for all *men*" (5:18a);
- "by the one *man's* disobedience the many were made sinners" (5:19a).

The "old self" that was crucified with Christ and died with him is the person that was united with Adam—that is, the natural person we were before our union with Christ. In that person "death reigned" (5:17a) because Adam's sinful nature had control, causing that person to deserve condemnation. But now, for those of us who are united by faith with Christ, that "old self" is dead. Because we are united with Christ who died, the Adam-united person that we were is dead, too.

---

5. Notice the wording of this sentence is yet another version of the "not only . . . but also . . ." form of transition that is so helpful for signaling the strategy of the message to listeners (see *CCP*, 262–63).

The Death of the Old Self Frees Us from the Guilt of Sin

Why is the death of the "old self" a good thing? We can answer by remembering that any condemnation that could be brought against us is a consequence of breaking the law of God. But Paul makes a critical observation about such condemnation at the beginning of the next chapter: "The law is binding on a person only as long as he lives" (7:1). If a person is dead, then the law does not apply to him or her, and if the law does not apply, then there can be no condemnation of that person. This is Paul's point in the preceding chapter: "Sin is not counted where there is no law" (5:13). So if the law does not apply to dead people, and no guilt is assigned to those to whom the law does not apply, then no guilt can apply to those who are identified with Christ's death. Paul appropriately rejoices in a later chapter, "There is therefore now no condemnation for those who are in Christ Jesus" (8:1).

Consider how our own laws echo this truth. A few years ago, on the highway near our home, a truck driver got distracted on his cell phone, topped a hill, and plowed into a line of stopped traffic. He killed four people. Yet despite the tragedy and suffering for those he hit, the truck driver received no penalty—not even a traffic ticket. Why? He was also killed in the accident. We do not give traffic tickets to dead people. So also, the law cannot condemn those who are dead in Christ.[6]

The Death of the Old Self Frees Us from the Control of Sin

The death of the old self not only frees us from the guilt of sin; it also frees us from the control of sin. Paul says that "our old self was crucified with him [i.e., Christ]," not only that "the body of sin [i.e., the guilty part of our old self] would be brought to nothing," but also that "we would no longer be enslaved to sin" (6:6). How can the crucifixion of our "old self" free us from sin's control? The simple answer is that dead people don't sin. They don't do wrong things, and they can't be made to do wrong things. They're dead! And in the spiritual universe that transcends this temporal world, this declaration that God's people are no longer subject to sin's control and enslavement is good news that provides hope in our most desperate moments.

In one of my early pastorates, I had the sad task of conducting the funeral of a child who had accompanied her father on a tractor ride. Like many farm children,

---

6. Multiple illustrations are provided in this portion of the message not only to clarify, and not only to motivate, but also to provide listeners some relief from the dense thought that may discourage their continued attention.

she loved riding on the fender next to the driver's seat while her father drove. One day, on an unfamiliar field, the tractor unexpectedly hit a ditch and shook the girl from her perch, and she was killed in the fall.

After the funeral, I gathered with the family in their home for the traditional meal provided for out-of-town relatives. Their grief was profound, and as we ate, parents urged the children to be quiet, sending them to watch television in a corner of the room. What immediately appeared on the screen was a public service announcement warning kids about drug use. The warning depicted a young woman being lured into dark streets by seedy characters. To our horror, she looked amazingly like the girl we had just buried. A number of people in the room gasped in recognition of the resemblance, and we all expected the grieving mother to dissolve into fresh tears. Instead, she rose from her chair, shook her finger at the television, and said in a voice of defiant victory, "You can't touch my baby because she is with Jesus."

The mother was very, very right. Since she was now with Jesus, the daughter could not be controlled by any sin. This was true because of the daughter's physical death. But Paul wants us to understand that a similar truth applies to all believers because we are spiritually united with the death of Christ. Because our old self— that self controlled by our Adamic nature—is dead, we are no longer subject to the irresistible compulsions to sin. Certainly we may yield to temptation, but that sin is a choice of our freedom, not a consequence of our slavery.

The person that was enslaved to sin—and unable to resist its control—is dead. The application to our lives is immediate. Satan yet tempts us to believe that he has control over our hearts and passions. But we must face our temptations with the realities of Scripture, not the lies of Satan. The old self is dead, united with Christ in his crucifixion. In our unregenerate, Adamic nature, we were not able to resist the evil one; we were enslaved to sin. But for the believer, that former identity and reality is dead. We are now united with the death of Christ, so that not only is the guilt of sin inapplicable but also the power of sin is broken. We are not slaves to sin anymore because the old self who had that nature is dead.

Union with Christ's Life

But the glory of our union with Christ is not fully explained when we speak of being united with his death because that is not the full story of his ministry. He did not simply die; he also rose to life. This means that the implications of our union with Jesus are not fully described when we speak of our identification with his death. Since he is now alive, and we are united with him, then we are also united with his life. We are not only given a death certificate by virtue of our union with Christ; we are also given a new lease on life—new power for living.

Eternal Security[7]

We are free from the control of sin not only because we are dead to it in Christ but also because we are empowered by our union with the life of Christ. Paul writes, "Just as Christ was raised from the dead by the glory of the Father, we too might walk in newness of life" (v. 4). The power that we have through our union with Christ surpasses the natural inclinations and impulses that could give sin control in our lives. Paul emphasizes the supernatural power we have by first reminding us that we are eternally secure by virtue of our union with the one who overcame death: "If we have been united with him in a death like his, we shall certainly be united with him in a resurrection like his" (v. 5). The bonds of sin that once constrained us now cannot keep us from eternal life with Christ.

Present Ability

The benefits of our eternal security are not merely future. Our eternal security in Christ grants us temporal ability to live for him. Understanding of this present power unfolds as we follow the contours of the apostle's thought. Most of the content of verses 5–10 is directed toward giving believers a sense of security in an insecure world. Paul says that we can be assured of our eternal life because we are united with the one who was raised from the dead. Paul concludes, "Now if we have died with Christ, we believe that we will also live with him" (v. 8).

Such eternal security should make us willing to live for Christ today even when such commitment may require struggle, risk, and sacrifice. But all of that effort

---

7. Note that the subpoints in this portion of the sermon are progressive and parallel in syllable and sound (the second words of each of the subpoints rhyme), making it easier for the listener to identify each as a new idea proportional in importance to the corresponding subpoints. Such structural finesse may seem artificial or forced for new preachers, but these are actually the patterns of conversational speech that we naturally employ to convey meaning. Knowing how and when to employ them in preaching is a matter of feel and rhythm more than rules and regulations. Skilled use of such aural cues in an oral medium adds natural clarity to the sermon.

would be senseless if there were no hope of victory over the sin that assaults us now. So Paul also reminds us that we are united with Christ, "so that we would no longer be enslaved to sin" (v. 6). For our encouragement he adds, "So you also must consider yourselves dead to sin and alive to God in Christ Jesus" (v. 11). Life eternal is promised eventually (v. 5), but new life is already here because we are united with him (v. 4).

The same power that raised Jesus from the dead now indwells and empowers us. From other passages (e.g., Rom. 8:10–11), we know this power is the work of the Holy Spirit in us. The life-giving and sin-overcoming power of the Spirit indwells us because we are united with Christ, who rose from the dead by the power of the Spirit. By virtue of our union with Christ, we are alive to God through the power of the Spirit.

Full Identity

The full dimensions of what it means to be "alive to God" are apparent when we consider the full experience of Christ, with whom we are united. If we consider the aspects of our union in chronological order, Paul says,

- "Our old self was *crucified* with him" (6:6);
- "we have been united with him in a *death* like his" (v. 5);
- "we were *buried* therefore with him by baptism into death" (v. 4).

"Crucified, dead, and buried" are terms the Apostles' Creed applies to Christ. In this passage of Romans, the same terms apply to us by virtue of our union with Christ. But just as these terms are not the end of the Apostles' Creed, they are also not the end of the apostle Paul's encouragement for us. Jesus was not only crucified, dead, and buried; "the third day he rose again from the dead." And if we are united with him, that resurrection power is also ours. This is Paul's ultimate point: "Just as Christ was raised from the dead by the glory of the Father, we too might walk in newness of life" (v. 4).

Key aspects of the Passion Narrative (Christ's crucifixion, death, burial, and resurrection) are put before us in the terms used by Paul, and he indicates believers are united with Christ in each. This means that we are not only joined to Christ in the sense of being part of a club or family; we are also joined to his experience. In a way beyond natural explanation, we have been spiritually united with Christ in all the aspects of his dying and living. So when we face the difficulties of sin and circumstance in this life, we need not feel either abandoned or weak. We face what Christ faced with the sense that we can endure and ultimately conquer because we are united with him who already did so.

United with Christ, we experience all the events of his passion:

- Through our shame and pain, we suffer the travail of his crucifixion scorn, mockery, betrayal, exposure, terror, and deprivation.[8]

- Through our struggles and failures, we die with him—experiencing labored breath, a stopped heart, people losing hope in us, and loved ones losing confidence in us.

- Through our loss of significance and pride, we are buried with him, our feet immobilized beside his, our cold hand against his cold hand, powerless despite past strength, and with darkness inescapable—all around and our only friend (see Ps. 88).

But none of these mortal experiences are Christ's end or ours. The sin creating all that shame, pain, and darkness did not have ultimate control over Christ and does not determine the fate of his people. We are not only united with the One who was crucified, dead, and buried; we are also united to the One who rose from the dead, ascended to God, and by his Spirit indwells our hearts. Through him we not only have eternal security and present ability; we also have his full identity to serve God the Father with both.

Jesus is our identity, our security, and our strength because our old self is dead and his life is ours through our union with him. But simply possessing his identity, security, and power may not be sufficient incentive for us to turn from sin. Instead, these indicatives (what is true of us) may only make us vulnerable to the accusation of licentiousness Paul's critics advance. If you know you are loved, secure, and in control, why would you bother to follow biblical imperatives (what God

8. Note that each of these complex, parallel sentences begins with the same word. An English teacher, preparing students to write essays would not advise such redundancy, but in an oral medium such a mnemonic device provides welcome navigational cues through complex thoughts and provides rhetorical power for ideas that need to be emphasized. Note also that these sentences (which are tied together by the same beginning words) also contain forms of the key words (crucified, dead, and buried) that will be pivotal for the following point that this passage of Scripture echoes the Apostles' Creed. Thus, the parallelism not only groups similar thoughts; it also points to key differences in each of those thoughts that the preacher will next emphasize.

calls us to do)?[9] Paul answers by describing the new calling that motivates those truly united with Christ.

II. Our Union with Christ Gives Us a New Calling

Our Responsibility

Paul knows nothing of a life redeemed without responsibility to the Redeemer. The apostle clearly articulates the calling of those who bear Christ's identity. Paul says believers are to serve "as instruments for righteousness" (Rom. 6:13). He then explains what that means by stating our obligations negatively and positively.

Negatively

Because we have the ability to resist sin, Paul says, "Let not sin therefore reign in your mortal body, to make you obey its passions" (v. 12). He adds, "Do not present your members to sin as instruments for unrighteousness" (v. 13a). In essence, he says, "Don't give sin reign in your life, and don't contribute to its reign over others."

Positively

The apostle also tells believers how to contribute to God's reign. When Paul says, "Present yourselves to God as those who have been brought from death to life" (v. 13b), he reminds believers of their present status (the indicative of who they really are). They are not their "old self" living under the enslavement of sin. That existence is dead. Instead, they are alive with Christ and have his resurrection power coursing through their bodies. Thus, Paul says, "Present yourselves . . . and your members to God as instruments for righteousness" (v. 13c). Privilege has obligations.

Because we are united with Christ, we are expected to live for him. Incentive to do so comes from understanding the amazing impact that we can make as we live for him. Paul says that we are God's instruments of righteousness

9. The imperative/indicative discussion of previous parts of this book is furthered by the understanding that our union with Christ provides the status and strength we possess (the indicatives) to do what God requires (the imperatives). For further discussion of these indicative/imperative relationships, see CCP, 317–21 and 325–27.

because sin "will have no dominion" over us (v. 14) and because we should not let sin "reign" in us (v. 12). This dominion language reminds us of Paul's earlier language about competing spiritual realms: "If, because of one man's trespass, death reigned through that one man, much more will those who receive the abundance of grace and the free gift of righteousness reign in life through the one man Jesus Christ" (5:17). The implication for the immediate passage is clear: By being "instruments of righteousness," we are helping to turn back the reign of sin that has had dominion since the dawn of humanity. Our righteousness is not simply a matter of individual distinction; we are participants in the divine crusade of redemption that is turning back the dominion of sin over the whole of creation. As those who are united with the resurrection power of Christ, death has no more dominion over us, and through us death's reign is being reduced over the whole of life.

Our Power

Because we are united with Christ, the apostle presumes that we have the power to act on the imperatives he gives. When he says, "Let not sin therefore reign in your mortal body" (6:12), because you "have been brought from death to life" (v. 13) and "sin will have no dominion over you" (v. 14), the apostle is declaring the power of Christ we possess. Our minds may whisper that we have no power to resist sin, and our experience may convince us that we are weak before temptation's assaults, but Paul addresses us as those who have the power to do as he says—because through our union with Christ we do!

My wife, Kathy, is usually very gentle in expression, but there are moments when I have come to expect some steel in her voice. One of those moments is when one of our children is despairing of accomplishing a task that they have the ability to do. An example would be when it's two a.m., and the chemistry project due the next morning is going badly. I may hear a daughter cry, "I just can't do this. I'll never get it right. I am so dumb." That's when I expect to hear my wife's voice toughen as she provides the strength for a child's resolve with words like these: "Now you listen to me. You are not dumb. God gave you the brains to do this. You can do this, and I will help you. Now let's get to it." With similar vigor, the apostle Paul reminds us of the power we really do have through our union with Christ so that we will honor the calling of righteousness he gives.

Our Motivations

We have Christ's calling to be instruments of righteousness and Christ's power to fulfill that calling; all that remains is the willingness to do as we can.[10] Paul provides such motivation with words that surround his description of our calling.

God's Face

Paul reminds us that honoring God's imperatives honors us before God. Paul instructs the Romans, "Present yourselves . . . to God as instruments of righteousness" (v. 13). We live before the face of God (*coram Deo*). All our lives and actions are present before him. Thus, one of the reasons that we act on the instruction and ability that we have is to honor the One before whom all things exist. The Puritan John Owen wrote that one of the motivations of righteous living originates from understanding that ungodliness is simply not "fitting" for a person called to live for the glory of God. The Father who redeems us and loves us looks on, so we present ourselves to him in ways that befit the status he gives us.

I compare this befitting motivation to the way that chaplains in training at our seminary conduct themselves on days when we honor their service to our country. Those who may on ordinary days be a bit disheveled in T-shirt and jeans, instead stand erect with shoulders back and chin squared on the days that they wear their uniforms. Before onlookers these servicemen conduct themselves in a manner befitting the identity of those called to represent their country. So also believers who understand their calling as instruments of righteousness by virtue of their union with Christ are motivated to live as befits their status before God.

Christ's Rescue

The awareness of God's view of us is not meant to stimulate dread, cowering, or hiding. The One who looks on is the One who "brought you from death to life" (v. 13). We offer ourselves as instruments of righteousness not only because God looks on but also because he has given his Son to rescue us from

10. For discussion of how grace creates motivations and affections that compel holiness, see *CCP*, 312 and 320–23.

death. Our service is not merely a matter of personal honor but even more a matter of profound gratitude. We long to serve Christ because he loves us and gave himself for us.

Owen preached that all sin is ultimately lack of love for God. By recalling the rescue that Christ provided for us at the cost of his blood, we stoke the fires of love for him that warm our affections for his service. The math of the mind may yet seek to sway us to sin for a season with the argument that God will forgive us later, but the stronger chemistry of the heart motivates us to love and honor the One who gave his life to rescue us for eternity.

Our Freedom

The final motivation for righteousness is as contemporary as it is powerful. New York pastor Tim Keller says that today's preachers have to recognize that simply condemning certain behaviors will not turn from evil a culture that has lost its moral compass. Identifying certain behaviors as "bad" may simply sound judgmental rather than corrective. An alternative, which may be more persuasive and just as biblical, is to warn people that unbiblical behavior is enslaving.

Consider the sad life of singer Amy Winehouse. Her rebel lifestyle probably won her as many fans as did her amazing voice. Few of her followers found her "bad" behavior off-putting. She did not lose fans until her substance abuse made her start missing concerts and forgetting lyrics. So much did her addictions control her that her father attributed her death to her trying to detoxify too fast. The substances that enslaved her would not release her even when she tried to leave them. The tragedy for her fans was not her wild freedoms; it was her enslavement to her habits. More than being "bad," being controlled is the sin of this age. Loss of freedom rather than shame for sin is the great demerit.

This repulsion to enslavement is not necessarily a wrong motivation for righteousness. Such a motivation is well within the ethic of the apostle Paul, who urges believers not to obey their bodies' passions (v. 12), or come under the dominion of sin (v. 14), or be its slaves (vv. 16–17). For those who are feeling the compulsions of sin and who doubt that they can ever be free of its enslaving bonds, the opportunity to be free is strong motivation to exercise the power of our union with Christ.[11]

11. Note that there is a proper love of self (as one loved by God and treasured by him) that should motivate us to seek freedom from enslaving sin (see *CCP*, 322–23).

Conclusion

With wonderful power and grace, the apostle Paul assures us that believers are participants in God's grand plan to bring his reign of righteousness over the whole world. He swells our sense of purpose with the privilege of being colaborers with Christ in God's plan of redemption, and then urges us forward with the knowledge that we serve before the face of God, in the love of our Rescuer, and freed from the slavery of sin. Through the grace of our union with Christ, we possess security beyond sin, ability over sin, and incentive to fight sin. Such grace is not a license to sin but real power to overcome it. The power does not originate in us, but by virtue of our union with Christ, such power flows through us and remains in us despite our natural weakness.

In October 2011 an older Iowa couple experienced a tragic automobile accident. Norma and Gordon Yeager had been married for seventy-two years. She was ninety; he was ninety-four. As they were being treated in the hospital, they continued to hold hands on adjoining beds. Gordon passed away still clinging to Norma. His breathing stopped and he became ashen, but his heart monitor continued to register. The beating on the monitor continued because Gordon was still united with Norma. With her hand holding his, it was her heart that registered through him.[12] In a similar way, though we have not the power to overcome the dominion of death, by our union with Christ his life becomes ours. Norma passed away soon after Gordon, but the resurrected Jesus is alive in us. By our union with him, he gives us his power to fight sin, and by his great love for us, he gives us the loving motivation to fight with and for him. As a consequence, where sin increases, grace abounds even more, to give us the will and the power to live for the Christ with whom we are united forever.

12. Christina Ng, "Iowa Couple Married 72 Years Dies Holding Hands, an Hour Apart," ABC News, October 19, 2011, abcnews.go.com/US/iowa-couple-married-72-years-dies-holding-hands/story?id=14771029#.UMUHrbambTU.

Preach the Word

The last few sermons of this book have focused on how the grace of God provides motivation and power for Christian obedience. As we conclude, we do not want to neglect a means of grace God provides that also empowers his people and is the reason for this book. The preaching of the Word is a divinely ordained means by which God ministers the truths and presence of his Son to his people in order to equip them to serve him.

The sermon that follows focuses on the spiritual power of preaching. This is an example of an expository sermon prepared for a lengthy passage of Scripture. The sermon does not attempt to cover the entire passage in depth but focuses on those portions that address a specific topic: the power of the Word of God preached.[1]

The Scripture introduction[2] narrows the focus of the message and alerts listeners that the full text will not be "exhausted."[3] Rather, the larger portion of Scripture is read (and touched on in the message) to give proper context to the verses that

---

1. This sermon was originally preached at the national conference of the Gospel Coalition in 2010 and was originally published in *Entrusted with the Gospel: Pastoral Expositions of 2 Timothy*, ed. D. A. Carson (Wheaton: Crossway, 2010).

2. For a further description of Scripture introductions, see the author's *Christ-Centered Preaching: Redeeming the Expository Sermon*, 2nd ed. (Grand Rapids: Baker Academic, 2005), 244 and 249–51; hereinafter *CCP*.

3. For further discussion of "exhausting the text" and "covering the territory" in expository messages, see *CCP*, 118–19 and 156.

will be highlighted. This narrowing of focus allows the preacher to remain "expository" regarding those aspects of the text that touch on the declared purpose of the message. Although the traditional ethic of "covering the territory" of the text in an expository sermon is not followed, the sermon remains an exposition of those aspects of the text declared to be the focus of the message.

The sermon would lose its expository credentials if the message did not reflect the truths established by the context of the text. Thus, at the same time that the Scripture introduction narrows the scope of the passage that will be expounded, the preacher explains that the Scripture reading has been broadened to give listeners proper context for the verses that will receive focus in the sermon.

Preach the Word

2 Timothy 3:16–17

Scripture Introduction

In a recent letter to supporters, China mission leader Sam Ling wrote: "The church in China is feeling the impact of neo-evangelicalism and post-conservatism. . . . Overseas Chinese seminaries are evolving into post-conservative schools. The church is losing her orthodoxy. . . . We must call the church to faithful adherence to . . . the inspiration and inerrancy of Scripture." These are amazing words. Within two generations of the explosion of Christianity in China, there is now an erosion of confidence in Scripture. We should not be amazed at such a thing. This is not a new problem.[1]

In 2 Timothy 3:10–4:5, for example, the apostle Paul writes to his protégé Timothy—in the same generation that the gospel came to Ephesus—to exhort the young preacher to continue teaching that the Bible *must* be believed. False teachers have already crept into the church, eroding confidence in the Scriptures. This early reality reminds us that every generation—regardless of the orthodoxy preceding it—must determine anew the answer to the question, "Will we believe the Bible?"

---

1. One reason to use illustrations is to "disarm hostility," if the preacher anticipates opposition to the matter being addressed. I recognized at this conference that there would not be unanimity regarding the nature of Scripture but that there would be unanimity regarding the mission of the gospel. Thus, an illustration that used the priorities of mission to introduce a defense of the Bible's integrity and power seemed fitting (see *CCP*, 230).

To answer this question for our own time, we should consider again Paul's focus on this issue in chapter 3, verses 16 and 17 of this passage. To discern the full import of these verses, however, we will also need to consider key ideas in surrounding verses. Our understanding will grow as we read the full text, remembering that Paul has just warned Timothy what false teachers say and do.

Scripture Reading

Read with me 2 Timothy 3:10–4:5:

> You, however, have followed my teaching, my conduct, my aim in life, my faith, my patience, my love, my steadfastness, my persecutions and sufferings that happened to me at Antioch, at Iconium, and at Lystra—which persecutions I endured; yet from them all the Lord rescued me. Indeed, all who desire to live a godly life in Christ Jesus will be persecuted, while evil people and impostors will go on from bad to worse, deceiving and being deceived. But as for you, continue in what you have learned and have firmly believed, knowing from whom you learned it and how from childhood you have been acquainted with the sacred writings, which are able to make you wise for salvation through faith in Christ Jesus. All Scripture is breathed out by God and profitable for teaching, for reproof, for correction, and for training in righteousness, that the man of God may be competent, equipped for every good work.
>
> I charge you in the presence of God and of Christ Jesus, who is to judge the living and the dead, and by his appearing and his kingdom: preach the word; be ready in season and out of season; reprove, rebuke, and exhort, with complete patience and teaching. For the time is coming when people will not endure sound teaching, but having itching ears they will accumulate for themselves teachers to suit their own passions, and will turn away from listening to the truth and wander off into myths. As for you, always be sober-minded, endure suffering, do the work of an evangelist, fulfill your ministry.

Sermon Introduction

Los Angeles was burning on the evening of the first Rodney King verdict. Many of us remember why. During an arrest, a video camera had recorded white policemen beating King, an African American, and those officers had just been exonerated.

The predominantly black neighborhoods of South Central Los Angeles exploded in retaliation and riot. The rage was vengeful, violent, and indiscriminate. News cameras filmed a group of young men dragging a Hispanic worker from his truck, knocking him to the ground, and brutally beating him.

Into that angry mob waded an elderly, black minister named Bennie Newton, whose name will forever bring honor to the office of pastor.[2] Risking his own life, Pastor Newton repeatedly stepped in the way of those who were delivering the blows. He took the punches and kicks on his own back and legs. He shouted above the curses of the attackers, "This man has done nothing wrong! You must stop this. You must stop this!" And eventually they did stop. They turned away in disgust from an old man, who had faced their fury with nothing more than a Bible in his hands.

Why did he have a Bible? Surely it was a symbol of his office, but it was also a statement of his faith that, whether facing life or death, he would entrust himself—body and soul—to what this book attests. Why bank so much on a book? We have to answer that question because *what we believe about this book will determine what we say and do to safeguard those whom God puts in our care.* If there is erosion of faith in this generation, it will be because we who are church leaders forget the nature of *the Book.* Forgetting the nature of the Book is so easy to do. This letter written in the first generation of the gospel of Christ makes clear our tendency to forget the nature of God's Word. And so that we will not forget, the apostle Paul reminds us in this letter to Timothy of the nature of the Scriptures. He tells us that in them we *hear the voice of God, see the hand of God, and know the heart of God.*

I. Hearing the Voice of God (v. 16a)

Hearing the voice of God requires a foundation of belief in what the Bible says about itself. Paul says in our passage that the Bible is "breathed out by God" (v. 16). These words translate the Greek term *theopneustos,* which means "God-breathed." In theological circles we refer to this as the doctrine of biblical inspiration.

2. I would not normally feel it important or good to specify the ethnicity of a pastor (or any other person) in an illustration. However, such identification of the "hero" of this illustration seems appropriate in order to offset the negative description of other African Americans, especially since they are described by me—a white preacher (see illustration cautions in *CCP,* 202–4).

The Meaning of Inspiration

A few years ago, an accreditation team came to Covenant Theological Seminary, where I have served as president, to examine us for the renewal of our license to operate. The head of the accreditation team was the dean at a major Midwestern university. He met with me early in the visit and asked me to identify some of the distinctions of our school. I said to him, "One of the key commitments we have is that the Bible is inspired." "That's great," he said. "I think the Bible is inspiring too." I had to smile and say, "That's not exactly what I mean."

What *do* we mean when we say that the Bible is inspired? The Greek term actually refers to "expiration," breath being breathed out as one speaks. When you speak, you feel your breath come out as the words are expressed. So Paul contends that when Scripture was written, God was breathing out his Word. Just as God breathed life into humanity at creation, so, Paul says, God breathes spiritual life into the Scriptures so that we could be new creations.

Exactly how men could write words that reflect their situations and personalities and yet still be God's Word to us is a mystery. We don't understand it entirely, but elsewhere Scripture describes the process. The apostle Peter writes, "No prophecy of Scripture comes from someone's own interpretation . . . but men spoke from God as they were carried along by the Holy Spirit" (2 Pet. 1:20–21). Paul states the consequence of this process when he commends believers at Thessalonica for receiving his message "not as the word of men but as what it really is, the word of God" (1 Thess. 2:13).

Augustine summarizes well the import of these truths by saying simply, "Where the Bible speaks, God speaks."

The Significance of Inspiration

Because it is God-breathed, Scripture is God's very Word to us. This is not just an abstract observation for academic discussion; it is one of the most precious truths Christians possess to survive and thrive every day.

Implications

In everyday life and in the greatest trials of my life, God speaks to me in his Word. When I believe what the Bible says about itself, I have the privilege of hearing God's voice.

At a young people's meeting, a fresh-out-of-seminary youth pastor I know attempted to impress his group with the wonder of the divine inspiration of Scripture. He gathered the teens in a circle, put a chair in the middle, and handed out Bible verses printed on cards to everyone in the circle. The person sitting in the middle chair was blindfolded and asked to tell the group some problem he or she was experiencing. Then, someone in the circle was supposed to read an applicable Bible verse that dealt with the problem. The idea was that because the person in the middle chair was blindfolded, he or she would perceive the verse being read as though God himself was speaking through the words of Scripture.

The youth leader thought this was a really clever idea. The kids thought it was really dumb. None of them would talk about a problem more significant than how to get an A on Mrs. Bailey's math quizzes—and there really wasn't a good Bible verse for that. The whole thing was going miserably, and giggles rather than the voice of God predominated.

Then a new girl, who had been sitting on the periphery, volunteered to sit in the middle. The giggling subsided a bit as she was blindfolded because no one knew her well enough to tease her. Then she spoke: "I am so miserable. I don't know if I can stand my life anymore." No one knew what to say or do; most just looked down in embarrassment. But one boy looking down saw the verse in his hand and read, "God is faithful; he will not let you be tempted beyond what you can bear. But when you are tempted, he will also provide a way out so that you can stand up under it" (1 Cor. 10:13 NIV 1984).

"No one cares for me," said the girl. But then another girl in the circle read, "I have loved you with an everlasting love; I have drawn you with unfailing kindness" (Jer. 31:3 NIV).

"You don't understand," said the girl in the blindfold with a voice now desperate. "My parents kicked me out last night and said, 'Never come back!'" Then someone read, "I will never leave you nor forsake you" (Heb. 13:5).

They took the blindfold off the girl. She was crying and through her tears asked, "Why doesn't God *really* talk to me that way?"

The youth pastor responded, "He just did. Because the Bible is inspired, it is God's very Word. God *did* really speak to you with those verses."[3]

---

3. Again, it is important to remind preachers that the primary reason to illustrate is not to clarify but to motivate. If the preacher concludes that because a matter has been very clearly explained it does not need an illustration, then many opportunities will be missed for listeners to experience the emotional power and

Even those of us who are much more mature in our faith can be foolish about what we think we want from God. We think that life would be so much easier if God would just miraculously write his words in the clouds or speak in the thunder. But if he wrote in the clouds, the words would blow away, and if he spoke in the thunder, his voice would fade away. So instead, by the prophets and apostles, God asks, "Would you mind if I just wrote my words down for you in the Bible, so that you could have them wherever you go and whenever they are needed?" Inspired Scripture is the greater miracle. God has given us his abiding Word so that we are not without his voice in all the trials and temptations of this life. In the Bible, we proclaim, God yet speaks to his people.

The leaders of the Reformation expressed these truths with particular power. Martin Luther said, "The church is God's mouth house." When the Bible is proclaimed in the church, God is yet speaking through the church to his people and to the world. In the Second Helvetic Confession, the Swiss Reformers made this point in very strong terms, saying, "The preaching of the Word of God is the Word of God." To the extent that our preaching is true to Scripture, God's words yet echo in the church. God's voice is available to his people—even when it comes through our human mouths—when we are faithful in preaching his Word.

John Calvin expressed the truth of inspiration in words so strong that were it not Calvin who spoke, we might question if such things should be said. He said, "God has chosen so to anoint the lips and tongues of his servants that, when they speak, the voice of Jesus yet resounds in them."[4]

We are accustomed in Reformed circles to thinking that Christ is the ultimate audience of all we preach; we are less accustomed to thinking that Jesus is the *speaker*. When our words are true to his Word, Jesus yet comes and ministers to his people in the preaching of the Word. The human instrument is used, but Jesus speaks. That little plaque that appears in so many churches behind the pulpit for only the preacher to see ("Sir, we would see Jesus") could well be altered to say, "Sir, we would hear Jesus." God's voice is present to his people when we speak the truth of his Word in the pulpit, in Sunday school, in the counseling office, or in

---

spiritual weight of the truth. Such whole-person understanding of the meaning of the text is important, lest listeners know in their heads but not in their hearts what God communicates in his Word (see *CCP*, 178–86; and the author's *Using Illustrations to Preach with Power*, rev. ed. [Wheaton: Crossway, 2001]).

4. John Calvin, *Institutes of the Christian Religion*, 4.1.5. For similar comments from Luther, see Edward F. Markquart, *Quest for Better Preaching: Resources for Renewal in the Pulpit* (Minneapolis: Augsburg, 1985), 83–84.

a child's bedroom. However great are the challenges we face, we have this great comfort in proclaiming God's Word: we are not alone. By his Word and Spirit, Jesus is with us and in us, speaking to his people as we say what the Bible says.

What I am contending—because the Scriptures attest the same—is that when we speak the truths of the Word of God, we are not simply speaking *about* Jesus, nor are we simply speaking *for* Jesus. We are speaking *as* Jesus.[5] Through us, Jesus is yet ministering to his people by the Word he has inspired. The syllables are in the sound of our voice, but the Spirit applies the truths of the Word to the hearts of God's people in such a way that Christ himself is present to speak his Word to their hearts.

Expectations (vv. 10–14)

Because Jesus speaks to his people as we speak the truth of his Word, there are expectations that naturally follow.

Purity.[6] Since we are speaking as Jesus, we should commend his words in how we conduct ourselves. We are speaking "as though God were making his appeal through us" (2 Cor. 5:20 NIV). So, as those who speak with Christ's voice, it is legitimate to ask, "What would Jesus do?" Paul answers that question for Timothy in preceding verses: "You . . . have followed my teaching, my conduct, my aim in life, my faith, my patience, my love, my steadfastness. . . . Continue in what you have learned" (2 Tim. 3:10, 14). Paul reminds Timothy that he is to "desire to live a godly life in Christ Jesus" (v. 12) and that he is called to be a "man of God" (v. 17).

The quality of our lives does not make the Word of God true or endue it with power. The Word is inherently true and powerful, but by our lives we can either add static to what God is communicating or provide a clear signal. We should not let present, legitimate demands for authenticity and transparency convince us that the call to godliness is old-fashioned or ineffective. In preaching the Bible, we who have the Word of Christ in our mouths are charged to commend it with the purity of our speech, habits, and motives. Do not let anyone convince you that the people of God do not desire godliness from their leaders. True piety is not passé. While

5. The statement would be inappropriate without the surrounding content that clarifies its meaning. Such clarification will not, however, keep the statement from sounding startling. The statement is a form of hyperbole that can be put to good rhetorical use in preaching when not used too often or left without qualifying explanation.

6. These sub-subpoints are very briefly stated and in alliterated terms to allow them to be heard as separate ideas without significant additional explanation or organization.

no one wants sanctimonious religiosity, God's people need to know the gospel is real and frees us from our sin. The leaders of God's people communicate the hope of the gospel by speaking and living so as to honor the Jesus we voice.

Persecution. If we speak as Jesus, we should expect that we will experience what he did: persecution. Paul appropriately warns Timothy, "You, however, have followed my teaching . . . my persecutions and sufferings that happened to me at Antioch, at Iconium, and at Lystra" (vv. 10–11). These were the cities of riots and rocks, where crowds were stirred up against Paul and stoning followed. Now Paul says, "Indeed, all who desire to live a godly life in Christ Jesus will be persecuted" (v. 12).

Many of us still sing an old hymn containing these words about the path of suffering: "It is the way the Master went, should not the servant tread it still?" If Christ experienced persecution when he spoke for God, we should not be surprised that we would experience the same when we speak for him. From outside the church and inside the church, attack will come against those who speak Jesus's words. I say this not to frighten but to forearm. When you face persecution for faithfulness, do not presume that you have done something wrong or that your situation is strange. All who are faithful will face challenge. You are not alone in suffering. You have not failed because you face pressures. "Indeed, all who desire to live a godly life in Christ Jesus will be persecuted."

Power. With wonderful pastoral wisdom Paul follows this warning about persecution with a promise of power. We are not alone *in* suffering for God's Word, and we are not alone *when* suffering for God's Word. Paul says to Timothy, "I charge you in the presence of God and of Christ Jesus, who is to judge the living and the dead, and by his appearing and his kingdom: preach the word" (4:1–2).

We should be able to read this verse with new understanding when we recognize that Christ is present in the preaching of his Word. The reason that Paul can charge Timothy faithfully to proclaim the Word in the presence of God and Christ Jesus is not simply because they superintend all human activity from some heavenly perch but because God and Christ Jesus are present in the Word preached. The presence of the living Lord stimulates a second key thought: if Christ is present, then it must be with resurrection power. Though he died, Paul says, Jesus will appear to judge the living and the dead. If he who has power over death itself is present in the preaching of the Word, then vast spiritual power accompanies those who preach. This does not spell an end to all trouble, but it does indicate that God's Word will accomplish what he intends as it is faithfully preached (Isa. 55:11).

If a United States military officer cannot launch an atomic weapon without orders from the president, think how powerful must be the force unleashed that requires a charge from God and Christ Jesus! Yet this is precisely the power that is at work in us when we preach God's Word. Knowledge of this power gives Paul reason to urge Timothy to "be ready in season and out of season; reprove, rebuke, and exhort, with complete patience and teaching" (2 Tim. 4:2). Because the Word of God has such great power, we can speak its truths in season and out, expecting it to perform God's purposes.

In addition, because the power is in the Word and not in us, we can say whatever needs to be said with "complete patience and teaching." Because the Word of God has power (the Greek term is *dunamis*), then like dynamite it should be handled carefully. This means that we can afford to be patient to "complete" our teaching. We do not have to try to make the Word effective by human manipulations, extraordinary eloquence, or intimidating zeal. We should never take the approach that the Word cannot work if we aren't on our game. The power for spiritual change is in the Word faithfully preached, not in the preacher properly wound up.

At the same time, because the Word is so powerful, we can be very bold. We do not back away from truth because some may reject or ridicule us. We are able to speak without fear or favoritism because of the power the Word contains. We can also afford to be compassionate in manner and expression when appropriate because God does not need us to strong arm or manipulate his truth so that it will convince others. We have the Word of Christ, so it is right that we express its truths in the manner of Christ—with courage when needed and with compassion when needed. In either case, we expect the power of Christ to be present because his voice is echoing in ours.

Because the voice of Jesus is present in the proclamation of the Word, we are not alone when we preach, nor are we powerless. The One who brought creation into being when he spoke still speaks with the power to make new creatures in Christ Jesus through the faithful proclamation of his Word. What a comfort and what an encouragement to "preach the word"!

II. Seeing the Hand of God (v. 16)

When we faithfully proclaim the truths of the Bible, not only do we have the privilege of hearing God's voice; we also get to see his hand. Seeing the hand of God also requires a foundation of belief in what the Bible says about itself. The belief that needs to be affirmed can be determined by asking the question, "How much of the Word of God is inspired?" The answer of Paul: "*All* Scripture is breathed out by God" (v. 16a). All that is Scripture has the same origin: the inspiration of the Holy Spirit. There is a necessary implication: that which has been inspired by God will reflect his character.

A great place to see God's character reflected in his Word is Psalm 19:7–9. In this passage the psalmist is describing the nature of the various aspects of God's Word. But if you did not know that the writer was describing the Word of God, what would you think was being described? Focus just on the descriptive terms to answer the question.

> *The law of the LORD is perfect,*
> *reviving the soul;*
> *the testimony of the LORD is sure,*
> *making wise the simple;*
> *the precepts of the LORD are right,*
> *rejoicing the heart;*
> *the commandment of the LORD is pure,*
> *enlightening the eyes;*
> *the fear of the LORD is clean,*
> *enduring forever;*
> *the rules of the LORD are true,*
> *and righteous altogether. (Ps. 19:7–9)*

Were you only to consider the adjectives, what would you think is being described? You would think *God himself* is being described. He is perfect, sure, wise, right, pure, clean, enduring forever, true, righteous altogether. That's the point. The Word of God reflects the character of God, since he inspires it. This means that the Bible is perfect, sure, wise, right, pure, clean, enduring forever, true, and righteous altogether—and for this reason it can be entirely trusted as the hand of God to guide us where we should go and to direct what we should do.

Theologians refer to this principle of the absolute trustworthiness of God's Word as the doctrine of biblical inerrancy. When we say that the Bible is inerrant, we must quickly add that our interpretations of it are not without error. Elsewhere the apostle Paul will remind Timothy that he must study to be a godly workman who is "rightly dividing the word of truth" (2 Tim. 2:15 KJV). We can make wrong "divisions," but this acknowledgment does not deny the inerrancy of Scripture; it simply calls us to be skilled interpreters.

Further, if God's ways are not our ways and his thoughts are above our thoughts, then we should not be surprised that there are passages that stretch our knowledge. We can make mistakes simply because we do not understand enough. But saying that we can mess up is something entirely different from saying that God's Word is mistaken. Paul says, "*All* Scripture is breathed out by God." That means that all that God has given as his Word reflects his perfect character. Whatever truth the Bible teaches is true.

The spirit of the age, of course, challenges this doctrine of inerrancy and points to supposed contradictions or inaccuracies in the Bible. But virtually all of these can be answered by reasonable investigation from a mind that believes God has inspired Scripture. This matter of "believing investigation" needs to be emphasized. We should not think that by logic or science we can irrefutably rebut every possible objection to Scripture. While there are many sound arguments to defend the truth of Scripture, there is always the possibility that someone will come up with an argument or discovery that we haven't considered yet. At that point we base our doctrine of Scripture not on the sufficiency of our logic but on the faithfulness of our God. We trust him ultimately to reveal what is true not because we can prove it to be so but because he has proven *himself* to be faithful.

The great preacher Charles Spurgeon once said that anyone who would trust Scripture must be willing to be thought a fool for twenty years before science will prove him right. In general, I like and agree with this sentiment, but still we need to be wary of the assumption that reason will serve to confirm all that Scripture attests. We must not forget that logic supports our faith but is not its sole pillar. The Westminster divines struck a good balance when they said that by its many "incomparable excellencies" the Bible "doth abundantly evidence itself to be the Word of God; yet, notwithstanding, our full persuasion and assurance of the infallible truth and divine authority thereof, is from the inward work of the Holy Spirit, bearing witness by and with the Word in our hearts."[7] By Spirit-induced faith as well as by reason-driven logic we believe the Bible to be entirely true.

7. *Westminster Confession of Faith*, I.5.

If this belief in the absolute truth of Scripture sounds naive and simplistic, please recognize that it is far more logically consistent than the arguments of those who claim that the Bible is a "good book" despite its many flaws. Many of us were trained in our college years to use the "three Ls" in responding to those who said that Jesus was just a good man. We said this could not be the case because Jesus claimed to be the Son of God. If he said this knowing he was not, then he was a *liar*. If he believed he was the Son of God when he was not, then he was a *lunatic*. But if he said he was the Son of God, and he really was, then he really is the *Lord*. In light of the claims he made, Jesus could *not* have been simply a "good man."

The same logic applies to the argument that the Bible is just a good book, though a flawed one. The Bible claims to be the Word of God—more than three thousand times some form of the phrase, "Thus says the Lord," appears within its pages. Either this is a colossal lie, or it is sheer lunacy, or the Bible *is* the Word of the Lord. The Bible cannot be just a "good book."

Release from the Idolatry of Self [8]

If the Bible is not the infallible Word of God that it claims to be, then not only should the Bible have no great significance for us, but God himself disappears from us. A professor once responded to a student who was challenging the total truth of Scripture by taking a pair of scissors from his desk drawer. "Here," said the professor to the student, "take this pair of scissors and cut out everything that you don't think should be in the Bible. But you should recognize that by the time you are done picking and choosing what should be included, the only wisdom that you will have left is your own."[9]

Whenever we become the judge of what the Bible should say—when our Scriptures are only our best cut-and-paste job—then we substitute our wisdom for God's. In my mind's eye, I imagined that by the time the student was done with his

---

8. The goal of the material in this and the following subpoint is not so much to further the conceptual understanding of biblical inerrancy as to have listeners "feel" the impact of its rejection on their spiritual lives. The consequences of not having a reliable Bible are not merely intellectual but deeply spiritual and relational.

9. Readers of all the sermons in this book will recognize this illustration from a previous use (in Example Sermon Six). This repetition indicates a dynamic all pastors experience: using a good illustration more than once because it powerfully serves the purpose of multiple sermons. Prudence, experience, and good record-keeping, however, should keep a good illustration from becoming overused or a cliché of one's ministry.

scissors, his Bible looked like a string of paper dolls, and each doll looked like the student. Each was a reflection of the student's own wisdom and opinions. Thus his Bible was simply a reflection of himself, a creation of his self-idolatry from which belief in God's inerrant Word frees us.

Release from the Isolation of Self

The great sadness of having a Bible that reflects only our own thoughts is not simply the elimination of divine wisdom but the elimination of divine presence. There will be times in all of our lives when the darkness closes in and we cry out for God. But if our Bible contains only the content of our own wisdom, then the only sound that we will hear when we call out in the darkness is an echo of our own voices. Though it is usually described in academic terms, inerrancy is our freedom from a suffocating aloneness—the inevitable prison of being shut up with one's own judgments as the only guiding companion in life. Without a Bible that can be trusted beyond our own wisdom, God disappears from our lives and human opinion alone determines what is right and wrong, proper or foolish.

But God has not disappeared. To the contrary, by his Word our Lord yet guides us with his hand in the darkness. The apostle says that the Word is "profitable for teaching, for reproof, for correction, and for training in righteousness" (2 Tim. 3:16b). Each of these words reflects Paul's understanding of the essential truth of all Scripture:

- *Teaching*: The Bible leads us in the path of truth.[10]
- *Reproof*: The Bible knocks us from the path of error.
- *Correction*: The Bible returns us to the path of truth.
- *Training in righteousness*: The Bible directs us in the application of truth, taking us all the way down the path of God's will for godly living.

10. Students of preaching profit by remembering that only four things can be done to explain a text. You can repeat it, restate it in different terms, define (or describe) it, or provide a proof of its meaning. The first two of these explanations are the most common and need not be added to if they make the meaning clear and convincing. Sometimes preachers seem to believe that they must make what is obvious sound scholarly in order to show that they are serious about exegeting the text. However, regular indulgence of the inclination to make what is simple seem complex will rob God's people of the confidence that they themselves can understand God's Word (see *CCP*, 103–4, 109–10, 119). In the case of the words being explained in this portion of the sermon, the form of explanation is simple restatement, which also provides adequate definition.

Through these means our Lord provides his unerring hand to lead us through the darkness of our world. He extends *his* hand through the veil between heaven and earth to guide us with the truths of Scripture every day, everywhere, in every situation we must face (1 Pet. 1:3, 21).

III. Knowing the Heart of God (vv. 15 and 17)

When you have the voice of God to comfort and the hand of God to guide, what you really have in Scripture is the heart of God on display. As with the voice and the hand of God, knowing the heart of God also requires a foundation of belief in what the Bible says about itself. Paul tells Timothy to "continue in what you have learned and have firmly believed, knowing . . . the sacred writings, which are able to make you wise for salvation through faith in Christ Jesus" (2 Tim. 3:14–15). The Bible reveals God's heart for his people by telling them of the salvation that is provided for them through faith in Christ.

Yet these "sacred writings" to which Paul refers could only be what we know as the Old Testament, written before Christ's coming—for most of the New Testament had not yet been produced. How could these Old Testament writings make Timothy wise for salvation through faith in Christ Jesus?[11] One answer is that the Old Testament Scriptures contain predictions of the coming of Christ. But there is a more comprehensive answer. Paul tells Timothy that the Scriptures have been given "that the man of God may be competent, equipped for every good work" (v. 17). The word "competent" in this phrase is a translation of the Greek word *artios*, which means "complete." An important implication results from understanding Paul's statement that the Scriptures are given to "complete" us: *we are incomplete apart from the provision of God.*

How are we incomplete? That has been made apparent by what God has already revealed about himself in his Word. He is perfect, sure, wise, right, pure, clean, and righteous altogether (see again Ps. 19:7–10). At the same time, Scripture reveals something quite different about *us*. Echoing many Old Testament texts in this

---

11. To this point, this message is an orthodox presentation of the doctrine of Scripture, but redemptive truths are lacking. If the sermon were to end here, it might serve the dogma of the devoted but would do little to minister to the souls of God's people because there has been no reference to the grace of God, which is necessary for us to be able truly to honor and serve him. Thus, the *redemptive orthodoxy* of this message rests on the *exposition* that follows regarding God's provision of his grace through his Word (see *CCP*, 273–80).

passage, Paul reminds us that people naturally "will not endure sound teaching, but having itching ears they will accumulate for themselves teachers to suit their own passions, and will turn away from listening to the truth and wander off into myths" (2 Tim. 4:3–4). In short, God's nature is holy and ours is not. There is a great disparity between God's nature and ours that requires God's provision in order for us to be rescued from our spiritual "incompleteness."

Because the "sacred writings" are always revealing God's perfections and our incompleteness, they are consistently pointing us toward the necessity of faith in someone beyond ourselves to rescue us from our spiritual destitution. If we will simply ask two questions of any passage—what does this text tell me about God, and what does this text tell me about humanity?—then we will always discover redemptive truth glimmering.[12] All Scripture directs us toward faith in Christ, for he is the ultimate message of all the "sacred writings." Thus, when Paul tells Timothy, "Preach the word," the apostle necessarily charges the young minister to proclaim Christ (the Incarnate Word) as the aim of all he preaches.

Our work as proclaimers of Scripture is never done when we have told God's people the duty and doctrine a passage may teach. If people are left to think that they are right with God because they *do enough* or *know enough*, then they are ultimately looking to their own strength and wisdom as the source of their salvation. They must always look toward the Savior and trust in his provision even as they respond in obedience to God and thirst for knowledge of God.[13] Surely this is why Paul tells Timothy, "Always be sober-minded, endure suffering, *do the work of an evangelist*, fulfill your ministry" (4:5). Though Timothy has a mature ministry in Ephesus, he still must proclaim the good news that is in Christ Jesus in order to fulfill his ministry.

12. For further discussion of how these two questions function as "spectacles" enabling us to see redemptive truth in any text of Scripture, see *CCP*, 284–86 and 308–9.

13. Students often ask, "What is the proper place for redemptive truth to be expressed in a sermon—beginning, middle, end, or throughout?" Each strategy has its place, depending on the nature of the text and the nature of the situation. Sometimes it is best to lay a grace foundation and build imperatives upon it; sometimes it is best to give the imperatives and then show how grace provides the motivation and enablement for their fulfillment; sometimes an ironic twist best drives home the redemptive truth; and sometimes redemptive truths are best woven throughout the message. There is not a single best place for redemptive truth in all sermons. The point to emphasize as we conclude this book is that the sermon should not end until the grace has been given its place in the message (see *CCP*, 310–11). "Apart from me you can do nothing," said Jesus (John 15:5). We should not send God's people out into the world to glorify him without God's grace to enable them (see *CCP*, 273–74 and 295).

Conclusion

How do we remain Christ-focused in all we proclaim? The answer lies in the realization that *all* Scripture is *always* revealing the voice, the hand, and the heart of God. *And when you have the voice, the hand, and the heart of God, you have Jesus.* He is "the radiance of the glory of God and the exact imprint of his nature" (Heb. 1:3). Being faithful to the full message of Scripture is presenting Christ, for whom the human heart thirsts. And understanding that Christ is the message of *all* Scripture explains why God's people so thirst for God's Word.

Many of us cherish the words of the psalmist, "As a deer pants for flowing streams, so pants my soul for you, O God" (Ps. 42:1). We may forget how the psalmist says that thirst is satisfied: "My soul is consumed with longing for your rules at all times. . . . I open my mouth and pant, because I long for your commandments" (Ps.119:20, 131). Why would anyone long for God's commands? Because when those commands are rightly understood as revealing the caring voice, guiding hand, and saving heart of God—leading us to understand our need and God's provision—then we thirst for what God's Word teaches.

I have never had a more powerful impression of how the human heart thirsts for the Word than when a friend explained how he came to a saving knowledge of Jesus Christ. He was an ordained minister in a church that considered the Bible only as a work of men that should be critically dissected for its occasional truths amidst its primitive religious expressions.

By mistake my friend got hooked into a tour of Israel that got him and his girlfriend traveling with a bunch of evangelical ministers and their wives. One day the tour took them to the Garden Tomb, one of the places in Israel reputed to be where Jesus was buried and rose from the dead. The ministers decided to celebrate communion at the site. Since my friend had stayed in the background for most of the tour, the others decided that now was the time for him to do his share of ministering. He was asked to conduct the communion service. He did so. But as this unbelieving minister distributed the elements representing Christ's body and blood, and as he said the Words of communion in the place of Jesus's resurrection, my friend was struck not only with the hypocrisy of what he was doing but also with the reality of what Christ had done.

When the service was over, the other ministers continued touring the site. My friend did not. He went back to the tour bus and waited with almost frantic desperation for the others to finish their sightseeing. He says, "For the first time in my life I was thirsty for Scripture, and I felt I would die if we did not get back to the hotel as quickly as possible so that I could read my Bible." There are streams of living water in the Word that satisfy the thirsty heart with God. For this reason the apostle Paul says clearly and passionately, "Preach the word."

"Preach the Word." This should be our privilege and passion, knowing that when we do so, we share the voice, the hand, and the heart of God with thirsty people. Whether they know they are thirsty or not, their heart's cry is always, "Give me Jesus." How do we do that? Preach the Word.

> *When I am alone, give me Jesus. How?*
> *Preach the Word, and his voice will minister his presence.*
> *When I am afraid, give me Jesus. How?*
> *Preach the Word, and his hand will guide my path.*
> *And when I am defiled, give me Jesus. How?*
> *Preach the Word, and his heart will cleanse my soul.*
> *Give me Jesus. How? Preach the Word.*

General Index

adoption, xxi
African American tradition, 56, 58, 69n22
allegory, xiii
alliteration, 56, 81n9, 223n6
"Amen," as pulpit dialogue, 60n7
analytical questions, 12nn22–23, 15n28, 43, 188n6
anchor clause, 7n10, 21, 24n2
antinomianism, xvii
Apostles' Creed, 208, 209n8
application, xxiv–xxvii, 10n18, 119–20n8, 157–58
  grace-based power in, 122n9
  and illustrations, 47n12
  situational specificity in, 189n7
  unrolls imperatives, 189n7
Auden, W. H., 199
Augustine, 220

baptism, 164, 202–4
"Battle Hymn of the Republic," 64n14
Belarus, 139–40
"be like" messages, 110, 117n6
Bible
  arrangement of material, 141, 143n1
  genres of, xiv, 141
  inerrancy of, 226–28
  inspiration of, 220–23
biblical theology, xiv, 71, 127, 132n5, 133n7
billboards, 7n11, 7n14, 15n28, 25n4, 61n8, 64n13, 77n3, 163n2
biographical sermons, 110, 114n5
blood of Christ, xxvii
Braddock, James J., 175
bridges, xv, 74

Brown, Steve, 53, 126
Burke, Kenneth, 59n5

calling, 210–14
Calvin, John, 100, 148, 222
Carey, William, 134–36
Cassels, Rosalie, 68
Chalmers, Thomas, xxvi
Christian liberty, 191, 201
Christian life, 157, 173, 184, 189–90
citation in sermons, 113n1
civil rights movement, 61n9, 63–68
command/parable/narrative interplay, 141–42
commands, 141, 157
completeness, 230–31
conclusion, 176n11
"context is part of the text," 74, 128
Covenant Theological Seminary, 220
"covering the territory," 216
covetousness, 172
credit in sermons, 113n1
crescendo at conclusion of sermon, 56, 69n22
cross, xix

dead ends, xv, 90
deductive sermons, 4, 22, 39, 42n3
descriptive to normative movement, 82n10
despair, xxviii
desperation, 149–51
dialogue style, 56
didactic text, 4, 22
discipleship, xviii
doctrinal statements in Prophets, 90
dying to self, 162–63

Scripture Index

239